W9-CQN-637

Speaking of the Short Story

Speaking of the Short Story

Interviews with Contemporary Writers

*edited by Farhat Iftekharuddin,
Mary Rohrberger, and Maurice Lee*

University Press of Mississippi / Jackson

Copyright © 1997 by University Press of Mississippi
All rights reserved
Manufactured in the United States of America

00   99   98   97   4   3   2   1

The paper in this book meets the guidelines for permanence and durability of the
Committee on Production Guidelines for Book Longevity of the Council on Library
Resources.

Library of Congress Cataloging-in-Publication Data

Speaking of the short story: interviews with contemporary writers /
edited by Farhat Iftekharuddin and Mary Rohrberger.
    p. cm.
Includes index.
ISBN 0-87805-970-9 (cloth : alk. paper). — ISBN 0-87805-971-7
(pbk. : alk. paper)
    1. Short stories, American—History and criticism—Theory, etc.
2. Short stories, Commonwealth (English)—History and criticism—
Theory, etc.   3. Short stories, Latin American—History and
criticism—Theory, etc.   4. Authors, Latin American—20th century—
Interviews.   5. Authors, Commonwealth—20th century—Interviews.
6. Authors, American—20th century—Interviews.   7. Short story.
I. Iftekharuddin, Farhat.   II. Rohrberger, Mary.
PS374.S5S68   1997
813'.0109—dc21   96-54886
                                    CIP

British Library Cataloging-in-Publication data available

CONTENTS

C all it short-story hyphenated or short story unhyphenated, the popularity of the genre has persisted since it first appeared. Practitioners continue to discuss the short story in such individual and sometimes idiosyncratic ways that the form seems to have been kept alive by its own magical ambiguity. The short story, as distinguished from the story that is merely short (tale, fable, parable, sketch), has its beginnings, most agree, in the early nineteenth century, with the short fiction written by four major writers: Washington Irving, Nathaniel Hawthorne, and Edgar Allan Poe, in the United States, and Nikolai Gogol, in Russia. An examination of the stories written by each of these men suggests very strongly that Hawthorne's "My Kinsman, Major Molineux" is the prototype of stories to follow, creating what Brander Matthews, American short story writer and critic, called a new genre. Strangely coincidental is the fact that it was in a review of Hawthorne's *Twice-Told Tales* that Edgar Allan Poe set down what is everywhere considered to be the first theoretical statement concerning the form that Poe called "tale," but that later came to be known as "short story." Poe emphasized length, saying that the story needed to be short enough to be read in a single sitting or else it would lose its effect on the reader; he emphasized coherence, saying that every word had to fit into one total design. And perhaps most important, Poe emphasized the role of the reader as cocreator since meaning was submerged beneath the obvious surface of the stories. Hawthorne's stories made use of what is known as a typical plot line, moving from exposition to conflict and climax and then falling to a denouement. Such a plot line ordinarily makes use of extraordinary events: a man takes a walk in the forest and meets the devil ("Young Goodman Brown"); a man kills his only son and is thus released from sin ("Roger Malvin's Burial"); a doctor creates his own kind of garden of Eden (or evil) and tries to people it with his own version of an Adam and an Eve ("Rapaccini's Daughter"). These kinds of situations call for symbolic readings, and indeed everything in a Hawthorne story can be said to be symbolic where image patterns coalesce to help determine meaning. Most symbols in such stories can be classified as "common" symbols signifying that a storm, a forest, or a clearing in a forest has connotative meaning generally understood within our culture.

Although this kind of story dominated the nineteenth century, certain changes and variations did take place during that time, making the transition to modernism a natural consequence of the short story's development. In the first place few nineteenth-century writers made use of the plot structure known as Freytag's Pyramid, a completely balanced movement from exposition to denouement. Most short story writers elongated the rising action and brought the climax nearer to the end of the story; thus, a story like Poe's "The Fall of the House of Usher" exhibits just such a structure, the climax occurring toward the very end of the story when Lady Madeline makes her second appearance and Usher finally realizes what he has done. The ending of the story follows immediately when the house of Usher collapses and falls into the black and lurid tarn. Besides variations in the plot structure, other changes took place that marked the transition to modernism. Melville, for example, in a story like "Bartleby, the Scrivener," brought the short story into a contemporary time frame and experimented with the use of point of view, thus increasing complexity by means of shifting perspectives. Where Hawthorne used the omniscient author almost exclusively and Poe seemed to favor a fairly uncomplicated first person narrative, Melville provided limited viewpoints where differing perspectives often hid the truth.

Early in the twentieth century three writers—James Joyce, Katherine Mansfield, and Sherwood Anderson—began writing stories that shifted both form and content, bringing the story squarely into the developing modernist perspective. Exposition disappeared; traditional plot lines gave way to *in medias res* beginnings. Falling action and denouement disappeared. Climax became (following Joyce's use of the term) epiphany. Even the appearance of closure was eliminated. Truncated plots became the norm, and the surfaces of stories involved everyday people in everyday events: a boy becomes abnormally upset because of a conversation he overhears at a bazaar ("Araby"); a young girl wakes up anxious about the wind ("The Wind Blows"); two sisters find it difficult to handle their father's death ("The Daughters of the Late Colonel"); a father becomes fixated upon making an egg stand on its end ("The Egg"). In these kinds of stories, although common symbols continue to be used to help direct meaning, authors are more prone to create their own symbols in context; thus, a reader has to determine the meaning of the wind, for example, by patterned references to it throughout the story. Following in the footsteps of Joyce, Mansfield, and Anderson is just about every major writer of the first half of the twentieth century—Hemingway, Faulkner, Welty, Porter, Toomer, to name a few. This is not to say that the "traditional" story disappeared and the "modernist" story took over, for such is not the case at all. Traditional stories with fully developed plot structures continue to be written alongside of modernist stories even with the advent of postmodernism which brought with it distinct philosophic assumptions about the "real."

About midway through the twentieth century postmodernists arrived with dramatically changed metaphysical assumptions about the nature of the real and insisted that a realistic representation of the human condition could only be achieved by the use of fragments, as in the short stories of Donald Barthelme. Some of his stories consist of catalogues of items with seemingly no relationship to each other, and others make use of grotesque situations: a grown man suddenly back in grade school ("Me and Miss Mandible"); a large balloon suddenly appearing in the sky with no indication of where it came from or its present purpose ("The Balloon"). In the story "See the Moon," Barthelme insists on the use of fragmentation to depict contemporary reality: "Here is the word and here are the knowledge knowers knowing. What can I tell you? What has been pieced together from the reports of travelers. Fragments are the only forms I trust. Look at my walls, it's all there." To understand works that depend on fragmentation as a method of representation, readers are forced to conceive the whole at once, to observe the collage rather than the individual components of the story. Other writers of the postmodern mode claim that since traditional history is unreliable as a means of understanding humanity, self-reflexivity is the necessary direction to take, as in the works of John Barth and Robert Coover. Barth's "Lost in the Funhouse" may be the prototypical story in this mode. This story is a story about telling a story about telling a story about telling a story that, at the same time, is telling several stories and analyzing how to write them. Coover utilizes this self-reflexive narrative form in "The Babysitter." In this story, a plethora of points of view participate in the telling, including a television set whose channels are constantly being changed. Further, to confound the realm of the possibly real, many of the sections are imagined, having the same level of reality as the stories on the television set. These authors, then, achieve continuity within their stories primarily through the exploitation of language and through spatial rather than linear connections between each segment of the stories. Thus, art became artifice.

The form of the short story experienced two other significant changes at the hands of magic realists and minimalists. Magic realism, most obvious in the works of Latin American writers such as Gabriel García Márquez and Isabel Allende, has also been employed by authors from other parts of the world such as the Indian/British writer Salman Rushdie. The most noticeable feature of this technique is the seamless merger of alternative reality with conventional reality. In fact, in magic realism the defining line between these two notions of reality is so blurred that characters within the texts move freely between the two realities and often exist simultaneously in both. Thus, the real and the magical worlds become interchangeable or one. Magic realist writers accomplish this transference or merger of multiple realities through a combination of cultural myths and mysteries extracted from folklore, superstition, and the occult, along with empirical information and experiences that are a part of contemporary reality. Gabriel García Márquez's "A Very Old Man with Enormous Wings" and Isabel Allende's "Walimai" are perfect examples of such mergers of the real and the magical. The ease with which magic realists merge the "unreal" with the "real" stems from the notion that both the rational world and the mythical and mysterious worlds are a part of our human collective consciousness; all is one. In fact, the genesis for many a myth, superstition, and occult experience lies in the rational, for the mysterious often breeds from the empirical. The umbilical cord that bridges the rational and the extensional world in fiction is of course the imagination of both the author and the reader.

While magic realism calls for narrative excess, minimalism demands exclusion. A phenomenon that started in the late 1970s, minimalism is an offshoot of realism and is marked by a major reduction of the experiential into a minimalized representation of it. Art in this narrative style reflects life through symbolic and metaphoric compression. Minimalists select details from contemporary surroundings and convert those elements into referential icons that then operate as vehicles for meaning. Through a process of cognitive association, limited discourse is said to allude to the macrocosm, which is contemporary life itself. Thus, fast-food enterprises, department stores, all prefabricated material, commercials, and commercialized life on TV become the symbols and metaphors of minimalist writing. A casual mention of shopping at K-mart, for instance, then becomes the vehicle that defines the socio-economic standard of the character involved, along with a myriad of associative behaviors both personal or social that contemporary readers can recognize as part of their own experiences to which they can attach meaning. The stories in Raymond Carver's collection *What We Talk About When We Talk About Love* are perfect examples of minimalist writing. Although Carver rejected being tagged a minimalist, his own description of his writing style attests otherwise. Commenting on his impatience with writing a novel, he states, "It has much to do with why I write poems or short stories. Get in, get out. Don't linger. Go on" ("On Writing" in *The New Short Story Theories*). Although he adheres to this "get in, get out" principle in all of his stories, Carver aggressively applied this principle in the stories in *What We Talk About When We Talk About Love*. Besides being marked by sparsity of narrative content and extensive use of cultural icons to carry meaning, several of the stories in this collection were considerably reduced in length, like "Sacks" and "The Third Thing That Killed My Father Off," (previously published as "Fling" and "Dummy" respectively in *Furious Seasons and Other Stories*); the objective was to cut "everything down to the marrow, not just to the bone" (Carver, *Fires: Essays, Poems, Stories*).

When a story is categorized as either traditional, modern, postmodern, magical realist, or minimalist, the difference pointed to is mostly one of fictional framework; the intent and the art behind the fabrication are seemingly alike. Very often, however, there is the tendency to group writers in one slot or another, overlooking other similarities. Most authors reject categorization and view themselves as members of what Rudolfo Anaya calls the "collective consciousness." Indeed, in their definitions of the short story as a distinct genre, short story writers from Poe and Hawthorne to the most recent contemporary writers have more in common than in difference. Brander Matthews, in "The Philosophy of the Short Story"(1901), developed his theory regarding this genre from Poe's famous review of Hawthorne's *Twice-Told Tales*, insisting on a single character, event, emotion, and situation to create the unity of effect that Poe demanded. Mary Rohrberger in "Fiction Writers on Writing" (*Critical Survey of Short Fiction*, McGill, 1981) points out that what is absent in Matthews's theory is "Poe's suggestion, not stated overtly but clearly implied, that the story radiates a whole that is not described but suggested, that story becomes metaphor." Hawthorne points to this "suggested" or "metaphoric" quality in defining the romance in his preface to *The House of the Seven Gables* (1851), when he states that the romance in pursuing "the truth of the human heart" has a "right to present that truth under circumstances, to a great extent of the writer's own choosing or creation."

Hawthorne's observations regarding the romance have uncanny similarities with the philosophies of modern writers. Joseph Conrad states that writers should use imagination "to create human souls to disclose human hearts" (from a letter printed in *The Indispensable Conrad*, 1951). William Faulkner talked about the "human heart in conflict with itself" in his Nobel Prize speech (1950). Ernest Hemingway, using his iceberg theory in *Death in the Afternoon* (1932) to define the short story, points to what is hidden below the surface where the author can express what is "truer . . . than anything factual can be." Sherwood Anderson, deriding "plot stories," claims that the "unreal is more real than the real, that there is no real other than the unreal" (*Sherwood Anderson's Memoirs*, 1942). D. H. Lawrence in *Studies in Classic American Literature* (1923) speaks of "art-speech" as the "only truth." In fact, Lawrence's comments (in defining the tale) that "the curious thing about art-speech is that it prevaricates . . . it tells such lies . . . and out of a pattern of lies art weaves truth" and "never trust the artist, trust the tale" are remarkably similar five decades later to what Isabel Allende has to say about story writing. "I think that everything is true, that fiction is just a way of saying something that is truthful from the very beginning. What is fiction? A bunch of lies, but it wouldn't work if those lies didn't come from a very honest truthful place inside you." These observations have a re-markable similarity to those of Hawthorne's insisting on "the truth of the human heart" a hundred and forty-three years ago.

In the history of the short story, theoretical and philosophical observations about it have come often from practitioners of the genre as well as from scholars and critics. In different syntactical and metaphorical ways authors provide clues to the intrinsic genetic similarities that exist within this elusive genre. Canadian writer Clark Blaise reaffirms Anderson's fear of "plot stories" when he states in this volume, "I'm very impatient with traditional narrative. Conventional linear narrative simplifies too much. Readers are in dialogue with stories. They are asked to project from the details on the page something that is not on the page." Blaise's words remind us of Hemingway's iceberg concept, and Allende's observation that "I only give them half the story. The other half has to be recre-ated or created by the reader, and that is the space we are going to share."

Practitioners from Poe to Allende, from Mansfield to Arias have made state-ments similar to Faulkner's that in any hierarchy of genres, poetry stands at the pinnacle followed by the short story. Novels are easier, writers declare, because mistakes can be hidden, but in a short story there is no place to hide the wrong word, the wrong tone, the lack of a clarifying metaphor. Short story writers voice their attempts to understand the genre through discursive language and the use of metaphors, and many of them also believe that some kind of mystery is at the base of each example of the genre. Hence, scholars and critics with their careful explications of the text point to these kinds of literary multivalence to be found in short stories. Such endeavors by both writers and critics have contributed to a common thread, to take the short story seriously as a genre worthy of study and in need not only of definition but of foregrounding in the literary panoply. This collection of interviews with authors and scholars of diverse ethnic and national backgrounds informs us of a broad spectrum of issues regarding the short story, particularly issues of theory and the viability of this genre.

The interviewees, in defining the short story and in speaking of their individual writing processes, reveal diverse theoretical opinions about the character of the genre: some offer views reminiscent of Poe's definition of the tale and others demand a new perspective. Many contemporary writers emphasize the primacy of form. Charles E. May insists, "Writers are most interested in form because they know that form is what makes literature." This perspective is echoed by Richard Ford, who thinks of his stories as constructions and notes that "their logical sequential nature is an achieved quality: the process of first putting one thing next to one thing, then putting the next, all of which creates, if you're lucky, the illusion of a cohesive story." For Ellen Douglas, cohesiveness is a matter of unity of subject, tone, and style. Regardless of the effort put into it, a story must "seem to have been written at one setting." Isabel Allende describes this effect in metaphorical terms: "A short story is like an arrow: you have only one shot, and you need the precision, the direction, the speed, the firm wrist of the archer to get it right." The writers interviewed here often express their own individual means of conceptualizing or beginning a story, and in doing so they frequently reveal what, in their view, is significant or important, about the genre. For Bharati Mukherjee, writing is a "matter of finding the most compelling metaphor, the most precise metaphor." Rudolfo Anaya sees each story as a gem: "[it] has to do with intimacy; the characters describe that." Often writers speak of their craft as acts of almost unconscious inspiration and imagination. Clark Blaise, for instance, notes that "with a short story, the beginning is the end. . . . If you yield to the magic of a beginning, which just seizes you, you can continue it." Judith Ortiz Cofer begins each of her stories with characters, a script, a scene, and a setting, and then, she says, "I allow them to enact." She adds, "The lines are so fine between my creative nonfiction and my fiction that the only way I can explain it is by intent." Arturo Arias, who thinks of himself primarily as a storyteller, also sees the similarity between his short story writing and other genres: "They're all stories. Even when I'm writing political science, it's a story." For Simon Ortiz, the story is "an expression, a human expression, of what is the world." He goes on to address the importance of storytelling for Native Americans, pointing out that "without the oral tradition for indigenous peoples, there's no cultural continuity." The story, therefore, "enhances and engenders what one's connection is to the rest of the world." Still other writers seek to expand the possibilities of the genre and develop their art outside of or in resistance to the traditional forms of their predecessors. Leslie Marmon Silko, in assessing the aims and accomplishments of postmodern and contemporary writers notes, "They're trying to escape the strictures of the formal story form." She herself admits to having abandoned the confining limitations of "classical" rules, and she vows, "I'm not done making trouble with the short story form."

Any discussion of the viability of the short story is complicated by the many concerns embedded in this issue, and the views of authors and scholars are just as diverse as their definitions of the short story. Some are excited about the direction that the genre has taken while others are less optimistic. While Susan Lohafer acknowledges the renewed interest in the short story and the efforts on the part of many practitioners to organize as a movement, she cautions, "The more established we become as a field, the more we begin to lose some of the very characteristics which drew some of us—certainly me—to this study in the first place. I mean a certain quirkiness, a maverick quality, a resistance to any ideology." To sustain the short story, stories must not only be written, but taught as well. Addressing the social/pedagogical issues, Charles May says, "I don't feel on the defensive against the current anti-formalist approach. For me there is no content without form. . . . So, if I look at stories more formalistically than a lot of critics do, who are more interested in stories as containers of social ideas, or reflection of social ideas, it is because—whatever those social ideas are—they're still the result of some artifice, some fiction-making, some creative process." At the same time, Susan Lohafer warns against "pre-formulated responses": "Nowadays, nobody would think of forcing the meaning of a story into a didactic moral; but we do, routinely, channel its impact into well-worn grooves of cultural criticism." Another key component within this discussion of viability is the willingness of major publishing houses to employ the same vigor in publishing and promoting collections of short stories as they do novels. Rudolfo Anaya expresses serious doubts regarding the interest of publishers in bringing out and promoting the genre: "The publishing world doesn't publish short story collections. Until that changes, the future is not optimistic." He, like many other contemporary writers, feels that this neglect is even more pronounced in the case of ethnic literature: "You find few stories by Chicanos, Chicanas, Native Americans, or other ethnic groups. If you check the catalog of major publishing companies, you will not find collections of stories by minority writers." Ellen Douglas, who for a while, turned from short stories to novels, believes that that situation is slowly changing for the better. "You can sell a collection of stories and you can find some limited market for them in magazines. So . . . after twenty-five years of not writing any stories lately I've begun to do it again." The surge in the publications of short story collections in the 1990s is a hopeful indicator that may quell, to an extent, some of the concerns raised by Anaya, particularly when Anaya himself has recently signed a very lucrative contract with Warner Books.

The interviews in this collection were conducted in June 1994 during the Third International Conference on the Short Story in English, sponsored by the Society for the Study of the Short Story, the University of Northern Iowa, the University of Iowa, Iowa State University, and the literary/scholarly journal, *Short Story*. The primary focus of this conference is to bring together prominent and emerging short story writers, critics, and scholars of the genre into a forum that addresses every facet of the short story, from craft to theory to pedagogy. As a result, authors such as Isabel Allende, Richard Ford, Bharati Mukherjee, Rudolfo Anaya, Leslie Marmon Silko, Simon Ortiz, Amy Tan, Amiri Baraka, and Sonia Sanchez, among others, addressed their views regarding the genre along side critics and scholars like Mary Rohrberger, Charles E. May, Susan Lohafer, Wilson Harris, Austin Wright, Alan Reid, and Shirley Lim. The short story has and will continue to thrive as long as authors, scholars, publishers, and readers remain collectively engaged in the aesthetic creation and appreciation of this genre. *Speaking of the Short Story: Interviews with Contemporary Writers* should appeal to all literary audiences but particularly to those who write, teach, and attempt to define the short story. This collection is unique because it brings together—under one cover and within a multicultural framework—discussions regarding all facets of the short story genre from short story devotees be they writers and/or scholars. Even those scholars and critics advanced in the critical study of this genre will find in this book specific philosophies, ideologies, and theories from both national and international authors and critics as they define individual stories and derive individual theories.

Speaking of the Short Story

Isabel Allende

Farhat Iftekharuddin

I sabel Allende, a Chilean, was born in Lima, Peru, in 1942. Her career covers a wide range of experiences including journalism and teaching. She has taught at the University of Virginia, Charlottesville, Montclair College, New Jersey, and as late as 1989, she taught creative writing at the University of California, Berkeley. She is the author of the international bestsellers *The House of the Spirits* (1981), *The Infinite Plan* (1991), *Of Love and Shadows* (1984), *Eva Luna* (1987), and *The Stories of Eva Luna* (1990). Her latest book is *Paula* (1994), a memoir of her heartbreaking experience watching her daughter die a prolonged death. Her novels *The House of the Spirits* and *Of Love and Shadows* have been adopted into motion pictures. Her works have been translated into more than 27 languages and have been bestsellers in Latin America, Australia, and the USA. She has won numerous literary awards including Books to Remember Award, American Library Association (1996), Critics' Choice Award (1996), Author of the Year, Germany (1994), Book of the Year, Germany (1994), and Panorama Literario Award, Chile (1983). She currently resides with her husband in California.

Iftekharuddin: Critics have drawn comparisons between your works and other Latin American writers. They readily compare Gabriel García Márquez's *One Hundred Years of Solitude* with your novel *The House of the Spirits*. Some feel that it is a remake of Márquez's novel replacing patriarchal authority with emphasis on matrilineal strength. How do your respond?

Allende: I belong to the first generation of writers of my continent who have been brought up reading other writers from Latin America. The previous generation, which we have called the "boom" generation, included such writers as García Márquez, José Donoso, and Carlos Fuentes. The phenomenon of the "boom" started in Barcelona. I was very privileged to be a part of the readers of the writers of that time. I grew up reading them, and when I started writing, I think that all those wonderful words, those images, that tone to narrate our continent was so deeply rooted in me that it just came right out in a very natural way. It was not my intention at all to create anything ironic about *One Hundred Years of Solitude* because I really admire that novel very much. I have read it a long time ago, and I don't remember it very well. But comparing *The House of the Spirits* with *One Hundred Years of Solitude* in the way that it is compared is totally unfair.

Iftekharuddin: What were the compelling reasons for writing *The Stories of Eva Luna* after the novel *Eva Luna*?

Allende: Well, several reasons. The first one was that many people questioned, when I finished the book, that Eva Luna is a storyteller, this is her story but where are the stories she tells? I had never considered the short story genre because I think it is very difficult. At the time, after I finished *Eva Luna,* I divorced my husband in Venezuela and went on a crazy lecturing tour that brought me to the United States. I ended up in northern California where I met a man and fell madly in love, so that's the reason too. I had to move to this country following a passionate heart; it was a very hectic time. The only advantage of short stories is that you work in fragments. I thought that since I had to go on working, the only thing I could do then was something brief. So, I thought that writing short stories that Eva Luna didn't tell in the book was a good idea.

Iftekharuddin: Almost every story in *The Stories of Eva Luna* has an epiphanic ending. Is this sudden awareness simply an awakening on the part of the character, or is there an imbedded socio-political message?

Allende: I don't try to give a message in anything I write. Sometimes there is a sort of surprise for me too because the characters come out with these endings; they come out with these things that happen to them in spite of myself. In some stories, I seem to know from the very beginning what the ending will be, but I know it at a gut level; I don't know it intellectually. If I would have to tell you the story before writing, I wouldn't know, but when I start writing, everything seems to flow in a very natural way and ends up in a surprise for me, except in one of the stories. It's called "The Little

Heidelberg." When I finished that story, my mother read it and said "I like the story, but this is a crappy ending." I thought she is right; there is something wrong with this ending. She couldn't tell me what was wrong, but I realized that I had not followed the instincts of the characters; I had tried to impose a happy ending, and it didn't work. So I just let the characters talk for themselves, and I got a very strange ending that is difficult to explain, but that's what they wanted.

Iftekharuddin: Was that the only story where you felt that you were being an intrusive author?

Allende: Yes, except for one other. The last story in this collection, which is the most elaborate story in the book, is called "And of Clay Are We Created"; and it is based on a real story. In 1985, there was a volcano eruption in Colombia and a little girl was trapped in the mud, and she died there after four days of terrible agony. I saw her on television in Venezuela, and I wrote this story. When I finished the story, I realized that I had tried to tell the story from an intellectual point of view, very passionate but it was my mind working. And then I realized that it wasn't the story of the little girl; it was the story of the man who was holding the little girl. So I rewrote the story once more, and when it was finished, I realized that there was something phony about it too. It wasn't the story of the man who was holding the girl; it was the story of the woman who is watching through a screen the man who holds the girl. This filter of the screen creates an artificial distance but also a terrible proximity because you see details that you would not see if you were actually there. And so, the story is about the change in the woman who watches the man holding the girl who is dying.

Iftekharuddin: Do you feel that aspiring short story authors should attempt to create that kind of a screen in order not only to distance themselves but also give themselves the ability to be introspective without being intrusive?

Allende: I think each author has a different approach. You cannot give a formula or a recipe because it won't work. What works for one story may not work for the other story. I think that in a short story the most important thing is to get the tone right in the first six lines. The tone determines the characters. In long fiction, it's plot, it's character, it's work, it's discipline—a lot of stuff that goes there. But in short stories, it's tone, language, suggestions—it's inspiration. So I don't have a recipe. That's why I don't like to write short stories; I hate them. I like to read them, but I don't like to write them. I would much rather write a thousand pages of a long novel than a short story. The shorter, the more difficult it is.

Iftekharuddin: Why don't you elaborate on what it is exactly that you find difficult about writing short stories?

Allende: The fact is that everything shows. In a novel, you can have a lot of knots and bad stitches, and if you are lucky, the charm of the tale will carry the book, and the reader will be trapped in the plot and in everything that happens there; it's like a party, an orgy. A short story is not; a short story has very brief time, very condensed concentrated plot, if there is a plot. The subtleties are important; the suggestion is important. You work with the reader's imagination, and your only tool is language, and there is no space or time for anything else. Everything shows. This is how I compare these genres: the novel being a very elaborate tapestry that has a lot of details, and you embroider it with threads of many colors without even knowing what the finished design is. A short story is like an arrow; you have only one shot, and you need the precision, the direction, the speed, the firm wrist of the archer to get it right. So, you do it right from the very beginning or just abandon it. Get it right the first time. How does one do it? I think that's where inspiration comes in, the muse. That's why I feel so uncomfortable with short story writing because I am not an inspired person; I am a hard working person. I don't mind spending twelve hours a day for a year writing fiction, but if I need the inspiration and I don't have it, I feel very distressed.

Iftekharuddin: Do you feel the impulse that it is time to write another short story?

Allende: I have not felt the impulse since 1987. But it may happen again in my life, depending on the circumstances. People are always asking me for short stories for some reason. The publishers don't like short stories. They think that they won't sell. However, the students seem to like them a lot. I get a lot of letters from them, and they always ask me for short stories. And you know what? The movie people want short stories because it is much easier to create a movie from a short story than from a novel.

Iftekharuddin: In the short story titled "Interminable Life," you write:

> There are all kinds of stories. Some are born with the telling; their substance is language, and before someone puts them into words they are but a hint of an emotion, a caprice of mind, an image, or an intangible recollection. Others are manifest whole, like an apple, and can be repeated infinitely without risk of altering their meaning. Some are taken

from reality and processed through inspiration, while others rise up from an instant of inspiration and become real after being told. And then there are secret stories that remain hidden in the shadows of the mind; they are like living organisms, they grow roots and tentacles, they become covered with excrescences and parasites, and with time are transformed into the matter of nightmares. To exorcise the demons of memory, it is sometimes necessary to tell them as a story.

Is this your definition of short story and also your process of writing short stories?

Allende: This is how I feel about fiction writing. I have had a tormented and long life, and many things are hidden in the secret compartments of my heart and my mind. Sometimes, I don't even know that they are there, but I have the pain—I can feel the pain; I can feel this load of stories that I am carrying around. And then one day I write a story, and I realize that I have delivered something, that a demon has come out and has been exorcised. It's not something that I do consciously, except in very few occasions, but when it happens, it's such a relief. That's how I feel about fiction. Some people do this in therapy, some people do it in meditation, some people do it drinking. My way of getting rid of the pain, my way of exorcising and understanding the world is writing fiction. Maybe that paragraph is about that; it's about all the demons and the angels that I have inside that I don't know that I have, and I have to bring them out into the light and talk to them and see them in the light.

Iftekharuddin: What are the sources of the experiences that you describe in your stories?

Allende: Most of them come from things that have really happened. Newspapers, television, radios, those are the great sources of inspiration for me. For example, that story we were talking about "And of Clay Are We Created" is something that I saw on television. Sometimes, it is something that I see very briefly in the news, and I start asking myself questions about it. In *The Stories of Eva Luna,* there is the story—I don't remember the title ["If You Touched My Heart"]—of a woman who is kidnapped by a man and put in a cellar where she spends fifty years. She never talks to anybody and becomes like an animal in the darkness. When she is finally rescued, she is transformed, sort of, into a horrible beast that has spent all her life in that cellar. I got this from a spot on television (in the news) in Venezuela. A jealous man had kidnapped a young woman and put her in a cellar where she spent fifty years. I saw her on television when they brought her out wrapped in a blanket. That was it; she was never again in the news. So, I started asking myself, why did it happen? Why didn't she scream? Why didn't she try to get out? How did she survive? By asking myself those questions over and over again, the story came out; the motivations of the story were in those questions. Other times, it's people who tell me things, and I look behind whatever they have told me. They tell me something that they think is a story, and I realize that that is not the story. The story is something that lies behind that or beyond that. Often, it's something that I guess. I have one story called "Our Secret." It is a story of two young people who meet, make love, and in the lovemaking they discover that both have been tortured in the same way. The experience of torture has marked them so profoundly that they can't completely make love and cannot relate to the world; they have been destroyed. This came from something that I saw once. I had just met a couple of young people, Chileans, in Venezuela. I saw that both had similar marks on their wrists. At the beginning, I thought that they had tried to commit suicide. Then I realized that they were both from Chile, both were exiles, and both were from the same generation: I started asking myself more and more questions about them. Finally, when I came up with the story, I thought this is just pathological. I am imagining these awful things; this can't be true. Later, I confronted my theory with the reality of their lives, and it was true.

Iftekharuddin: How do you then cloak fiction with truth or truth with fiction?

Allende: I can't trace the boundary. I think that everything is true, that fiction is just a way of saying something that is truthful from the very beginning. What is fiction? A bunch of lies, but it wouldn't work if those lies didn't come from a very honest truthful place inside you. Why do you want to write that story? Why do you want those characters and no other characters? That plot and no other plot? Because you are tapping into something that is your own experience, your own sentiments, your own emotions, your past, your biography, or a collective soul. And because you tap into that, the story is true and it works. When you don't, you have created this artificial fiction that is reassuring—the romance novels, the thrillers, and the mysteries—which are genres that don't work with truth, but they are also categorized as fiction, entertainment. But we are not talking about that; we are talking about something that is much deeper.

Iftekharuddin: Is Agua Santa your mythical town like William Faulkner's Yoknapatawpha or Sherwood Anderson's Winesburg, Ohio?

Allende: No, I feel much better with an undetermined place and undetermined time. I like the ambiguity when the story happens in a landscape that the reader can invent. If you think about it, the only thing that you know about Agua Santa is that it's hot. You don't know anything else about it; you don't know where it is; you don't know how it looks or how many people live there because I want that place to be not my mythical place, but the reader's mythical place. And that's the same treatment that I give my characters. Very seldom is there a physical description of a character in my writing because I want the reader to create the character. So I only describe what is absolutely essential for the story. The fact that a person is retarded, or has a harelip, or is very tall is told because, in a way, that is important to the story; otherwise, I wouldn't even say that. I don't even mention the age; you don't know whether they are young or old.

Iftekharuddin: How about those characters who are highly sensuous. There is overt sexuality in stories such as "Wicked Girl" or "Toad's Mouth." Are you asserting the notion of female body as text in these stories?

Allende: I wouldn't say that my stories are sexual; I wish they were. I really would like to write erotic novels. Unfortunately, I was raised as a Catholic, and my mother is still alive, so it's difficult. However, I feel that there is a part of me as a person that is extremely sensuous and sexual. Through that part of me, I can express certain truths that I cannot express otherwise. When I say sensuous, I don't mean sexual: for me sensuous includes food, texture, and smells. In all my stories and novels you will find smells because that is extremely important to me. A few days ago, I was given a doctorate in Maine, and the person who was putting the hood on me smelled wonderful. I got totally distracted; I couldn't think of the fact that I was receiving this doctorate, only of his smell. I would have followed that man to the end of the world because he smelled a certain way. Smell is very important to me; it's like nature, like sounds.

Iftekharuddin: In your stories the real and the hyperbolic blend. That puts you into the field of magic realism. You also have an acute female sensibility that we can detect. Some have observed the parodying of perhaps Pablo Neruda and Marquis de Sade. If you were to characterize yourself, would you call yourself a feminist writer?

Allende: Yes. First of all we should agree on the term feminist. Right now it is loaded with negative meanings for a lot of people. Because I am a woman and because I am an intelligent woman, excuse my arrogance, I have to be a feminist. I am aware of my gender; I am aware of the fact that being born a woman is a handicap in most parts of the world. In only very privileged societies, very privileged groups, have women achieved enough freedom and enough awareness to be able to fight for their rights. But in any circumstance, a woman has to exert double the effort of any man to get half the recognition. I want my daughter, my granddaughters, and my great granddaughters to live in a more gentle world. In a world where my son, my grandsons, and my great grandsons will also live in a much better place and where people can be companions and partners, where sex can be something that we will both enjoy greatly, and where love for ourselves, love for each other, and love for this planet will prevail. I think that is what being a feminist means, the awareness and the strength to fight for what you believe.

Iftekharuddin: The epigraph to your novel *The House of the Spirits* is a poem by Pablo Neruda where the poet raises the questions, "How long does a man spend dying?" Addie's father in Faulkner's *As I Lay Dying* may have already responded to that when he said that "the reason for living was to get ready to stay dead a long time." How would Alba, Eva Luna, or even you, respond?

Allende: I don't know about Alba or Eva Luna, but I know what I would respond. I think that the reason to live is to learn. We come here to experience through the body things that the spirit could not experience otherwise. So we need this body, and we have to transform this body into a temple of learning. It is difficult because our culture does not promote that at all. But I try to use my senses, my imagination, my body, my mind, and all the things that I have in this life to make the spirit grow. That's what we come for. If you think about it, there is silence before we are born and silence after death; life is just a lot of noise.

Iftekharuddin: Elvira in *Eva Luna* tells Eva, 'Your mother must have had a liquid womb to have given you that inventiveness you have to tell stories, little bird." Is that the secret of writing short stories?

Allende: That's one of the many dirty tricks. It's amazing. Sometimes these things just occur to me, and I write them down without ever thinking that anybody will even notice. For example, I write a food recipe. I just make it up and then people call me and say it didn't work. If I provide a beauty recipe saying that if you do this or that, it will make your hair blond, people believe it, but it's not true. It's just part of the tricks, and after all, all wombs are liquid when you are pregnant.

Iftekharuddin: Going back to the issue of asserting yourself as feminist, what is it that you don't want readers to view your work as? I hope it's never negative in the sense of not reading a piece of literature simply because it is viewed as feminist—that would destroy the essence of literature.

Allende: I don't know. Each reader has a different approach. I want my readers to be entertained. I want to grab them and seduce them into the reading. I want to invite them to this wonderful place where we can share a story, and I only give him or her half the story; the other half has to be recreated or created by the reader, and that is the space we are going to share. Sometimes in the stories there are political elements, social elements, feminist issues, or environmental issues. All the things I believe in come out, but I don't want to deliver messages. I don't have answers; I just have the questions, and I want to share the questions. On the other hand, labels are unavoidable when you have critics. Critics are terrible people. They will label you no matter what, and you have to be classified. I don't want to be called a feminist writer, a political writer, a social writer, a magic realism writer, or a Latin American writer. I am just a writer; I am a storyteller.

Iftekharuddin: Scheherazade not only saved her life through her stories, but also received the recognition of the Sultan. In essence, she brings herself into existence with words. Is Eva Luna your protagonist who brings "the female" into existence through words?

Allende: Yes. I also think that in a weird way Eva Luna is me or I am Eva Luna. She is a storyteller, and she creates herself; the reader doesn't know if he or she is reading Eva Luna's biography, what Eva Luna invents about herself, or the soap opera that she is writing. So there are three levels of writing and understanding this novel. I believe that in a certain way that's how my life has been. If you ask me to tell you my life, I will try, and it will probably be a bag of lies because I am inventing myself all the time, and at the same time I am inventing fiction, and through this fiction I am revealing myself. So these are the three levels through which my life happens. I can't say who I am because the boundaries, as I said before, between reality and fantasy are totally blurred.

Iftekharuddin: Are those the three levels that readers must also keep in mind when they read the collection of stories, *The Stories of Eva Luna*?

Allende: Don't keep in mind anything, just enjoy it.

Iftekharuddin: I think you are looking at a critic here.

Allende: Critic, just enjoy it.

Iftekharuddin: What do you think your narratives lose in translation?

Allende: My books have been translated into twenty-seven languages that I know of, but I also know of other translations that have not been authorized, for example Vietnamese and Chinese. I have no control over the official translations, let alone the ones that are not authorized. In English, French, and German, the translations I know are very good. Now, every time that I read aloud in English my own stories, I feel very uncomfortable. I think the translation is great; sometimes it sounds much better than in Spanish, but it's another story. I can only be myself in my own language. It's like making love, you know; I would feel ridiculous panting in English. I really need to express it in my own language. When I play with my grandchildren, it's always in Spanish. There is something that is playful and sensuous; it happens at a gut level, a very organic level that can only happen in your own language; it's like dreams.

Iftekharuddin: Is there something you cannot write about, a "demon of memory" that you cannot "exorcise"?

Allende: I don't know because I have been trying to exorcise them all and in the long run, I may achieve that if I have enough time, if I live long enough. I have a lot of demons. There are certain things that appear over and over in my writing that I can't avoid: they seem to be love and violence—two very strong issues in my life.

Iftekharuddin: You have written four novels and a collection of short stories. You have reached fame with these works. Is it time for another collection of short stories, you think?

Allende: You know, I have just finished another book that will be published soon. Now it's being translated. It's a sort of memoir. I think it's non-fiction; however, it reads like fiction. After finishing this book, I felt so exhausted, so drained, that I thought, well, I will spend six months without doing anything, and let's see what happens next. And there is a certain voice inside me saying why don't you just spend these six months thinking about short stories? But as I told you before, I really need inspiration and if it doesn't come . . .

Iftekharuddin: What's the title of this new work?

Allende: It's called *Paula*.

Iftekharuddin: What would you tell aspiring short story writers about writing short stories?

Allende: Don't. Write a novel; it's much easier—the longer the better. You will get a publisher, you will get an agent, and it will be much easier. It's much easier to write. Short stories are closer to poetry, to dreams than they are to long narratives. And I think that you need a very skilled writer. How many short stories can you remember? How many are memorable: How many have been transcendent? How many short story writers are really important writers only for their stories? It's because it's a very difficult genre, very difficult. So I would tell them, try with a novel first and when you have the skills, then you can write a short story. But people think it's the other way around. People think that if they can write a short story then eventually they will be able to write a novel. It's actually the other way around. If you are able to write a novel, someday with a lot of work and good luck you may be able to write good short story.

Iftekharuddin: You started off your career as a journalist. Has that made writing fiction easier for you, particularly the short story?

Allende: Yes, because I still use many of the techniques that I used as a journalist: for example interviewing people. As a writer of fiction, I believe that it is much better to research with interviews of real people who have experienced the event, whatever that event may be, than going to a library and looking at books. Through interviews you can come up with things that you will never find in a book. Journalists are in the streets hand in hand with people talking, participating, and sharing. Writers are very isolated people. They usually live protected under the big umbrella of a university or some institution, and they are disconnected from real life in the world. They end up writing for professors, students, and critics and forget that there is the world out there. So, my background as a journalist helps me in that way. And there is something else that helps enormously. As a journalist, you know, you have a few sentences with which to grab your reader, and you are competing with other media; you are competing with other articles in the same newspaper or whatever media you are using. So you have to be very efficient with language, and you have to remember that the first impor-tant thing is to have a reader. Without a reader, there is no text. Writers forget that; writers write for themselves. I am in that sense much more of a journalist. I will not write something that is just for myself except the last book which I recently wrote, a book that I wrote out of extreme pain. I could not have written anything else. When I wrote it, I was not thinking of publishing it. My daughter died recently; she was in a coma for a year, and I took care of her. During that year, everything stopped in my life. I had a year to revise my life, to ask myself the questions that I had been avoiding and go through the most excruciating pain. I think that I am still in that tunnel of pain, but the fact that I finished the book has been like a catharsis in many ways. So, when I started writing *Paula,* my only goal was to survive; that is the only time that I have written something without thinking of a reader.

Rudolfo A. Anaya

Farhat Iftekharuddin

Rudolfo A. Anaya was born in 1937 in a village named Pastura in eastern New Mexico. Anaya is an author, playwright, and editor. He is best known for his award-winning novel, *Bless Me, Ultima* (1972). His other works include *Heart of Aztlan* (1976), *Tortuga* (1979), *The Silence of the Llano*, short stories (1982), *The Legend of La Llorona* (1984) and *Lord of the Dawn: The Legend of Quetzalcoatl* (1987). He is the co-editor of a collection of essays, *Aztlan: Essays on the Chicano Homeland* (1989). Anaya has recently signed a six-figure book contract with Warner Books. Warner has already published a 1994 illustrated, hard-cover edition of the classic novel *Bless Me, Ultima*. Other works by Anaya by Warner Books are *Alburquerque* (reprint of 1992 novel), *Zia Summer* (1995), and *Rio Grande Fall* (1996). Long overdue, Rudolfo Anaya is now recognized as a major, powerful, contemporary Mexican American writer.

Iftekharuddin: Do you feel that Mexican American literature is gaining more prominence in American universities?

Anaya: Recently it seems that some of the high schools are beginning to take our texts into the schools. For some time now, some teachers at the university level have introduced our works. There is a new interest in multicultural literature, so teachers are now searching for our titles and new writers in the field of Mexican American literature.

Iftekharuddin: To what would you attribute this pronounced interest?

Anaya: I don't think it's pronounced. I think there is the beginning of an interest. I think the country has just awakened to the fact that it has within its borders people of different nationalities and different heritages. In our region, the fact that there is more immigration from the south of the border has awakened people. In large populated states such as Texas and California, teachers are looking for literature that they can share with their Chicano students, perhaps literature that has more relevancy to their daily lives. So, that has caused a new interest at the teaching level.

Iftekharuddin: You have written several novels and a collection of short stories. Do you feel more comfortable writing in the long form or in the short form?

Anaya: I feel comfortable doing either one. The question is, which one am I more often in? I think that most often I am writing novels. Having discovered my love for the novel, it's difficult for me to leave that genre. I love the short story, and I am aware of the differences. One idea calls to be a short story and another the novel, but most often I like the larger exploration, expansion, and development that the novel allows as opposed to the short story which has to be more of a gem.

Iftekharuddin: Perhaps you could elaborate on that and give us a definition of what the short story is?

Anaya: When I get the image or the idea for a story, it dictates to me what it will be. It will either be a short story, a play, or a novel. The image, the idea, and the characters tell me almost immediately what they are going to be in. Are they going to be on stage? Do they have much to discover about their lives that should be revealed through a novel? Or will the character say "look at me only for this instant in my life or for this theme, for this one time." For this more intimate and shorter look I use the short story. For me, the short story has to do with intimacy; the characters describe that. It has also to do a lot with setting. An important element for me is the voice, the voice that I hear that tells me how to write the story, how the story should be narrated. That voice is different for a short story and a novel.

Iftekharuddin: In a review of Hawthorne's *Twice-Told Tales,* Poe made several key observations about the short story. He stated that below the surface of stories "a strong undercurrent of suggestion runs continuously." Regarding brevity, he said readers must be able to read a story at one sitting or the story will lose "the immense force derivable from totality"; the story must have a "unique or single effect"; it must contain a "pre-established design"; and that the reader must read it with a "kindred art." Do you agree with any or all of these statements? Is there one more of Poe's observations that you would emphasize over the others?

Anaya: Parts of Poe's definition are applicable, and I suppose that there are writers that have read Hawthorne and said that is how they want to write. Any one of Poe's elements could be blown up and become central. Minimalism has reduced the short story to one paragraph which you can read in one sitting. Is that what Poe had in mind? Of course not. For me the crucial element in the story continues to be the haunting by the voices that ask to have their story told; that voice translates into characters. Who are the characters that come to me and for what reason? In a novel you can have multiple characters and much development. In a short story, it's usually one person, one voice that I hear, and it says "tell my story."

Iftekharuddin: Are these compelling "voices" the impulse that made you decide to write the collection of short stories *The Silence of the Llano.*

Anaya: In each story that I write, there is a singular character whose story has to be told. I concentrate on the story of a character and let the elements of fiction work themselves out.

Iftekharuddin: How do you see the future of the short story as a genre?

Anaya: The publishing world doesn't publish short story collections. Unless that changes, the future is not optimistic. We should be grateful to small presses that continue to publish collections of short stories. If you look for magazines that used to include short stories, they're not around anymore. What we need to do if there is to be a brighter future for short stories is to get more aggressive as writers with magazines and publishers and ask why they are not publishing short stories. Why aren't those markets being developed? There is a market where short stories can be promoted, but I think the publishing industry thinks it's not a paying market. This presents a greater problem for minority writers whose works don't get published in the more respected publications. You find few stories by Chicanos, Chicanas, Native Americans, or other ethnic groups. If you check the catalog of major publishing companies, you will not find collections of stories by minority writers. I know there is a great need in the schools for stories by minority writers. Teachers have a need, but they don't have the collections. So, there's a lot of work to be done.

Iftekharuddin: What role do you envision Mexican American authors playing in promoting the future of the short story?

Anaya: I think our role is limited because we ourselves have only recently had access into some of the major trade publishers. We have been relegated either to publish with our own small presses or with the small independent presses around the country. So, it comes down to the question of who has the palanca as we say in Spanish, the leverage. We keep emphasizing to publishers that we have a lot of writers who have produced a lot of exciting work, and that they have a responsibility to look at that work and begin to recycle those stories back into the schools because there is a large population now of not only Mexican Americans, but also Asian Americans, Native Americans, and representatives of other countries who are dying to get stories by minority writers. They are eager to encounter part of themselves in the stories, a reflection of what the story brings to them. Both as writers and educators, we have to work to remedy the situation.

Iftekharuddin: What are the sources of the experience that you describe in your stories?

Anaya: The primary source has to do with the fact that I am a New Mexican. A great portion of my growing up has been fashioned and molded by the oral tradition and values of my community. I listened to stories as a kid; this was before we had television and very little radio. We were exposed to a great deal of storytelling. That oral tradition fed my imaginative self. Sometimes it is dreams; sometimes it is the subconscious; it is that place where the spirits enter to speak. If you have an "openness" to creation, you hear those voices. Most of that has to do with my environment. I write about the people of New Mexico and their experiences. I like to explore the value system, the beliefs of my community. We are the first generation of Chicano writers. We had no Chicano literature in written form when we went to school. It's important for us to go to our oral tradition and use it to infuse our literature with our values, and share what we write with the community.

Iftekharuddin: The oral tradition of storytelling is in decline. How do you feel that is going to impact Mexican American writers? Where do you think they ought to turn for their inspiration?

Anaya: One always turns within. There is no where else to go. You have to listen to yourself, and then you write out of that experience. I think one of the things that affects both our literary and oral tradition is the fact that we have been able to swing back and forth between those two traditions. Those of us who write in the Chicano community are the storytellers; we are the *cuentistas*. Tradition has not really been broken; we have only stepped from an oral storytelling setting around the kitchen table to writing it down on paper and sharing it with a wider community.

Iftekharuddin: To what extent do you rely upon mythology?

Anaya: All of my work is infused with the mythic: questions about good and evil, our origins, our stories, our legends, our heroes, our heroines. These interest me because they shaped me. Growing up in a small Hispanic village near the river in a very open country, in a very Catholic world, filled me with the need to explore the mythic. So, the symbols that I develop, whether they be in the novel or the short story, not only enlighten me, but also enlighten my characters. For me, writing is a way of enlightenment. At the time that I write a short story, not only should my character come to a brief, perhaps momentary, illumination, but so should I the writer. That is perhaps one reason why I write; in the exploration of the character, I also come to that brief enlightenment, that epiphany that helps me along in my path of life.

Iftekharuddin: In your article "Aztlan: A Homeland without Boundaries" from the collection of essays that you edited titled *Aztlan: Essays on the Chicano Homeland,* you state that "myth" is our umbilical connection to the past, to the shared "collective memory." How are you defining myth here? Also, the "collective memory" you speak about, is it the "collective memory" of Mexican Americans or the "collective memory" that all of us share from our pasts?

Anaya: The collective memory is shared by all of us. We are connected to our ancestors because of a common link. Our births are connected to the first cell that had stirred somewhere on earth, and further back to the first moment of the creation of the cosmos. We share in that consciousness. As we evolved, we told stories, and the stories that we told a million years ago, whether they were just sounds or scratched on the cave walls, are part of our inheritance. The symbols that began to be laid down for us to orient ourselves to each other, to the earth and to the universe are part of that mythic element. They speak to something deep within ourselves that helps us to understand ourselves and to connect us. That connection is important; I don't subscribe to the fact that we are alienated human beings, that some-how this is the first generation on earth. I think that's nonsense. We have ancestors; we have a history. In myth, we understand the symbols that help to center us, to orient us, and make us better human beings, better in the present moment and also better for the future.

Iftekharuddin: The female characters in your short stories, when they appear, exude tremendous strength, following anguish and pain at the hands of masculine characters. They survive nonetheless, and ultimately it is the male characters who seem to learn and to recognize the strength of the female characters. Is that deliberate on your part to first point to the traditional thought that the Hispanic female is subordinate to the Hispanic male, and then assert that is time to consider the Hispanic females as equal to their counterparts?

Anaya: It works on many levels. It has to do not only with my immediate cultural ways and traditions that I observed growing up in a Hispanic culture, but also with the fact that the writer reflect not only the immediate but also on the universal. When I explore the feminine, and the feminine is not just the woman of my culture, the feminine is the universal. How does the feminine play a role in my own life? I have often asked myself why so many of the guides in my works are women. I think because the feminine has an intuitive side that is more in touch with our mythic elements than men that I meet in my life. So, most often, I am attracted to the knowledge of women and what they have to share. It's something that I find natural to explore.

Iftekharuddin: In your collection of short stories, *The Silence of the Llano,* you deal among other things with the plight of the less-fortunate Mexican Americans and their struggle with assimilation. Your protagonists have little or no formal education, yet they speak with wisdom that often-time surpasses knowledge acquired through education. Whose voices are we hearing in these stories?

Anaya: I think that as much importance as we give to formal education and as much as we wish our children to acquire a liberal education because it is a means to survive in any society, we sometimes forget that people without that education have also acquired the substantial knowledge that we need to know ourselves, a kind of spiritual knowledge that all people posses whether they are formally educated or not. If some of my farmers, *vaqueros* (cowboys), or men and women who are from the working class speak with that kind of wisdom, it is because I have heard that wisdom in my community, from my parents, uncles, aunts, grandfathers, and neighbors. As a child, I was in awe of them because they taught me to look into something that is deeper than formal education. The yearning that I had for spiritual fulfillment came as much from those people as from the philosophers and writers I read as an undergraduate student. I never underplay the role of the people I write about; I think they have as much wisdom as anyone I know.

Iftekharuddin: What is it that you always keep in mind while writing a short story? That is, if you were instructing creative writing student, what would you tell them?

Anaya: I would tell them to listen to that character who wants a story told. We are the medium of those flashes of insight, images, or words that come to us and suddenly illuminate another person's life. As we extend ourselves to write about that life, we have to keep the character who initiated the insight in mind. The idea of the characters and how they visit us and how we become not only the dream-catchers, but also the character-catchers of the universe is important. So the writer has to open up to receiving those stories. If you can just sit down and be enraptured by someone whose story you know you have to tell because that's your responsibility, then you can learn narration and dialogue.

Iftekharuddin: When students approach you with the question, should I write a short story or should I write a novel, what do you tell them?

Anaya: That's a difficult one. As I explained earlier that the idea for the story, often generated by the character, brings its form with it. I always seem to know whether it is to be a play, a novel, or a short story. I don't think you can teach that; it's something that you have to be open to. The character will guide you into the events that will become either a short story or a novel. I get the impulse to write, and I know what it's going to be. I don't dictate it. It comes to me in the package that the character brings.

Iftekharuddin: Are your stories didactic in nature?

Anaya: Yes and no, in the sense that everything is didactic. If my writing is my way of knowledge, my way of exploring myself in the universe, it has to be didactic. What I find that illuminates me in the story that I wrote, I hope also illuminates the reader.

Iftekharuddin: What's next for Rudolfo Anaya?

Anaya: I am working on three novels, believe it or not. One will come out in the summer of '95, and one in the summer of '96. Both of these are in manuscript form needing revision. In the meantime, I jumped into this short little novel which I call *The Prophet*. It's about a man who is a prophet and comes to a city to teach. It's didactic.

Iftekharuddin: Is there a voice telling you to write short stories again?

Anaya: My short story voice has been in abeyance for a while. I have been writing children's short stories, which is a form, I think, of the short story. In the past year or two, I have written over a dozen, and I have two coming out next year in children's picture books. So, the short story voice has taken a little curve into the realm of children. I want to write for them and share my ideas and characters with them.

Iftekharuddin: I think then, you are going back to oral tradition because children love being read to.

Anaya: That's very true. I find that more and more in the schools that I visit. A lot of the invitations that I am getting now are from elementary schools, and I love it. I take my little collection of stories, and I go down and sit in a circle with the children and read. That is the oral storytelling. Whether one uses the manuscript or not, the oral tradition is alive and well in this kind of a classroom setting because one is sharing with the children.

Iftekharuddin: Those stories then become a part of their collective memory.

Anaya: Absolutely.

Arturo Arias

Cheryl A. Roberts

Arturo Arias is professor of Humanities at San Francisco State University. He is co-writer of the screenplay for the film *El Norte* (1984), and his most recent book in English is titled *After the Bombs* (Curbstone Press, 1990). Author of four novels in Spanish—*After the Bombs* (1979), *Itzam Na* (1981), *Jaguar en Llamas* (1989) and *Los Caminos de Paxil* (1991)—and winner of the Casa de Las Americas Award and the Anna Segher's Scholarship for two of them, he is a specialist on ethnic issues, a subject that is a central theme in both his fiction and his academic work. He has recently completed a new novel in Spanish—*Cascabel*—and two books of literary criticism, one on Guatemalan 20th century fiction, *La identidad de la palabra,* and another one on contemporary Central America fiction, *Gestos Ceremoniales.* He is also preparing another novel in Spanish, *Sopa de caracol* and an academic book on Central American systems of thought.

Roberts: I wanted to start with a little of your own background and ask how you became a writer. What led you to become a writer?

Arias: Well, I always liked to write, or rather, I liked the storytelling aspects that eventually one writes down, since I was a child. I lived in a middle class family in Guatemala City and like most middle class families at the time, because times have changed—that was the '50s—my family had two live-in maids, and the maids were both Mayan. When I was a little kid, my parents both worked, so I lived with the maids most of the time, and they would always tell me these wonderful stories. I loved the storytelling aspect of it. And ever since I learned to write, which must have been like nine, I began writing stories. Obviously, I wasn't thinking of being a professional writer, but I was writing stories. And then, eventually, when I was a teenager, like 16 or 17, and had to decide what I was going to do with the rest of my life, I had a moment of choice and epiphany. I said, "I'll just study literature and the hell with anything else. If I starve, I starve." And my mother said, "You will starve, son." And I said, "That's ok, ma." She's told me that she and my father decided to start saving money, just in case I couldn't make ends meet. But they were supportive. They never told me I shouldn't do it. And then, I began writing in a more systematic way, and it just took off from there.

Roberts: So you started with stories that would be considered short stories, so is that why you selected that genre? You've written a novel, at least one.

Arias: Well, to tell you the truth, I'm more of a novelist than a short story writer. They might be stories, but they're like shaggy dog stories, so they become very long. I actually have published four novels, I have a fifth one that's finished, and I'm presently working on my sixth one. But only one so far has been translated into English.

Roberts: *After the Bombs*?

Arias: *After the Bombs*. And *Los Caminos de Paxil* is in the process of being translated; I don't know if the title will be *The Paths to Paxil* or not, but at least that's the working title. So far that's all of mine—well, there's short stories in different anthologies of Central American fiction floating here and there, but I do work more on the novel than on the short story.

Roberts: What interests me especially is how Guatemalan history has influenced your development as a writer, particularly the 1944–54 Revolution and then the Counterrevolution. Does this provide primarily a setting or is this the actual theme, is this what you really want to talk about?

Arias: Well, that's certainly what I talk about. It's a process: it's not only the '44–54 period. That's what's there in my first novel, in *After the Bombs*, and what happened in that period informs the subsequent history of Guatemala and by extension, the subsequent history of my own literature. It's very central to the degree that I feel that in many countries in Latin America, and Guatemala is certainly no exception, political events shape people's lives and identities. And not just at an abstract or ideological level, but at a very personal level. I remember that happening in my family. My father was a minor functionary in the Arbenz government. He did not disappear, as does the father in the novel, but he did lose his job and we went through very hard economic times. My family always in secret, because of repression, spoke against the military dictatorship. My father taught me to hate the military, to espouse democratic values, and to resist authoritarianism, principles of patriotism, nationhood, and all of that. But that happened on a very daily basis in my exchange with my parents and uncles and aunts, since down there the family is not nuclear but extended—I interacted almost daily with all of them—in almost a conspiratorial sense. We were always taught that what you say in the house, you cannot say in public or we'll all get in trouble and things like that. So that informs a great deal of what your own identity is. And you begin experiencing that reality yourself in one way or another. I did not live the anecdote, for example, that appears of the rape scene in *After the Bombs,* but other friends did. And I lived analogous situations that were scary enough. To give you one concrete detail, the first time ever I had a date as a teenager, that my father lent me his car. It's hard enough to simply have your father's car and to have your first date without having to do it in a context like Guatemala City! So here I'm going with my date to wherever we were going and there is a military control. They immediately put machine guns to our heads and asked us to step out of the car. They searched the car to see if we have any subversive materials or weapons. They find none; then they start searching us to see if we have any weapons and in the process of searching my date, they begin fondling her and molesting her. It did not get to the extremes that I say in the novel, but it was uncomfortable and unpleasant enough for both her and myself. And the sense of impotence and anger, of like, there's nothing I can do, because they have the weapons and the power. Of course that was the end of the date. We went home. She was traumatized, she was crying. So those things affect you at a very personal level. It's not just the abstraction of the regime; it's a cumulous of daily events. And obviously they become a primary source for literature, but it is because of that I think that Guatemala is no exception. If you're born in South Africa, prior to what's happened now, or in any other authoritarian regime, there's really no separation between daily life and politics. They just become totally enmeshed into one, and so when you are writing, even about that which is most personal, it becomes political.

Roberts: And there's no real effort needed to elevate an incident like that into allegory, because it is, in a way, already allegorical.

Arias: It is.

Roberts: People are impotent—there's nothing they can do.

Arias: Exactly. Absolutely.

Roberts: In the part of the book called "Funeral for a Bird," I notice that the story starts out with Max naming things, being obsessed with the names of things. What's the significance of that?

Arias: Well, I think that there's a lot of power in words, which is one of the themes that also runs in the book. That scene to me will tie up with a much later scene where Maximo is with Ana Marina and tells her that he will build a cathedral of words and in the word, everything, outside the word, nothing, and that with his words he will make the generals disappear. To me there's that continuity about the role of language. Language is what basically frames, not only your identity but the world in which you live, the world in which you operate. And so the first step for me in that is to learn the names of things. To learn, ok, this is a radio, this is a TV, this is a university building—to learn the basic stuff that gives a sense and meaning both spatially and temporally to the world in which you operate. And then you come to understand the reality in which you live; even if there is some matter out there, it's basically the names you give to things and how you relate to things through words. And that process of learning, to me, is basic for someone who will eventually become a writer, which is certainly the case of Maximo in the novel. So to begin to name becomes important. But then there's the other side, to make it slightly more complex, which is that one of the allegories of the New World is, of course, that you're always naming things. When the Spanish conquistadors arrived, they named things. Then when Mayans resist, they rename things and go back to the old names before the conquest. And so naming becomes also a means of empowerment. It's charged with symbolic meaning. And that is very, very present in our daily life. Just little things, like in 1992, for us it wasn't a celebration of the 500th anniversary of the conquest of the Americas, but it was rather marking the passing of a civilization, and the encounter of two worlds, if you want to be diplomatic about it. But in how you name it is where meaning resides, and how you relate to that particular reality. And so that's where I'm trying to go with that.

Roberts: And important, too, is who has the power to do the naming.

Arias: Exactly.

Roberts: At the same time, from a linguistic viewpoint, the ability to name things gives you power, but it also limits you since once you learn certain names for things you may in fact be unable to see them from any other perspective, which means that the more languages you speak, and you speak at least three—right?

Arias: I speak four.

Roberts: Do you speak a Mayan language?

Arias: No, no, I don't. I speak Spanish, English, French, and Portuguese. And I do not speak a Mayan language.

Roberts: I thought maybe the maids had taught you. . . .

Arias: I should, but I don't. No, the maids didn't teach me. They spoke to me in Spanish and Quiche, which is the language I would still love to learn. It's so difficult that I've never gotten around to it. In fact, I have used Quiche phrases and even whole paragraphs in some of my later novels, but I've always done it working with a Quiche Mayan with me.

Roberts: Let me revert to something I was thinking of earlier, which is who are you writing for?

Arias: It's a good question. I think that primarily for myself, secondarily to leave traces of civilization, I suppose, about Guatemala. The obvious answer would be I'm writing for the Guatemalan people. And that would be a very nice, comfortable cliché answer, except that the Guatemalan people don't know how to read. Guatemalans are 80% illiterate and of the 20% that know how to read and write, their reading ability doesn't go beyond the third grade elementary level for most of them. So the Guatemalan people who could actually read me—not necessarily that they do read me—but that could actually read me is like 2, maximum 3% of the population. So to a large degree, my audience, in a very, very funny way, which I think is particular to small places like Guatemala that are almost invisible dots in the universe, is international, is kind of telling the rest of the world that there is such a place like Guatemala. You know, just now with the death of Jacqueline Kennedy Onassis, in the news they replayed the ending of the song of Camelot, in which it says how you gotta tell the world that there was once a place named Camelot and it was like this and like that. And that kind of echoed in me, because that's how I write, to tell the world that there was once a place called Guatemala, that was like this and like that, and whose passing I always suspect, because it is such an unviable entity as a nation. And it is in such a process of implosion and self-destruction, even ecologically to—What used to be one of the greenest and most beautiful countries on earth is now beginning to become barren ground—that I can conceive Guatemala passing in my lifetime. To some degree, my literature is like a little monument to what was once, to leave a trace of its existence for whomever might want to pick up those signals in the future. If there is a future.

Roberts: I would like to know who your heroes are in terms of writing. Who has influenced you?

Arias: Well, there are so many that it would become a long, long list. So trying to abridge it a little, I would say that a major figure is Julio Cortázar, because Cortázar encompasses both of the things that I've tried to do, which is on the one hand, be a very serious writer and take literature seriously. Seriously not in lacking humor—on the contrary—but in developing the craft of fiction in as thorough and solid a way as possible while being someone who politically is very present in terms of bearing witness, in terms of solidarity, and in terms of militating, when need be, without ever embracing dogmatism or anything of the sort, and in fact remaining always very critical in naming its danger even within the Latin American left, to give it a name. And so I've always admired that overall trajectory of his and the fact that he loves humor and he likes the surrealist. And I like to do a literature that is humorous. I like what he said once in an interview, that humor was the most serious thing there was. And so he's a major figure and he influenced a Salvadoran poet named Roque Dalton whom I admire very much, too, who is also a very, very funny poet, who became a guerrilla fighter and was killed in the '70s and left one great posthumous novel that has not yet been translated to English. It would be called *What a Poor Little Poet I Used to Be.* It's a satire, a very humorous satire of young Central American writers who are adrift, who are mainly bohemians and drink a lot, quote lines from poets, and who basically are going nowhere. I like him very much, too. And I think from Central America, he's been a figure. Then of course there's a grandfather figure or if you prefer a father figure, that I also have to kill in order to find a place for myself under the sun—Asturias, who without question looms very big in there and casts a giant shadow. I don't like all of his stuff, but his best still awes me—*Men of Maize, Mulatat.* So those would be names, but when I was a young writer, Joyce was also a very important figure. I really nurture myself through the modernists, especially Joyce and Proust, very significant writers that I've admired. And even though now I don't go back and reread them as often as I did when I was in my 20s, they certainly are markers in my life passage.

Roberts: You've sort of internalized them.

Arias: Absolutely.

Roberts: Although I don't think there is a definitive agreement on what makes a short story, lots of critics suggest that there's always some unifying theme, that there's a singularity to the story, which may represent any number of things, but the story itself tends to be a sort of unity which expresses one thought. What would be that one thought in "Funeral for a Bird"?

Arias: Well, it's a good question, but I think that in "Funeral for a Bird," it would be the inability, if you will, of the children to come to terms with the enormity of the atrocities amidst which they live. So they have to bring that down to a scale in which they can deal with it. You know, they're surrounded by corpses, and so corpses lose meaning. They become anonymous. But the one bird that they see, it's small and it's something that they can deal with. That gives them the means of expressing all the grief and all that feeling that they simply could not express given the enormous magnitude of repression. Not only could they not literally "carry all those corpses," but I think all human beings have to deny to some degree a great many atrocities when they become too unbearable. You have to bring it down to something small and meaningful in which you can express it all and bring it all out. I think that symbolically that's what the children do in burying the bird, ignoring all those corpses that litter the streets and just picking up the one bird and burying that one bird.

Roberts: Would you say that the same theme comes through in the story of "Woman in the Middle"? That there's a sort of denial?

Arias: Yes, I think that there is that. One of the running themes, not the only one, but one of the running themes in a lot of my fiction is how to come to terms with the magnitude of the violence in a country like Guatemala. How do you deal with it? Or how do you deny it and try to escape from it? which becomes the other side of the coin. But I do think that that's very much central.

Roberts: I could see pretty clearly how the violence of the Counterrevolution, the invasion and so on of 1954, appears in these stories. Would you say that the violence today with left and right wing guerrilla and death squads is a different sort of violence?

Arias: No, I think it's the consequences of it. Basically, the invasion of '54, to tell the story as shortly as possible, brought about 31 years of military dictatorship. That dictatorship, in its turn, thus generated a process of resistance, that at first was just passive and ultimately became armed, and that brought about a civil war. The civil war did not resolve the crisis because neither side won militarily. By virtue of exhaustion of warfare, a negotiated pact had to be done and that began in the mid-1980s. Even though a real peace treaty won't be signed until maybe next year, the process of negotiating the conflict began in the mid-1980s. But a lot of the contradictions that were generated by both the period of dictatorship and then the civil war—contradictions such as discrimination against and racism against the Mayan population, the enormity of the atrocities followed by no accountability, no commission of truth afterwards, the fact that the repressors are still in positions of power—all of that has thus generated now a sort of war of attrition. It is no longer right vs left, in the classic sense, as it was in the early '80s, at the peak of the civil war. Now it's just anybody against anybody, settling their own accounts on their own. And so now you have a situation in which there might be, for example, an old leftist who moves back to Guatemala and the military tells him it's cool, no problem, we have nothing against you. But then there's an old sergeant, somewhere out there, that really dislikes this person for past deeds and then one day comes and kills this person. It wasn't that the army ordered this person murdered, and it wasn't part of a total plan of repression that happened ten years ago. Now it's just this very selective, almost random process, which makes it even harder to some degree. Because at least ten years ago, fifteen years ago, you knew on which side you were, and therefore you knew who would come after you and you could deal with it. Now it's much more gray, much more fragmented and ambiguous.

Roberts: Not the absolute polarization, but members of small groups . . .

Arias: Absolutely. But I do think that the whole thing is the legacy of '54, without question, because what '54 did was prevent the real creation of a democratic nation. It bottled up that process and polarized it for way too long.

Roberts: Do you blame the United States in part or in whole?

Arias: For '54? Yes. Which doesn't mean that I go about today, 1994, yelling "Down with yanqui imperialism!" But certainly for '54. One of the sad aspects about it is that we were victims of the Cold War, because truly Guatemala was like a fly roaming around an elephant. It's such a tiny country and so fragile and powerless, but in the context of the Cold War and the hysteria of the '50s and McCarthyism, it was a process that could not be tolerated and so the U.S. fomented that whole process. Without the U.S. there would have been no invasion—there would have been always a local right wing that would have eventually had to accommodate themselves to the process that was in place. And since what was in place then was what we would now call a social democracy—it was never a revolutionary left in power—

they would have eventually settled in their own place. But that's precisely what was prevented from happening. The invasion, without question, was a consequence of how the U.S. saw the world, the entire world, as a bipolar rivalry between the U.S. and the U.S.S.R. at that time, and in which no space could be left alone. Of course, the U.S. learned its lesson in Vietnam, too; it was part of that whole process.

Roberts: It may have. It may not have learned anything. Let me get back to your work, although I think that the history is fascinating, and of course has a lot to do with your work. You mentioned some of the themes that your writing revisits. Are there themes that haven't been mentioned yet that you wanted to talk about?

Arias: Well, themes have evolved in my work in various ways, but I think that one that begins to appear in *After the Bombs,* that might be implicit in "Woman in the Middle" but is certainly in my other novels that have not been translated yet to English, is the significance of Mayan culture and the implications of racism in Guatemala. Though we've used the image of Guatemala being like South Africa, we could now say like apartheid South Africa, since South Africa has changed. Guatemala still has not in this respect. It is a society, not of black and whites, but of mestizos and Mayans, which operated in analogous fashion. Mayans are thoroughly discriminated against and prevented from enfranchising themselves and perceived as a threat by the majority of the mestizo population—obviously not everybody, but especially the sector in power. That has really been also a central issue in the unraveling of Guatemala and the whole process of empowerment and growth of Mayan consciousness and reaffirmation of Mayan culture. I think that despite the enormous setbacks and the extremely high price that Mayans have paid for this process, since they have put most of the dead, they are in an ascendancy. Their movement is reaffirming itself more and more. I think that the fact that Rigoberta Manchu won a Nobel prize in 1992 is just one symbol of that whole process. And I do think that if it doesn't get dealt with in Guatemala, we will have another civil war and this time it'll be a racial war. When things become polarized, even people like myself who would obviously cast their lot with the Mayans but who are not Mayans—I am mestizo—would have to stand on the sidelines, because when that becomes polarized, you just can't be in the middle. And that's a topic that continues to operate in my work as I move on into newer novels. Another issue that I think appears in a clearer way than in *After the Bombs* in my latter work is men-women relations. They concern me, on a personal basis, but also on a larger basis—the nature of eroticism and of male-female relationships in a context of a traditional machista society and how that has begun to evolve and change, too, because it has. That's also an issue that appears in a more explicit and reflective way in my latter novels. And the last thing, a newer theme that's beginning to emerge recently, is the collapse of the Latin American left in the sense of loss of utopian dreams and people who believed in the revolution almost as a mystical experience, who all of a sudden are bereft of their beliefs and who are cast adrift and who now are wondering what to do with their lives and with themselves and lost at sea. I know people who have gone into alcoholism and into drugs, into sexual binges, just kind of lost, not knowing where to turn next. And into religious fundamentalism. That's a newer theme that's beginning to appear in the novel I'm working on now, but also in the one that I've just finished that hasn't come out yet in Spanish either.

Roberts: That would be your current work. We've talked primarily about you as an author, but what about you as a critic?

Arias: Well, there's that. One of the funny things about Central America literature is that there's very little criticism about it. In general, I don't think that there's abundant criticism about Latin American literature. Nonetheless, the amount of criticism that does exist about the major Latin American countries—Mexico, Argentina, Chile to some extent—simply dwarfs anything that might exist about Central America. As a result, I have—not only because I make a living at it, but because I see it as the other side of myself—the need to do a critical evaluation of Central American literature and to make it come into existence from a critical point of view. It's funny, it's almost like an invisible literature to the degree that it's not addressed critically, it doesn't exist. It's not in the bibliographies, it's not on the MLA panels, it's not named, and so it has to be named. That's the process in which I'm engaged as a critic and to which all my work, my recent academic work, has turned, which is also difficult. I just finished a book on Guatemalan fiction and it's so specialized that it's very hard to publish. It's the Catch-22 of the entire process, but it has to be done, nonetheless—to be named, to be placed on the literary map and to be recognized. One of the things that I see especially from the optic of the First World, both the U.S. and Europe, is that only the larger Latin American countries are ever recognized—again, using Mexico and Argentina emblematically—or else single individual writers that for one reason or another have had international recognition—García Márquez, Vargas Llosa, Isabel—but never placed in the context of their own literatures. You know many people in the U.S. or Europe might have read García Márquez but they haven't read a single other Colombian writer, nor do they know how García Márquez fits within the structure of Colombian literature.

Roberts: I think he's generally even just called a Latin American author.

Arias: Exactly—not even Colombian.

Roberts: Which might be interesting, for Central America, although geographically a small place, is extraordinarily diverse. Guatemala must have the most homogeneous Mayan population and Costa Rica is largely—

Arias: The most homogeneous Hispanic population!

Roberts: Not even Mayan at all.

Arias: In the sense of derivative of Spain.

Roberts: And British Honduras, now Belize, which doesn't even speak Spanish.

Arias: Exactly.

Roberts: And so trying to critique or to comment on the body of literature must be fascinating, looking for the things that unify it and still recognizing the diversity.

Arias: Yes, and especially naming the heterogeneity, because it's there, and recognizing heterogeneity as a defining characteristic of it.

Roberts: Really, that is unique in Latin America.

Arias: Absolutely. And one really interesting aspect too is that now there are a lot of really good women writers—Giaconda Belli in Nicaragua, Claribel Alegria from El Salvador, Gloria Guardia from Panama, Carmen Naranjo from Costa Rica—who are doing major work and who have placed the Central American woman at the center of the literary scene but here, that's still not—Claribel is just beginning to exist here. But she's the only one so far.

Roberts: It's remarkable.

Arias: Absolutely.

Roberts: I think we're running out of time. Is there anything else that you would like to say about your own work, on your own interests?

Arias: I have so many; it's hard to narrow down because there are so many things I like to do and have done that at times it's hard to fit within definable categories. I've published in anthropological journals and in anthropological books. I co-wrote the script for *El Norte,* which has been my one forage into cinema. I've published political science articles. For someone who looks at it with the eyes of a specialist in the traditional academic sense, I must be an extremely weird and esoteric character—I do fiction, I do criticism, I do social sciences, I do philosophy, but for me it's all part of the same. The issue is not the genre, but again, the naming of the reality of Guatemala, and sometimes you do it in different ways and you find different means of expressing it. But to me it's all the same, and it doesn't really make a difference. It does make a difference, but I mean it's not a contradiction to write, say, an essay that deals with politics of Guatemala for a political science journal and then do a novel and then collaborate in a film, because they're all dealing with the same process which is naming that reality, recording it, and trying to raise the consciousness of its existence to other people. One of the things that I feel about Guatemala is that, like Jews, we went through our Holocaust, but unlike them, that Holocaust is not recognized. It doesn't exist because it's not named. Yet we've lived it. We know our dead. And they really did die, but no one knows that in the rest of the world. To be able to bring that out, to be able to create a consciousness of that historical process for me becomes absolutely fundamental and that explains, I think, my own diversity, and having one foot in one thing and one foot in another, something else.

Roberts: But you think of yourself primarily as a novelist?

Arias: I think of myself primarily as a novelist, yeah, as a storyteller. They're all stories. Even when I'm writing political science, it's a story.

Roberts: And sometimes people learn better when it's in the form of a story than they would in another way.

Arias: Absolutely.

Ray A. Young Bear

Elias Ellefson

Ray A. Young Bear is a lifetime resident of the Mesquakie Tribal Settlement, which is located near the town of Tama in Central Iowa. He has taught at the Institute of American Indian Art, Eastern Washington University, and Iowa State University. His poems have appeared in numerous anthologies and magazines, including *Virginia Quarterly Review, Ploughshares, The Georgia Review, The Kenyon Review,* and *Harper's Anthology of 20th Century Native American Poetry.* His published works include two volumes of poetry, *Winter of the Salamander* and *The Invisible Musician.* His most recent autobiographical work, *Black Eagle Child: The Facepaint Narratives,* leads one on a "journey of words" through a world in which ancient knowledge clashes with modernity.

Ellefson: The academic world is in the midst of finding appropriate or nonoffensive language when addressing groups, such as the Mesquakie. I have seen the terms "Native American," "American Indian," and "Indian." Which term do you consider appropriate?

Young Bear: That's a very tough question because a lot of people are beginning to realize that any kind of labeling will stick with them for years and maybe even centuries. But one of the things I always say is to not be hung up on labels. I have no problem with either American Indian or Native American. Besides, etymology doesn't interest me. Writing is tough enough. Yet I have a great appreciation for people who know my tribal background and are able to call me Mesquakie.

Ellefson: What does it mean to be a Mesquakie? What is unique about the Mesquakie culture?

Young Bear: Well, I guess first and foremost, and this going back to how I present myself in a university or elementary classroom setting, I tell them that there are a lot of differences within our cultures. One the language, the spirituality therein as well as philosophy. These factors, as well as the history, separate a lot of people. The Mesquakie people, of which I am an enrolled member, are part of this area historically, and so we have beliefs that are animistic. Meaning we have a wide, unbridled respect for all earthly kinds of life, be it a tree, a stone, or a river. We believe implicitly they are very much alive, breathing feeling, sharing our existence.

When you try to convey that to an Iowa classroom or elsewhere, you end up with children and even graduates pondering whether trees are really alive. In a scientific context, they respond by saying "yes, they are," but for Mesquakies it goes beyond that. We believe in the presence of unseen forces, both good and bad. Once in a great while, they reveal themselves, but they are masters in concealing themselves in coincidence. Most Americans, I'm afraid, can no longer see how these unseen factors influence our day to day functions. That would be the greatest difference in being a Mesquakie, that animism is a unique philosophy to cherish and hold.

For the things that have happened to my wife, Stella, and myself, any American—I don't care how intelligent or skeptical—would probably check themselves into a mental ward. While it may be visually stunning to watch movies like *The Exorcist* or *Close Encounters of the Third Kind,* to be an actual witness or participant in a supernatural manifestation is nightmarish. Steven Spielberg is brilliant, but I doubt if he has ever seen a mega-UFO that fills the sky. We have. But that doesn't mean anything unless its image is embedded in your mind. In the same manner skeptics scoff at these mysteries, I believe it's silly to live without this kind of awareness. I equate it with vulnerability that is next to nakedness.

Think about this: when Catholics partake in the wine/blood of their Deity, I believe that is their belief. It symbolizes something that is concrete and unchangeable—for them. Although my late beloved grandmother barely understood English, she would sometimes go to the Presbyterian Church, the one that used to be here. She would say, "Ma ma to mo wa ki-i ni- *we ji -ya ma i a wa ni*. They are praying and that is why I am going. She respected that element of religion. I wish the same could be said for the

Euro-American polity that sought to annihilate us in the name of Christianity.

Ellefson: What else makes the Mesquakie people unique?

Young Bear: We are perhaps one of the few tribes in the United States who have actually purchased their land as opposed to having the government allot the land for us. In that aspect we are unique, for it was my great-great grandfather in 1856 who acquiesced momentarily to the Euro-American aspect of money. Money equals a deed. Today, unlike other tribes, we are property owners here in Tama county.

The real question that you should be asking, Elias, is this: With the multi-million dollar gambling novelty, are we still unique? In Mesquakie prophecy money is seen as negativity. In other words, the very act of acquiring land could be lost through similar means. If you buy, you can also sell. But most of our supposed leaders today have already sold themselves out—and the tribe. We may be considered one of the most conservative tribes in the Midwest, but that may be short-lived, when greed comes by way of clandestine agreements and unforgivable bureaucratic mismanagement, the chances of becoming a Hobblelegged Nation are great.

Incidentally, while I was originally in favor of having the Short Story conference held on the Settlement, I had second thoughts. My anti-gambling stance doesn't sit well with its bigwigs and all their underlings. Excuse me, my Mesquakie relatives, but when illiterates have dominant control over tens of millions of dollars of your money you can bet your ignorant little behinds it will be squandered. Heavy statement, yes, but they'll forget it when investigations begin.

Ellefson: In *Black Eagle Child* you write: "To be ignorant, uninformed, and oblivious to one's origins was to openly defy 'the one who created you' and invite adversity." What happens to a people who neglects its past?

Young Bear: Did I say that? Wow! I plead guilty to all of the above. In going back to some of the metaphors I use, they become culturally "hobble-legged." Sure, there are some people who have succeeded by living outside of the Mesquakie Settlement but for those who remain the responsibilities are immense. In my own case, compared to my late grandmother and my parents, I am a complete waverer when it comes to spirituality. I admit that forthright in my public appearances and my books, I'm no self-proclaimed expert on this subject but I report what I see.

Basically, in order to be the all-around circumspective Mesquakie you have to be attentive to all the factors of what it takes to be such. That's no easy feat. Sometimes this cannot be done to the fullest extent because we are all modernized. However, to the exclusive segment few who uphold the Principal Religion, I am humbled. To the hypocrites, regrettably, I am ashamed. And myself? There isn't enough space to list my excuses. But there are days when I wake up thanking my parents for not sending me to boarding school to study to be a casino commissioner or a tribal council member! (Laughs.) A joke! Seriously, I may not be all of who I should be but at least I have the credentials on who I am. Meaning my profession won't land me in federal prison for embezzling or racketeering.

In any event, we have all acquiesced to Euro-Americanism: by the way we dress, the way we eat, the way we act and so forth. Education, of course, has played a major role toward that regard. To openly neglect your origins, therefore, is to invite adversity that can take many forms. Punishment can be divine in origin for someone not living up to expectations. Punishment can also be sent through dark, mystical means. And I suppose someone can suffer by living away from "The Sett" (Mesquakie Settlement), suffer because the daily interaction with the clans is absent. That's what I see.

Ellefson: Are there any lessons you could teach Euro-American people, such as the Italian-Americans or Norwegian-Americans, regarding the importance of preserving one's cultural legacy?

Young Bear: Well, no, not really because each culture has its own set of principles, codes, and precepts. Not knowing how it is to be those people I really wouldn't have any advice to give other than to say that if you come from a background in which your ancestral roots are very close (so close that you can identify with great-great grandparents and so forth whether in the new or old country), then I applaud these people for making a strong effort to acknowledge their roots. Basically, this is what I stress wherever I travel.

Ellefson: How does your writing preserve your ties to your heritage?

Young Bear: Writing is very . . . How do I put it? In the 1600s—it is said—when we first had contact with the French emissaries-explorers in Wisconsin, we adopted the English alphabet. For nearly three centuries the Mesquakie people have been utilizing the alphabet. But we don't use it in the English context, rather we use it syllabically. Our tribal name, as an example is written out as *Me skwa ki* proper or The Red Earth People.

Contrary to the beliefs of many, writing isn't new. For me, writing is a personal link to the writings of my grandfathers. I have in my possession their journals that date back to the early 1800s. I therefore believe that "word-collecting" is genetically encoded in my blood. I marvel at the process itself because I wasn't comfortable with English until late high school, 1967 to 1969. Even then extraordinary luck was involved. To now find myself in the writing profession is astounding, but when I look into my roots, reading and translating my grandfathers' journals, I realize that I'm not far off from my late grandmother's expectations. Although she taught me to be wary of The Outside World, she was the one who saw there was a purpose to my work: keeping alive my grandfathers' writings. I bring the journals out on occasion with white gloves in dim light to let them breathe, to remind them we are still here. There is a magic there.

In the novel-in-progress I take this a step further. Edgar Bearchild, my alter-ego, is apprised he has been chosen to maintain his Six Grandfather's journals and to serve as a reminder to his Black Eagle Child tribe of ugly things to come, beginning from childhood.

These white people will destroy everything and they will cause the demise of humankind and Grandmother Earth, my grandmother warned as we awaited the orange school bus beside the frosty gravel road.

(Inevitable, I would later subscribe, Mrs. O'Toole of Doeingham—Doo-tin-hem—Junior High School was a conspirator, an agent of the Red Pedagogical Army. From her coffee and nicotine-stained dentures a message was spewed out. Propaganda. Another flag bearing a symbol but a flag just the same.)

And for this reason alone was I blessed with a mission, I recited aboard the orange school bus, to be the harbinger of prophecy, and angel of Earth's End . . . Ally of the Northern Lights . . . Me, an ocher seal-eyes poet in a tight flannel shirt, hole-ridden jeans, and Presbyterian Church-donated shoes."

Ellefson: When I looked at *Black Eagle Child* for the first time, I noticed that many sections are written in poetic form. Are these sections intended to be read as poetry or as short fiction?

Young Bear: That's a very good question. I don't have a solid answer. One doesn't really know the mechanics by which they operate. My work pretty much leads me around. Depending on the mood and since my background is poetry, by habit I favor the poetic format. Of course, I'm a firm believer that the various forms of writing are not that far apart. It all depends on the length of the sentence, the tone, and the message-intent. I operate in many different levels. Essays I love and nonfiction project entitled *The Red Earth Journals* has already been started. No poetic format there, though.

Ellefson: One of the central issues at the conference was establishing a definition of the short story. How would you define the short story?

Young Bear: How would I define a short story? Presently, I am working on a fiction manuscript entitled "Remnants of the First Earth." Anyway, my NYC editor and I have differences as to what makes a novel. But within my own experimentations, and since this is my first full-fledged effort to write a novel, I am not seeing the connections between the chapters right away. I view them rather as a group of stories, but eventually I will have to find the glue that holds everything together. That's a hard job because I am more impressed with the chapters which seem to be little stories. But in the long run editors are vital since they make out the checks. Yet, I'm hoping there's enough experimentation, enough of the real me, to make critics and scholars wonder for many, many years what I was doing.

Ellefson: What do you think your contribution in terms of form has been to the short story?

Young Bear: Right now, I have yet to make a contribution. After two decades of writing poetry, it's tough switching to fiction. Even more in my case. For almost the same amount of time I went on a self imposed exile from popular American literature. Yet throughout I struggled to get my poems accepted in elite magazines, anything east of the Mississippi. The score is zero. Ironically, and this wears me down sometimes, Indian-imitated poetry will radiate from these glossy pages.

Once I was confronted by a letter to an editor about this poetic injustice and he/she wrote back listing all the Indian-related publishing activities he/she had done. Which was simple self-validation BS. With the exception for a handful of Native American writers who've made the glossy pages, far more have been excluded. And why is that? Paternalistic ignorance.

So, about chipping in my two cents worth to the short story, I will give it a good try. For me, there's such a thing as an "optimistic rejection." This is embarrassing, but I have no qualms about mediocrity. Fiction editors are actually writing back, signing their names and asking to read more. If only I was prolific! How pathetic this must seem, me fishing beside the muddy bank of modern American Lit, radiant and hopeful from a mere nibble on the line. Maybe if I change my name to Bill "Burning Hot Sun," I'll haul in a winner. Hell, it's done all the time.

Ellefson: I think you answered part of this next question earlier. Who had the greatest influence on your growth as a writer?

Young Bear: My grandmother, no *ko me sa*, would be the first. From her I learned mythology, the language and customs. Secondly, I would have to say the Upward Bound program at Luther College in Decorah, Iowa. I am indebted to a program. Thirdly, it would be Robert Bly, a major literary figure, whom I met in 1969. Through him I was able to meet and correspond with a number of editors who eventually published my work. After Bly, it would have to be another institution rather than a person: Pomona College. From 1969 to 1971 I was a student there. I attended most of the poetry readings sponsored by this upper-middle class school. Since they could afford the top poets, I listened to everyone who was popular back then.

Ellefson: Which contemporary writers to you admire?

Young Bear: Today, it would have to be James Welch, Gerald Vizenor, and Louise Erdrich. The reason for that is they are related in part to the Algonquin/Woodlands linguistics family. Meaning that eons ago everyone spoke the same language. Somewhere we grew apart and the languages changed. But not much. Once in Northern Saskatchewan I communicated word-for-word with a Cree Indian elder. It was a beautiful experience. With the Kickapoo Indians who moved to Northern Mexico years ago, the same could be done. Supposedly, they speak the oldest form of Algonquin. Anyway, based on this ancient relationship, I have a keen interest with the writers mentioned. Of course, the last time I read and taught their work—in Iowa City—was 1989. I haven't read anybody since. But I like the movies that were made from the books by Amy Tan and Isabel Allende, *The Joy Luck Club* and *The House of the Spirits*. But then I also liked Charles Bukowski's movie *Barfly*. The only videotape movie I have ever bought. Guilty me.

Ellefson: During the conference, Amy Tan brought up an important issue affecting ethnic writers in America. Sometimes ethnic writers draw criticism for not adhering to politically correct expectations. Do you feel any pressure to present only positive images of American Indians?

Young Bear: No, I don't. In fact, I communicate through whatever affects me at that particular time. People often say I have a very embittered view about life in general. That may be true. Yet, considering all that has occurred to our tribal society—500 years of unparalleled inhumanity—I cannot help but be pessimistic. I am not sorry for not being upbeat and positive. When restaurant services, for instances, reach racist levels in the Tama-Toledo community, where I grew up as a student, it makes me wonder what else is going on. Even with the monolithic influx of money to these communities via the Mesquakie casino there is hate for us still. It manifests itself in small ways, like waitresses. It's rare when small town denizens respond to us in a trouble-free way. I'm not desirous of love per se; I just want to be treated better. With or without money!

It sometimes feels as if we're hurtling through the stars toward the 21st century. What shape we'll be in when we get there is questionable. My late grandmother used to say our shortcomings had all been predicted eons ago. Of course, this was sound advice for me as well. If and when things start reversing themselves, maybe then I can applaud the miracle of having survived this ongoing holocaust. But today I can't. Maybe I can regale when Mesquakie youth start speaking our language.

Also, one has to keep in mind that only five Native American writers— maybe one or two more—out of perhaps hundreds can speak, think, and write in their respective tribal languages. The rest, with all due respect, are either struggling to learn or else they simply have no need for it. To me, that's a sad commentary. Makes me almost want to question the validity of contemporary Native American literature. Considering that we have all been subjugated by a Euro-American polity, and considering that we employ English as the main vehicle of our thoughts, there's a contradiction. Simply put, if there's an outcry to portray things in a positive light, then it should begin by having the linguistically remiss learn their grandparents' language. They have a lifetime! As for successful Native American authors who have no need for their languages, maybe they could establish projects that help preserve and teach their languages to their people. Granted, they have earned their due but they shouldn't be too stingy. And what about me! What am I doing? If I had the bucks I'd donate willingly to any project that helps maintain our identity. In terms of giving back, though, Stella, my wife, and I through the Mesquakie song and dance group, have generated supplemental income for eighty artists since 1985. This, perhaps more than the writing, is a source of great pride. Seeing a ten-year-old dancer buy groceries, clothes, and even engine parts for the family is good. Should I ever reach the ethereal point where I am asked by The Creator what have you done? I sincerely hope this accounts for something. Wishful thinking, yes, I know.

Ellefson: I'm a young literary student with a new interest in Native American literature, so you have to forgive me for asking this next question. What place do "white" critics have in studying Native American literature?

Young Bear: That's a touchy question because many academicians who study our works are engaged in verbal warfare. To a point I can understand how Native American scholars would be defensive about this area, because we have been maligned in textbooks. Obviously, we would like to see Native Americans teach Native American literature. The same with our culture. For so long we have been dependent upon non-Native American scholars or critics to show us ways to appreciate our literature. But, I think we have reached a point where we have to break these "old codger school" associations. Now that would be the "PC" thing to do. Any literature that goes deeply within the tribal structure, through linguistics and religion, should be taught by someone who is intimate and familiar with these specific areas. That's also common sense. Right?

On another related level this is what Mesquakies have to watch. Nonrepresentation of their culture. Presently, there are academic types who are passing themselves off as Mesquakie scholars. These are people who have not done well within their areas of expertise. They are the epitome of hobbyism but they are more dangerous. They're slime, "K-Y jelly in suits." Some have the audacity to speak for us. In so doing they bring their personal troubles to the tribe. Some engage in self-promoting projects, using the tribe as the metaphorical icing on their ego-cakes. The sad part is, most Mesquakies cannot see they are being used. In one bizarre instance, one "overnight" scholar-instead of helping us—is now suspected of being involved in the unlawful sales of religious clan artifacts. Supposedly we have hired someone to recover these items. This job isn't for the meek-hearted, though. Another wannabe-scholar simply wants to exhibit his/her art pieces with us and will probably break proper representation laws in the process. Unbeknownst to national corporations and state public institutions who fund these escapades, laws are being broken at the expense of the Mesquakie tribe.

Ellefson: In *Black Eagle Child* you write: "Throughout the twenty years I have been involved with writing, I have attempted to maintain a delicate equilibrium with my tribal homeland's history and geographic surrounding and the world that changes its faces along the boarders." How to you maintain this equilibrium?

Young Bear: Simple, you have to become your own therapist. Literally. You have to suffer for a while until you reason things out, becoming in a sense your own psycho-healer. Being a writer, I sometimes feel as if the world is a giant concrete bridge that is balanced atop my chest and it's about to crash through. The reality is, it won't. There are other priorities in the offing that will need attending to—I know. Eventually. Writing therefore isn't everything. As you've heard, far more is involved to my life than books. I can dish out excoriation but I can also heed it.

This reminds me of something and it might be a good closure.

Once in my youth I flew across America on a plane with two other writers who chatted ceaselessly about literature, naming all the books they had read, written articles on, and so forth. Coming from a community where such gibberish is nonexistent, I remind myself of these contemporaries whenever I get lonesome for literary companionship. We may all be in the same "word-collecting" canoe, paddling in unison over a silver glacier-fed lake. But "if Miss Diane Chambers of the t.v. sitcom 'Cheers' ever strutted into the Why Cheer Pool Hall and put quarters up for a game, I'd rack the balls tightly. . . ." Nothing salacious here, please. Just quotes from the novel. My way of saying I like t.v. and playing pool.

Clark Blaise

Greg Wahl

C lark Blaise was born in 1940 in Fargo, North Dakota, yet is a Canadian citizen. He has been an innovator in both fiction and autobiography and is widely known for his combinations and permutations of the two genres. He is the author of three novels, *Lunar Attractions* (1979), *Lusts* (1983), and *The Border As Fiction* (1990); four books of short fiction, *A North American Education* (1973), *Tribal Justice* (1974), *Man and His World* (1980), and *Resident Alien* (1986); and three full-length works of non-fiction, *Days and Nights in Calcutta* (1977 with his wife, writer Bharati Mukherjee), *The Sorrow and the Terror* (1987), and *I Had a Father: A Post-Modern Autobiography* (1994). Currently, Blaise is Director of the International Writers' Workshop at the University of Iowa. His new novel, *If I Were Me,* was published in 1997. Biographical and critical sources for Blaise are the fall 1973 *Journal of Canadian Fiction* and the *New York Times Book Review,* September 29, 1974, and April 22, 1979. Further sources include *Quill and Quire, Authors in the News,* and *Canadian Fiction Magazine.*

Wahl: I'll get a question out of the way first that you're asked a lot, about rootlessness. Critics and interviewers have often billed you as a rootless wanderer. Now that you're back in Iowa at the International Writing Program, do you feel some sense of geographical or literary rootedness here?
Blaise: One problem with rootlessness is that I've had too many roots, that is, I have too many legitimate places to have come from, either lived in or

ethnically attached to, or, in some cases, politically moved towards. Iowa is the only place that I've lived in in my whole life that I have no claim on, or has no claim on me. I'm the only person in my family who's ever been to Iowa. So that in that ironical sense Iowa has the greatest claim on me because all other claims have proven to be false or all the other claims on me have proven to be illusions, and so I've committed myself to illusory homelands. Iowa has always been there as the place that gave me my degree, my calling, my wife—I met my wife in Iowa—and my most satisfactory job. It's the place where one of my children was born, it's the place where my children graduated from high school, so even though I can't claim an Iowa home, my children can, quite legitimately, and I suppose you can say that home is where your children are from.

Wahl: I love the story of you marrying Bharati Mukherjee on your lunch break on the first day of class . . .

Blaise: Thirty-one years ago.

Wahl: How has your marriage and your collaborative work with your wife affected your own work, in your recent works especially?

Blaise: It's been an expansion of my life. You generally marry someone with whom you're supposed to have a lot in common—that's the general formula for success in a marriage. And I went out and married someone who was, like, from another planet, so far as thirty years ago went. What did I know of India? Nothing. What did anyone know of India? Nothing. Especially, what did an American man know of an Indian woman? One never saw an Indian woman around. Okay, so I married one, and it meant that I had intimately involved myself with the so-called Third World. It meant that I had to now start seeing myself as having a stake in issues, languages, literatures, religions, that I had been able, conveniently, to ignore through the first twenty-two years of my life. Suddenly I had to take responsibility, in a sense, for those things, just as she had to start taking responsibility for baseball and things that were my own obsessions, so that coming, as we did, from opposite ends of the universe, we were like colliding protons on one of those accelerator tracks, until finally we had to be smashed head-on in order to sort of count the fallout and begin to reassemble ourselves after the giant collision. We had to really exchange nuclei, I think, somehow, in our core, before we could go on.

Wahl: Has that been manifested in your writing as well? Have you given up things and gained other things, as evident in fictions?

Blaise: I think it's quite clear. Bharati, of course, sets most of her work now in North America, and sees herself as an American writer, not as an Indian writer, not as an Asian American writer, not as an Indo-American writer, but purely as an American writer, and she's gone through the immigration process, which really is a signal that you are trying to change, that you have voluntarily accepted the notion of a new identity, otherwise you would stay here as a landed immigrant or as a green card holder all of your life. And the same thing with me. I've had to make less profound adjustments than she has, but nevertheless (and my job probably reflects it) I do travel the world, and I do consider any literature that does not embrace the world as being defective in some way, or at least as being shallow. I do, I think, also, embrace sort of the third-world notions that politics has a legitimate role to play in literature, in serious literature, and I've seen too much of the world's suffering and I've seen too much of the world's injustice, and just too much of the world's variety to be content with writing works that are entirely American or North American.

Wahl: That politicization, is that somehow related to the rise, or the spate, I guess, depending upon your view, of critical theory, and especially theories that are overtly political? Or do you think about that with your fictions?

Blaise: I don't think about it with my fiction, particularly, but I do think about the question of post-feminism, post-colonialism, post-Marxism, almost what I call post-deconstruction. The deconstruction model of criticism has tended to locate literary assumptions in a political nexus, so that political assumptions dictate literary values, and deconstruction continues to question so-called literary constructions until they reveal their political nature, or their political philosophy or prejudice, and I think that's a valuable undertaking.

Wahl: Do you worry about the dehistoricization that some people say goes along with that, especially given an interest in Third World literature? Many people would say it's important to remember the history of the Third World.

Blaise: Well, it's important to know the history of the Third World, if you're a historian, I think. If you're a fiction writer, in one sense, yes, you have to know everything, you can't ignore anything, and the more you know, probably the better writer you'll be. But I don't think you have to be historical in any restrictive sense, in an exclusive sense of being historically minded. I think what is more a danger in modern writing is the lack of a moral center, not a historical center, but the lack of a moral center, and I think that comes to us through a lot of the postmodernist influences that are on us, in other words, we go for shock, we go for shifting contexts, for quick changes, for cuts, for jumps, for the whole sort of CNN and MTV quality of mixed-voice narrative, in which we value transition, let's say, over continuity, and I think there is a problem. I've written, for example, on the problems of the Rodney King incident, and the tape of the Rodney King beating in Los Angeles, how, under postmodernist influence, you can take a tape that seems to be utterly convincing, utterly inculpatory, and run it in such a way as to make it an innocent document. In other words, you can get your policemen off by showing them beating a man who's helpless on the ground, and you do it by reversing it, by slowing it down, by segmenting it, by doing all sorts of postmodernist literary tricks. You therefore turn cinema verité into a kind of cartoon, and that's a danger we're finding in a lot of postmodernist-inspired literatures, just as we find it in postmodernist movies and other events.

Wahl: So for instance, would Kathy Acker be an example of that kind of cartoonish . . .

Blaise: I wouldn't want to cite Kathy Acker's work entirely, but I think that or Mark Leyner—there are a lot of works that are an adrenaline rush of reading, but there is a kind of a heartlessness to it as well. I think we need to have consequence. However we juxtapose, whatever our transitions, however rapid the shifting of scenes are in a work, consequence cannot be avoided. When consequence is avoided, then you end up creating a need for consequence that exceeds the original source, so you end up burning down Los Angeles. If you can't get consequence from narrative, it's almost like breaking an atom bomb. It's almost like fission in the sense that things fall apart and there's a much greater energy released.

Wahl: Speaking of narrative, it would be interesting to know, given your tendency toward a unified narrative, would it be fair to say . . .

Blaise: No, I don't think so.

Wahl: A traditional narrative, perhaps?

Blaise: No, I'm very impatient with traditional narrative, and I feel that it simplifies too much. The conventional, linear narrative is not, I don't think, anything I've ever tried to practice. I've always been looking rather restlessly for ways to tell a story that does justice to the complications and confusions I feel in my life, that I felt in my life growing up, or that I feel even today. And I want to write narratives that are true to so many of the things I know. In absence, my life has put me on a firing line in the world, where I have been in a lot of places and seen a lot of things, and met a lot of people who have enriched me enormously, and I want anything that I write to reflect that, not to avoid it or diminish it in any way. So to try to find a form that would be true or faithful to all the data that's in there, and all the data that's out there, and in me, is what's always been confusing to me. It's just that I don't want to take shortcuts.

Wahl: Have you settled, then, on what Barbara Lounsberry and others would term "autobiografiction"?

Blaise: Yeah, I have probably more than most people I know accepted the outline of my life as being appropriate either for autobiography or for fiction. I have found a kind of comfort zone in writing about a world that is controlled by a man like my father, and a woman like my mother, and a Canada that is hovering over the United States, and an America that is southern, or a Canadian reality that is French and English. And I've accepted, also, an Indian wife, quite often, or an Indian lover, whatever it may be, so that I have accepted the European strain that came in from my mother, I've accepted the French Canadian strain that came in from my father, and I've accepted, I think, the moral authority of their marriage, which was an improbable and unhappy and finally violent one. But it gave a great moral jolt to me, and it clarified the world into a very tension-filled universe. And, so long as I'm under the shelter of that marriage, imaginatively, I can imagine anything happening. So, I'm not dependent at all on autobiography for the content of my stories. I make up the content. But I am dependent on the authority, somehow. The authority for the imagination, the authority for the invention comes from reality, but not the content itself.

Wahl: Does that create, as one critic has suggested, the "demimonde," particularly in North American Education, where there's a space which author, narrator, and protagonist all occupy at the same time, or is the narration more straightforward than that?

Blaise: I think that's probably true, but I was just reading for a lecture I gave in Japan last week as a matter of fact; I lectured partially on Calvino's *If on a winter's night a traveler*. And there you have at the end, the central character, the author, and the reader, are all the same character, too. That kind of complexity in which you begin to see the world as composed of story, and of failed story, and the larger Ur-narrative is the thing that is larger than any of the individual stories that can be made up. And yet, you cannot get at the big narrative, except through a series of smaller narratives in which, inevitably, the reader of one becomes the writer of the next, and then the writer of them all finds himself wanting to get into the story, too.

Calvino did it, Kundera's done it—it may be essentially a European trick, but I've found my own way into it on my own. I think anyone who thinks seriously about trying to write fiction in the contemporary age is going to find that he or she is going to have to make up new ways of going about it. It's just not satisfactory anymore and it's not true, and it's not real to be playing Henry James games in the late twentieth century.

Wahl: The series of small narratives, then, that make up the Ur-narrative, become details—you've said that in your work you start with a detail and then embellish a story around it, so it's epiphanic in a way. Do you consider that a minimalist technique, or are you uncomfortable with that classification?

Blaise: Yeah, I'd be uncomfortable with that. I think minimalism, as I understand it, and as I read it and lived through it from a lot of people I knew who wrote it, is deliberately numbed; it's deliberately anaesthetized prose or reaction, and the characters in the minimalist story have walked through or survived a particular set of events that have left them without affect, without much reaction. We as readers are being asked to supply, in some ways, the affect, to supply the connections. The authors leave them out, or the editors of the authors force them to leave them out, whatever it may be. I've never been comfortable with that; I've always had an excess of affect, if you wish. I've always felt almost spongy with reaction to things. My problem has always been: too articulate, too much a control freak, wanting to say too many things, so I've never had the strong, silent, Ray Carver kind of response to things.

Wahl: You've mentioned also that your characters are all basically mother, father, or child characters and that the basic family unit is where you draw your characterization from. How have shifting values on what politicians call "family values" affected your characterization?

Blaise: Well, the whole word "family" has been so devalued and trashed by things like Denny's restaurants—"family" restaurants end up being hauled into court for racism. Family values in general, I think, are one of the last refuges of scoundrels. I've never really been interested in family values as such because I've never known them, I haven't seen them, you know. The values I knew were in fact true family values. They were a man and a woman and a child living through difficult times and places, and trying to make the longest and best go of it they could. That's the family value that I understand. Trying to impose, then, other sorts of values: how you look, how you act, how you speak, how you behave, where you work, and what political affiliations you have, all that is meaningless to me; I'm not interested in it. It would be wrong to think of father-mother-child as being very restrictive, I mean, those are prismatic concerns that—depending on how you turn the prism—throw out hundreds of shards of possible reactions. In my most recent book of stories, the father is a horse, I mean quite literally, is a mythic animal. The son is also a mythic creature. There is really no lack of variance for that father, that mother, and that child, or for the family unit. It can be in any time, any place, any variety of people. And so I don't feel as though I'm restricted to talking about a French Canadian father and an English Canadian mother and a boy living in Florida, as I was a long time.

Wahl: That brings up the question of other restrictions on characterization and voice. W. P. Kinsella came out very much against those who say that one shouldn't write in a voice ethnically or geographically or culturally other than one's own. How do you feel about that?

Blaise: Yeah, Bill Kinsella was, of course, in Canada, under a lot of strain at that time because of the appropriated voice rulings in the Canada Council. Canadian Indian writers were very upset about his many volumes of Indian stories. When I was reading in Canada a couple of years ago, I was reading a French Canadian story, and someone asked me from the audience, how do I feel about appropriating the voice of a French Canadian? Well, I've always thought of myself as a French Canadian, but the fact is, I was writing in English, not in French, therefore, by definition, I was appropriating a voice. And, I said, I thought that such people, such critics were trying to assassinate the imagination. I can understand, from a marketplace perspective, perhaps, someone getting upset that whites were taking non-white positions, men were taking women's position, whatever it may be, but from a writer's standpoint, there can be no interference with what the imagination tells you to write. I would not hesitate to write in any racial, any national, or any gender point of view. Probably, I would not do as well writing from a woman's point of view as a man's, probably I would not do as well writing in black- or red-face than in white-face, but that's not going to stop me from trying. I would have to accept the judgment of the readers on that. But I'm not going to accept the judgment of policemen or of literary turf-protectors who just want to control their own field.

Wahl: In 1987, you bemoaned the state of fiction in North America with a very few notable exceptions. Do you still feel that there's a dearth of good or interesting fiction?

Blaise: I think that what's happening is that we're in a state where we have many communities speaking and many fine writers within communities; I don't know that we have, right now, a kind of a social vision. I think the great novel of the '80s that I've read is probably *Beloved,* Toni Morrison's novel, which is, you know, a black, woman, 19th-century-set novel, very poetically written, and very politically indicting of American history. I don't think there's any book I've read that can match it in its depth and its beauty, and also, it must be said that it is deeply aware of, not flaws in black history, but problems in black character as well. So it's a very thoroughgoing investigation. How many great novels do you have to have in a decade to redeem the notion of the decade; I think her novel certainly does redeem a great deal. It hadn't appeared in 1987, so maybe it was there waiting. One year later it came out, and if I'd read it then, I probably would have said, "with the exception of Toni Morrison." I think there's a lot of good writing, but I as a white male—add all the others: white, straight, Judeo-Christian, educated, middle-class, white male, Euro-descended—cannot really feel at home as much as I at one time did with women's writing, with other kinds of ethnic writing, with gay writing, whatever it may be. I have been made to feel self-conscious about trespass. And that question you asked about Bill Kinsella is one example: how dare I trespass? It would be very unlikely that I would be asked to review a book from any one of those communities, and it would be very unlikely that I would accept a commission to review a book from any of those communities because I'm now suddenly aware that, what can I say? How can I judge? And what can I know about those worlds? So that I read in my field, in my ethnic field, in my bloodlines, if you wish, in my genetic field. And other than that, I read really outside of American literature entirely. Most of my teaching and most of my reading is in African and Asian and Latin American, Australian, Canadian.

Wahl: What's your classroom like?

Blaise: Well, I don't really have to teach so much anymore because I'm directing a program, so that when I teach it'll be just one course on a graduate level. I taught a course on what I call the exogenous English-language novel. That meant Salman Rushdie and Achebe and Gordimer, and Keneally and people like that. And then the last thing I taught was a workshop in autobiography. So I had Writers' Workshop students actually writing their autobiography, and I was trying to show them the difference between autobiography and fiction—even though the two may have similar origins in events in their own lives, that how you treat them is very, very different.

Wahl: Did your class arrive at some common denominator or a mark of that difference?

Blaise: I imposed it on them; we didn't arrive at it. I tried to impose it on them from the very beginning. Yeah, we did. I think we did. That they're opposites, fiction and autobiography. Autobiography is a record of consciousness and fiction is a record of experience. Autobiography does move toward resolution, to confrontation and resolution; fiction moves only to confrontation, it doesn't try to answer everything. There are a lot of subtle distinctions. I use them a lot in my book *I Had a Father,* my autobiography. I try to talk about the difference between fiction and autobiography in that book.

Wahl: I'm torn when I read your short fiction between recognizing a representation of dichotomies, for instance, American/Canadian, male/female; and between recognizing a kind of "blowing out the water" of those dichotomies. How would you guide a reader of your works who sees both of those things?

Blaise: Well, I guess we'd have to take it on a case-by-case basis, because a lot of those stories are records of my own confusions as I worked my way through . . .

Wahl: For instance, in your half of *Days and Nights in Calcutta,* the Indian/North American dichotomy you explore.

Blaise: Of course, that was non-fiction, that was reality, so I really was working through what anyone would feel in Calcutta, that on any given day you are in hell, or you are in a kind of blessed heaven, that is, you slowly learn to give up the sociological and the political baggage that you came with and learn to cherish individual human variety, and you start learning to move like a Bengali, that is to start moving in a Third World dramatic way where you engage each of the little separate incidents that make up a day, each of the little segments of a day, with a kind of personality and a kind of energy and a kind of dramatic flair, for human possibility that you simply are never called upon to exercise in North America. I mean, you go shopping here, you look for a good-looking thing under plastic to buy, and you put 'em in a plastic bag and you don't have to say a word in any of the shopping that you do. Well, you can't have that kind of shopping in India, I mean every mango that you buy is a negotiation. Everything you buy is a separate negotiation, with humor, with anger, and with a lot of self-consciousness, and a lot of care in every selection, and you simply carry that event to the point of exhaustion day after day after day with every single event. Nothing is without its full human load of possibilities, that's why I called it Balzacian—it's like reading a Balzac novel. Everyone is a hundred and twenty percent of a human being. Everyone has got an excess of personality, an excess of passion, an excess of cunning, maybe, and it calls upon you to have a hundred and twenty percent of what you ever thought you were capable of having. So that that became the pleasure, that became the challenge. But when you went there, you were looking for, "can't we just have a little peace and quiet, can't we just sleep in, can't we just rest, can't we just have a nice quiet meal?" The answer is, "no, you can't." So finally, you give up those North American expectations of convenience and speed and devote yourself to something else. And of course, the great pleasure that we take here in solitude, or privacy, or quiet, is the luxury you cannot get in India no matter how wealthy you may be. You cannot have privacy and you cannot have quiet.

Wahl: Austin Wright said that critical movements don't influence writers, but rather, other writers influence writers. Would you agree?

Blaise: Generally, yes. I think that maybe, though, I'm a little bit more theoretically vulnerable than most writers. I do read literary criticism, and I am a teacher, and I am a professor, and I read a lot of the stuff that goes on, and I enjoy, for the most part, going to literary lectures. I can remember distinct times in my life when literary criticism, literary theory, has in fact influenced me, very much, very definitely. There's a story in my first book of stories, *A North American Education,* called "The Salesman's Son Grows Older," and that story ended on just the noise of a windshield wiper on a car wiping snow off a windshield. That very decidedly rose from a lecture in Montreal by Tzvetan Todorov, the great structuralist at that time, in which he was making it possible in some of his critical comments on Henry James to see that there was an unspoken side. Structuralism was very good at that, in showing you the unspoken dichotomy, in a sense, in dialogue with the story. So you had the story on the page, and the reader was being asked to project from the details on the page something that was not on the page. And I was trying to do that, I mean I was really trying to reach outside the story in a sudden leap with those windshield wipers, those windshield wipers being in perfect synchronization with the heartbeat—I was trying to move from the outside to the inside. That very much came from the criticism. It didn't come from any other writer, it came from Todorov. I've had other moments like that.

Wahl: Do you have your own theory of short fiction as opposed to novel?

I don't know if I can say. I've written a lot on the topic, and I'm not finished talking about the short story. Some of the familiar definitions that Frank O'Connor has used and that others have used, from Edgar Allan Poe on up, are relatively true, I still think, about the unified effect, the single effect, and all the rest of it. But I've added a lot of wrinkles. In my own experience, a story is an attempt to capture, to recapture its own beginning, so that you take the first sentence or the first paragraph of a story, and what it really is is an attempt to understand a conflict. The rest of the story is an attempt to analyze, in fact, or to interrogate its own first paragraph. I think it's an interrogation of its own origin. The origin is utterly mysterious, seizes the writer's imagination almost in a way that he or she doesn't understand and then must work out, so that the ending is in fact the mirror image of the beginning. I think that the profundity of a story is really rooted in its ability to fully explore all the implications of its beginning, and I would say that the beginning is, up to a point (what I've called the "then" of a story) the moment in which the story shifts gears, announcing itself with a "then one morning, a phone call came," or "then one morning, a letter arrived," or "she looked out the window and saw people coming up the driveway," whatever. One of those moments that tells you in the beginning, towards the beginning of a story, "now the plot is taking over," now there is going to be a thickening of the plot. Well, that thickening of the plot is really not a thickening of the plot, it's really a plunging back into the beginning, but it's done in such a way that the reader's not aware of that.

Wahl: Is it evident when you begin writing that first paragraph whether it's going to be fully interrogated as a story, and will take shape as such, or rather as a novel, or as autobiography?

Blaise: No, I'm thinking of it purely as a story. I think if you're going to write a novel, you have so many other things on your mind that you know you're going to have to plunge on ahead, you can't afford to go back and interrogate the beginning. You're going to have to put so many other things into play. So many other balls are going to be in the air that the beginning is really nothing more than just an opening act. But with a short story, the beginning is the end, it seems to me. If you yield to the magic of a beginning, which just seizes you, and you can continue it—because I think most writers have an experience of having dozens of beginnings around that just couldn't be pushed—but if something in that beginning is pushing you, then, yes, you won't give it up, you'll know that it had a, that there was a crack in it somewhere that allowed you to see another dimension, so you'll stick with it. But some beginnings seemed interesting and rich, and you pushed it a little bit, and you saw that there was no reason to go further, that they yielded everything, they didn't need to go back.

Wahl: Has your association with so many international student writers in the Workshop affected your work?

Blaise: Oh, yes. The world of literature is like a rainforest, that is, every kind of genetic, every kind of flora and fauna, every kind of human possibility is out there in that rain forest. We only know the Midwest. We only know cultivated corn and soybeans, in literary terms. We don't know anything about the Amazon, or Africa. We don't know anything about the flora and fauna of Australia, for example. And so, every year, I'm confronted with having to read the works of thirty new writers from thirty different countries, all of whom are posing, to me, questions of almost simple identification. You know, "what is this thing? Is it a poem? Is it a story? Can you do this? You can't do that. You can't say that," and realizing that in many cases, you can. So it's been very useful. And the book that I'm working on right now is directly inspired by a writer who came into the program last year from Colombia, South America, and it's not magic realism at all, it's something very, very different. I'm continually grateful for it.

Wahl: Can you give us a preview of what your new work will be like?

Blaise: It's thirty short stories, but, first of all, they're not at all like the autobiographies we were talking about earlier. They're very brief stories—that's the influence of this Colombian that was very marked on me—and sincere, very linked as stories, almost like chapters of a novel. They don't have to fulfill the standard short story format of beginning, middle, and end. That is, story twelve might really end in the midst of story eighteen. They can have correspondences between one another that are quite interesting to me. They don't have to start with a conventional beginning, because they can piggyback on something earlier; they don't have to end within their own narrative, they can end in some other story's narrative. It's very new for me. I think of it as being very musical. I think these stories are like chords in a symphony, and so one chord is picked up by other chords later on, if you wish, in the symphony. I can have the illusion that a story that is only five pages long is really thirty pages long. And when I'm publishing them, I'm looking to publish three or four together as a group, as a setting, as a little mini-concert.

Judith Ortiz Cofer

Jocelyn Bartkevicius

J udith Ortiz Cofer was born in 1952 in Puerto Rico. She moved to the United
States in 1956. Among her awards are a National Endowment for the Arts
fellowship in poetry and the O. Henry Award for her story "Nada." She is the
author of *Peregrina* (1985), *Terms of Survival* (1988), and *Silent Dancing: A Partial Remembrance of a Puerto Rican Childhood* (1991), a memoir. Her works also
include *The Line of the Sun* (1991), *The Latin Deli: Prose and Poetry* (1993), *An
Island Like You: Stories of the Barrio* (1995), and *Reaching for the Mainland &
Selected New Poems* (1995). Her prose has also appeared in such journals as
Georgia Review, Kenyon Review, and *Missouri Review.* Cofer has also authored a
three-act play entitled *Latin Women Pray.*

Bartkevicius: You work in so many genres, how does what you write know
what it wants to be?
Ortiz Cofer: Well, you phrased the question correctly, because writing is
one area where I allow the subject to lead me. Some things want to be
poems, some things want to be essays, some short stories, and I don't fight
it. I have a rule that I break almost constantly: if I'm dealing with material
that is strictly—or mostly—based on memory, I try to use the creative non-
fiction form. I specify "creative" because my writer's imagination won't let
me stick to the strictly boring factual material. With *Silent Dancing* I followed an impulse. As I explain in the preface, Virginia Woolf said that you
can allow strong emotions to lead you, strong emotions leave tracks back to

moments of being. So my first step in writing *Silent Dancing* was to allow the memories to come and then shape them by using the techniques of fiction. Because I felt that I was trying to stay true to memory—although I do feel that that's about ninety-five percent impossible—I call those pieces creative nonfiction.

With the short story, even when based on very familiar material, as in "Nada," which is set in the barrio with women speaking (I can hear their voices), still, the situation is constructed. It was as if I said: "I have this setting, bring on the actors, I'm going to give them their lines and they're going to perform for me." So they weren't relatives whom I knew would behave this way or behave that way. I can't make my grandmother behave—I can do it but then I have to call it fiction, if I want her to behave other than Mamá. But these women who populate the barrio of my imagination appear in the short story. My imagination gives the characters a script, a scene, and a setting and then I allow them to enact what I feel should go on. So "Nada" and the other short stories are an attempt to tell a truth by creating material in which that truth can be enacted. I don't know if this is too circular, but basically, the lines are so fine between my creative nonfiction and my fiction that the only way that I can explain it is by intent. "Nada" is a fictional work, I didn't know a woman to whom this happened and I didn't know a woman who was the narrator, but I knew many women to whom many of the things happened and I condensed it all and created a narrator that was me if I had stayed in the barrio. But not me since I did not stay in the barrio. Does that make sense?

Bartkevicius: That makes a lot of sense. Would it be fair to say that with fiction you're starting with a memory and with an invented situation?

Ortiz Cofer: It would be fair to say but not always accurate. I would like to have a system, but in many instances I start with a known situation, something that actually happened. There's another story in *The Latin Deli* called "Not for Sale," which is about a young girl living in the barrio. Her father's very possessive, not unusually so, he's afraid for her and wants to keep her within the four walls of the apartment. I won't retell the whole story but there's a culture clash between the Puerto Rican father and an Arab salesman who wants to buy this girl for his son. The father keeps saying, "she's not for sale, not for sale." Well, this actually happened, and people will say, my daughter, for example says, "someone tried to buy you?" right before she laughs. And I say, well yes, actually, when I was fourteen or fifteen years old this man who was used to these deals in his own country (where it's actually not called buying, just exchanging goods for a woman, you know, for various reasons) wanted his son to come to America. Since we were American citizens he thought he'd pay my father whatever he wanted—merchandise, cash, sheep, goats, whatever.

I turned it into a Scheherazade story which is my thing, you know the story teller who inspires the story teller who tells the story. I base the story on what actually happened but not exactly as it occurred. I wanted the frame story, but at the time that it was happening to me I was not thinking this is a story of a future story teller. I used the situation (thinking no one was going to believe it was the truth anyway), and constructed a scene around it. What really happened took place in about ten minutes: This man came in and said, "I have a deal for you, I'd like to buy your daughter." My father said, "would you please leave my house immediately." The salesman kept raising the price and my father kept saying, "no it's not the money." It was an interesting third-world situation. I like to write about how culture clashes don't just exist vertically between white and brown and white and black, how sometimes the worst culture clashes happen between Cubans and Puerto Ricans or Puerto Ricans and Ecuadorians. Anyway, that story began with a known situation but I dramatized it; I made it into a whole story where it had been a ten minute incident.

Bartkevicius: I found myself wanting to say, "and your father especially." I feel like I know him from reading *Silent Dancing* and some of the essays.

Ortiz Cofer: Oh he was outraged, and the louder he got the louder the Arab man got too because he thought they were haggling. Now I can laugh about it. At that time we were thinking, Oh my God, what's going to happen here. An international incident.

Bartkevicius: Did you invent the bedspread in "Not for Sale"?

Ortiz Cofer: That's real and I still have it. I didn't know that it was my Scheherazade bedspread until much later, but I still have that bedspread. My mother made a mistake and put it in the washer and I have to mention this because the background is gorgeous; it used to be gold but now it looks like . . . I don't know, papyrus. And I mean it's strange, the threads have spread out. I have it now on a little couch in the room where I work, Scheherazade suspended. When I bought it, it was just this beautiful bedspread. Then I became addicted to reading the world's folk tales and fairy tales, and I would lie on that bedspread reading them. At one point I said, "It's Scheherazade!" Suddenly it occurred to me. So to clarify matters, in the story that realization happened the day I bought it, and that's why it's a story. I was just fourteen or fifteen, I wasn't making connections in the way that I make them now. Actually, it was later that I realized that the story-telling salesman sold me—or sold my mother—the bedspread which in turn I put into a story. So the story of the salesman and the bedspread became a frame tale in the same way as in *The Thousand and One Nights*. For me anyway, my version of it.

Bartkevicius: I really enjoyed reading that story because it's so rich with imagery. And as I read it I felt that it could be either story or essay; I didn't feel that I had to decide. In fact, that's one of the things I love about *The Latin Deli,* I could move from work to work without having to fuss over what genre I was reading.

Ortiz Cofer: Right. I asked for the press to arrange the book this way even though it was difficult for them. Booksellers want to know whether it's prose, poetry, or fiction. In act, it hasn't gotten many reviews for that very reason. They'll send it somewhere and get asked, "Which editor do we send it to?" Since it contains poetry, too, it's become no man's land. Very few people are daring to review it, which I find sad, because to me, writing is writing. I go from a story to a poem easily in that I'm covering the same material. One of the epigraphs from *The Latin Deli* is the line from Emily Dickinson, "Tell all the truth but tell it slant." I see writing essays, poems, and short stories as seeing the same material with different illumination. But it is a specialized society; it's very hard to write a book in three genres and have people pay it attention because they specialize in only one genre. I guess I stopped caring about that because in order not to have put the book together in that way I would have had to spend the last five years writing *only* poems, or *only* essays, or *only* short stories. Instead, I get up in the morning and write whatever the subject dictates.

Bartkevicius: So as writers we might get roped into a particular genre because of what shelf the booksellers . . .

Ortiz Cofer: Right! And that's not me because as a writer I am all three. When I wrote my novel, *The Line of the Sun,* I felt a very strong narrative impulse that kept me enslaved. I didn't stop writing poetry, but the novel was a different thing altogether. I wasn't trying to reflect on different things, I was just trying to tell the whole story without interruption, without going into other things. *The Latin Deli* and *Silent Dancing* are meditations. And meditations don't always come out in narrative form; sometimes they come out as a lyrical moment.

Bartkevicius: Does it take a lot of effort for you to buck that kind of pressure to write in a certain genre?

Ortiz Cofer: Well actually yes, but not so much the world's pressure because I'm not a money-making author. I think that if people were waiting to pay me a lot of money, I would feel the pressure to write a novel. I've had friends who are short story writers and if their stories are published in the *New Yorker* or whatever, then they're pressured to write a novel, because a novel really sells. A couple of them have told me, "this is not my area, but I'm being pressured." So because I don't make money for agents and publishers I am not pressured in that way. *I* decide what my next project is going to be. And I don't know, maybe I'm being simplistic in saying that it's a matter of money, but you do have a certain amount of freedom when you're a literary artist and no one is getting rich off of you. If no one is waiting to make money then you never know what is going to happen to your work. Publishing my work is a book-by-book thing; I send it out and hope that someone will take the chance to publish what I write. So I like to think that I can keep that kind of freedom because I can not imagine . . . I think I would just go blank if someone said, "write this way."

Bartkevicius: As you talk about genre, you remind me of Virginia Woolf who also said, I think, that writing is writing. She would often follow an impulse as she wrote. As a reader who also writes, I find *The Latin Deli* very refreshing, very liberating. It makes me sad to think that people aren't reviewing it if what's making them hedge is the very thing that I find liberating. You have written in *Silent Dancing* of Virginia Woolf as a mentor. Would you say she's a mentor chiefly in creative nonfiction?

Ortiz Cofer: She was a model in all writing. After reading *Silent Dancing* some people have said, "that's very strange because you credit Virginia Woolf and your grandmother." And I say that's exactly right because at my grandmother's house—this sounds like a cliché now because it's been said so much—but it was there that I learned how powerful story telling can be, it can change lives. When I was studying, the only woman that kept coming up in my required readings was Virginia Woolf. I had a chance to read her novels which I found very difficult and very challenging, but it wasn't until I read her memoirs, her essays, where she talks about her devotion to writing and how no one can dictate writing—that's a spiritual side of herself. What she said about memoir writing especially liberated me. She said your life is your life and you remember it in pictures—she called childhood a picture of a summer's afternoon. She remembered her mother not in factual details, but rather, by the print of a dress she was wearing one day when she laid her head on her lap, by the smells of the nursery, by all of these. I felt, well that *is* what I remember about my childhood, those moments of being. It was that one phrase of hers, "you must follow the tracks left by strong emotion to those moments of being." And I said, I can do that. I can follow those tracks back to those moments of being and those moments of being then became, I understood, the source of my poetry. That's why poetry follows the essays in *Silent Dancing,* the poems were written up to ten years before the essays, but it was by writing the essays that I discovered their origin.

Bartkevicius: The origin of the poems.

Ortiz Cofer: The origin of the poems. And that's why there'll be a poem that follows an essay. Sometimes it doesn't seem to relate to the essay, but there will be an image, and I'll discover where that image came from. An essay to me is a way to discover what you know, also what you don't know. I read my poems and said: Now what made me think of the woman who was left at the altar? As I wrote the essay I realized, yes, I heard my grandmother say it. And when did I hear her say it? When she was trying to teach us this. So the essay works for me as a time machine.

Bartkevicius: You've called Virginia Woolf and James Joyce time travelers.

Ortiz Cofer: Yes. Yes, James Joyce in *Dubliners,* a work that for me, meant everything. He took images of people in a city and gave us moving pictures. When I open his book it is like those movies where someone is looking at a book and suddenly the characters come alive. They're always there, and every time I read "Araby" I find something new. I mean I could memorize that story, it's so lyrical and beautiful. It contains the essence of first love and first disappointment in a way that I haven't seen matched anywhere else. And so it *is* very strange, because I'm a Puerto Rican woman, but my education is the education of the English major. I was an adult before I read Gabriel García Márquez, Isabel Allende, the Puerto Rican writers, and the Latin American writers and so my first influences were these people in English and American literature, particularly the southern writers, Eudora Welty and Flannery O'Connor. Later, when I read the Latin American and Latino writers, they also informed my writing, but I would say that I learned about the craft of writing from English and American literature, especially the women writers, the few that I could find in my outlines, because I came along when you might have one token woman in an American Literature syllabus.

Bartkevicius: I'm interested in talking about these very different people who are your mentors. In *The Latin Deli* you have that wonderful piece about reading literature in the library, about the Greek Temple.

Ortiz Cofer: Right, the Greek Temple in the ruins of an American city.

Bartkevicius: As I was reading that, I recalled *Silent Dancing* where you write about the women telling stories under the mango tree.

Ortiz Cofer: Right.

Bartkevicius: And listening to those *cuentos,* to your grandmother, and learning from your senses. Is there a conflict between learning from your senses in the oral tradition and learning in the library from the canon?

Ortiz Cofer: Well it wasn't so much a conflict as a necessary compromise. If you read *Silent Dancing* you know that my father was in the Navy. Every time he went off for six months at a time my mother would pack up and take my brother and me back to her Mamá's house. Her Mamá's house was crowded with people and children. And so we lived this life of the body; life was lived outdoors at that time in Puerto Rico. All the windows and doors were thrown open, people sat outside on porches and we talked. TV and the radio were minimal. That was an oral tradition; I would be playing and listening to the women talking. So it came into my ears, into my skin, you know, someone would bring out something and say, "Oh, the feel of this material reminds me of two years ago when . . ." And I would be playing, but I would be listening to how these women absorb memory and how they turned it into stories.

That changed radically six months later when I would go back to Paterson. We'd live in an apartment building where my mother feared the dangerous streets so we had to live indoors. Our main sources of information were either books or the TV. And so I went right through the Paterson Public Library once I was allowed—until age twelve you had a pink card, that meant you could not go to the adult section, then you got a blue card to go to the adult section. I just went right through it. They had a huge room, lined with the world's fairy tales. I want to go back to that library. It's probably a small room, and I was just a little person, but books everywhere. I just started out and read everything that I could find in the world's fairy tales, and I found out that the Cinderella story happened again and again; sometimes it happened in Africa, sometimes in China, sometimes in Spain. I would take home as many books as the library would allow. And I still remember that overdue fines were two cents a book. I remember that because I would have to keep my pennies since I didn't always get back to the library on time. I am more reliable now.

Bartkevicius: That shows.

Ortiz Cofer: Thank you. But the fact is that I had my library penny jar, and the private library police are probably still looking for me now. In "Not for Sale," I said that I heard Scheherazade's voice talking to me and voices talked to me in those books. It was never the same as Mamá's voice, but it was still story telling. And that's why I say at the end of "Not for Sale" that it's my own voice, now, telling the stories. It's not that I started writing early—I was no prodigy—but I started absorbing the material early. And I can't get away from the folk tales, they appear in my stories, like in "The Witch's Husband." I translate folk tales and stick them in my stories because they're still the primary source.

Bartkevicius: It was really stunning to me in that particular story, "The Witch's Husband," the great power story contains. You're supposedly there to lecture your grandmother, but she stops you dead by telling a story.

Ortiz Cofer: Right. She tells a simple little story, and the story is more powerful in its simplicity than anything that I could lecture her about. And that's the point. I didn't know that when I was little. I didn't know anything except that I loved being in Mamá's house and that I loved hearing her voice. But I was obviously absorbing it. And now I'm translating Puerto Rican folk tales and finding the wisdom contained in those stories. All the rhetoric that we have now, all the feminist rhetoric can be found in these stories usually told by women to other women to let each other know that they knew what it was all about, they knew where the power was. But it was just these simple little stories.

Bartkevicius: The stories that you tell seem very much part of a women's tradition. And I'm wondering how I'm going to put this, but there was Maria Sabida . . .

Ortiz Cofer: Maria Sabida and then Maria La Loca. I just wrote an essay about those two, about being a writer, called "Sleeping with One Eye Open," in *The American Voice*. I wrote about how I had two choices: I could either be Maria Sabida or Maria La Loca, the woman who was left at the altar. I reinterpreted the stories for my own purposes. Maria Sabida is the woman who marries the killer, you know, and she supposedly reforms him. But she's married to a killer and so she always has to sleep with one eye open. But it's not that the killer is necessarily a man or a husband, I say the killer is the angel in the house, Virginia Woolf's "angel in the house," anyone or anything that wants to keep you from your work. You have to sleep with one eye open because they will always try to keep you from your work. And so I consider myself a feminist but I don't consider myself a man basher. I don't think that everything is the responsibility of men. I chose to marry young, I chose to have a child. I *want* to have a child. And therefore, I cannot call her the angel in the house, I cannot call him that, you know. There are people who are oppressed, and then there are people who feel that they are oppressed simply because someone depends on them. When you allow love to enter your life, it also takes time. It takes time to love people. I don't mean to go off in that direction, but basically what I was trying to say in this essay, which was published in a feminist journal, is that the assassin husband is anything or anyone who deliberately tries to keep you from your work. Not because they love you but because their demands are unjustified. It can be any*thing* that you allow to keep you away from your work. And so you have to always have one eye open. The choice is to live like that, which puts a certain amount of pressure on you. If you're the artist sleeping with one eye open, you're always leading the examined life, and exhaustedly so.

If you're the woman who's left at the altar, you've allowed love or anything else to defeat you. You've been left at the altar. And I compare that to women who come up to me and say: "well I know that I could have been a writer, but I had a child, I had a husband, I had a job." Or they say to me: "I'm going to wait until my child starts college, my husband retires, whatever, to start writing." I compare them to the woman who has been left at the altar not because I'm unkind, but because writing is such a strong impulse, that I have seen women with a soul-deadening job and five children give up two hours of sleep a day to write. Or else you make that ultimate choice, you say, "what do I want?" and you make a choice. But living with this lie that I could have written . . . it really can make you a bitter person. My essay is about the choice. You can choose to be Maria Sabida, be exhausted all the time, because you do give up sleeping, or you are heartbroken because you do give up the people that you love but exhaust you. Or else you can just accept the fact that you are the woman who was left at the altar.

Bartkevicius: You write about the urgency to write.

Ortiz Cofer: Yes, like Grace Paley says, write only if you have to. And that doesn't mean for money. It means if, my God, if I could put all of the energy and anguish that I expend into real estate, I'd be rich. But I can't. In fact, this quarter, I gave about everything that I had, except about two percent, to my students. I taught lecture courses, and I had graduate students, and I read dissertations and everything else. For over fifteen years I've been getting up every day at 5 a.m. to write and this quarter I was getting up at 5 a.m. to read student essays. I was not able to be fully happy. It was like nothing . . . I got these awards, and it was what you would call a very good year for the recognition of my work and all that, and yet when I got the awards I would say: "I'm an impostor, how could they give me something for something I did years ago? I'm not writing now." And so it's not a virtue. I mean, I'm not saying I do this and so I'm better than the women who don't get up and write. Sometimes I envy them. Because I know that psychologically my vocation is to write. I was a good enough good Catholic girl to know—I asked the nuns what made them become nuns and they said, because they had no choice—it's called a vocation in the Catholic tradition and I see that writing changes me. Finally, this quarter I said, if I don't write a poem, I'm truly going to be certifiable. So I sat down and I worked on a poem, and people noticed. It wasn't that I went around bubbly—I'm a pessimist by nature—but it was a subtle shift, I was able to take other things. I was able to accept that extra committee meeting.

Bartkevicius: Writing sounds almost like meditation for you, a kind of centering.

Ortiz Cofer: It's not therapy. I think that art can be therapeutic, but I really do think that it is that momentary stay against confusion that Robert Frost . . . I live for those moments that are saved from confusion. And by confusion I mean overload, like today, I was late for this interview. I do pride myself in having overcome "my Latin time thing" and that's not by the way, a stereotype, there is such a thing as "Latin time," you know—you say we have an interview at 10:30, I show up at 11:00, you still haven't arrived with a tape recorder because you meant 11:30.

Bartkevicius: I was raised by an Italian so I lived in that time.

Ortiz Cofer: I'm not speaking for the other countries, I don't want to be sued. But hey, when my mother says be ready at eight for dinner and I am, she says why are you dressed so early? But the fact is, before I came to this conference I gave all my exams, I turned in my grades, and I had sensory overload. I came over here and blanked out this morning because basically the world is so demanding. But when I sit down to write a poem, time stops. I have to actually set an alarm if I'm going somewhere. And I know I'm not the only one this happens to; when you're involved in the world of images and symbols, you are in Rod Serling's "Twilight Zone." You are involved in a fourth dimension of time and you are time traveling. My poem was about my first job in Augusta, Georgia, and I was suddenly back at that sandwich shop and smelling everything. I'm a pragmatic; I'm not a romantic. It all has to do with a psychological process very close, very akin to association, where someone makes you recall things through association. So it's very much a process involved with physiology and psychology, no hocus pocus.

Bartkevicius: Back to the body again?

Ortiz Cofer: Well, yeah, you go back to an event or dig important things out of your mind, by simply focusing on your internal life, which is what you do when you go to a psychologist anyway. You allow someone else to unlock it. I tell my students, you want to know who you are, and what you know? Write. Writing is not self expression, it's self discovery. I have often started a poem thinking that I am about to praise someone, and say oh my God I better not show this to them. I did that to my mother, whom I love very much, but I started a poem called "My Mother's Hands," and I thought I was going to talk about how my hands have become my mother's hands. And it turns out that the poem ended with an image of the Borgia women strangling their lovers with silk threads. She's a small woman with strong hands and that lead me back to an understanding that what I remembered really was the strength of her hands, something that sometimes hurt me. I wouldn't have known that unless I had written that poem. I would have just thought, oh my hands look just like my mother's hands.

There was a session here yesterday on politics and writing. I basically believe that all serious writing is political because politics is simply the stand that you take in the world. I am for this; I am against this. This is not decent, that is not ethical; this is. Those are political choices even if they have to do with familial things. And so my story is about women in the barrio. But it is a political statement. It would have been a political statement even if it had been about women in the suburbs.

Bartkevicius: I don't know whether to call it an essay or a story, but the piece in *The Latin Deli* where you're going to the library.

Ortiz Cofer: That's an essay.

Bartkevicius: OK. I thought it was an essay but I didn't want to . . .

Ortiz Cofer: Well, I call the last half of the book personal narratives.

Bartkevicius: Yes.

Ortiz Cofer: I didn't want to intrude on the reader by saying these are stories, these are essays. But the book is divided into two sections, stories and poems and personal narratives and poems. Anything beyond the title "personal narratives," I consider creative nonfiction.

Bartkevicius: I had a lot of fun putting together pieces from the beginning section and from the end that deal with similar issues. Your "Advanced Biology" and "American History," for example.

Ortiz Cofer: They were both high school subjects.

Bartkevicius: I'm interested in what you're saying about politics. In the essay "American History," you run into Lorraine.

Ortiz Cofer: Right, the black girl.

Bartkevicius: You write of such a conflict, about how some of the people channeled anger into learning, and some of the people . . .

Ortiz Cofer: Into violence.

Bartkevicius: Yes, and when I read your writing, I think of it as political, but I don't think of it as angry. It's such a calm voice.

Ortiz Cofer: Well, as you can tell from meeting me, I probably cannot be described as demure or calm; I mean I have kind of a nervous personality. And while I don't know if it's best to be described that way, the fact is that when I write, there is a sort of mediating agency at work, whereas, in real life I can get very angry and immediately angry, and immediately remorseful. I'm being angry in my writing, but the mediating agency of memory and the image controls my emotions. I have come to a stage in my life where I believe that it's not necessarily conciliatory or pacifist to admit that some things are best looked at through humor, that some things are best looked at calmly. The fact that Lorraine, who happened to be black, wanted to beat me up because I did better at school, was a terrorist activity to me at the time. I really was terrified, especially because she lived on the way to the library; she was right in the middle of what I needed to get to. I thought of myself as very brave, and because I was a good Catholic girl all the time I would say, "if I die before I go to the library, I commend my soul," you know, I didn't want to go to hell. But now, as an adult I can actually say things like that and laugh about it, because we were two young girls. She was angry but it wasn't at me, it was at the positive attention that I got from the teachers because I was such a nerd and the negative attention that she got. It sort of perpetuated it, but the madder she got, the more negative attention she got. I see that now; I couldn't have seen that at the time.

I remember to this day how terrified I was about that situation. And yet I can't bring myself up to anger at Lorraine. I have often wished that I could remember her last name so I could go back and meet her. Maybe she's grown up to be a happy woman, a fulfilled woman. And then it fills me with anxiety to think that she might be in a prison somewhere because she could not channel her anger. I don't think that makes me a goody-two-shoes, believe me anyone who knows me knows that if I see prejudice in action, racism, whatever, my immediate response is just protective towards the victim and anger at the perpetrator. Yet with these things that happened early in my life, I have to make sure that I don't alienate my reader, not by being patronizing, but by putting these stories in a context that is familiar enough to them, two girls, you know, in a school situation, one of them channeling her needs one way and another one another way. That's a universal situation that people can read and understand; it's not just a black girl against a Puerto Rican girl. Now this happens all the time; it can be Vietnamese and Korean, black and white, and that sort of thing. No, I wouldn't call that playing on anger, but I do want the readers to understand that I'm talking about things that they should note and not allow to happen if possible. You know, if someone reads that essay and their child comes home and says something similar, maybe something can be changed so that two women don't grow up to hate each other because of a misunder-standing.

I don't know, I think that there is disappointment in some of what I write that things haven't changed enough. Also an acknowledgment that it's not always a vertical situation, that it's not always white against brown, white against black or black against whatever. Like in "Advanced Biology," I see it as a Romeo and Juliet situation with me wanting to be with this Jewish boy and his parents being opposed and my parents being opposed. That had nothing to do with the world at large. It had to do with barrio politics.

Bartkevicius: Politics that you were just learning at the time.

Ortiz Cofer: Right.

Bartkevicius: You seem innocent of the politics in the story.

Ortiz Cofer: Right, to me he was just a boy. I didn't realize that God and the Virgin Mary were going to come into play in this romance.

Bartkevicius: In *Silent Dancing* you write about looking for some ground from which to talk with your mother about the definition of "woman." You've mentioned Virginia Woolf's "angel in the house," and I think in that same essay she writes that we talk about a woman writing but we don't really know what a woman is yet.

Ortiz Cofer: Right.

Bartkevicius: Have you begun to discover now, after writing *The Latin Deli,* that definition of "woman" or are you still in search of it?

Ortiz Cofer: I'm still in search of it. I'm really in that last piece about the man who starts out life as a woman and no one questions his femininity. The names have been changed, but this came from a real story that my grandmother told me. I can hear her telling it; she always slaps her thighs and laughs because she says "and she used to put me between her knees and braid my hair." She looks at us and laughs and says, "and look at him now." She changes from "she" to "he" very naturally—doesn't bother her, you know, she was a girl with him and now he's a man and they don't talk in the same way. Things changed when he became a man. There was puzzling wisdom that came to me from listening to this old woman, about how we like to make categories that are so strict in the world. I am not naive enough to think that just changing clothes changes you, but I think changing attitudes changes you. A lot of my writing like a woman comes from being in the culture of women. What would happen if a little boy came up listening to these stories? Truman Capote has a couple of stories, that Christmas story that he wrote about being with an old aunt. I might be wrong and the critics might jump on me because I'm not a Capote expert, but he came very close to connecting with that thing that makes women tell stories in a particular way. I think that eventually I'm going to be wise enough to make the statement that I want to make—I'm not wise enough yet—which is, what if we stop thinking in terms of strict categories and just allow people to grow up exposed to similar things, not just boys with baseball and girls with stories. What would happen? Would there be a gender problem in the short story? Would we be discussing gender or could it just be short stories written by human beings? You know I like to write from the male perspective, there's *The Line of the Sun,* the whole first passage and me imagining myself as a Puerto Rican boy, which I was not allowed to be.

Bartkevicius: There's the story—or is it the essay, now I can't recall . . .

Ortiz Cofer: Now you're getting the point.

Bartkevicius: That we don't have to have strict genre or gender boundaries. In that story or essay, the girl dresses up in boy's clothes and then can't come to the dinner table.

Ortiz Cofer: Oh, that's a poem, "The Changeling."

Bartkevicius: A poem! Oh, yes.

Ortiz Cofer: I'm glad that happened in your reading; that means it all came together. That's part of what I'm saying; I explore that in that poem. The girl goes in and puts on her brother's clothes and comes out and tells war stories and the bloodier they get the more her father listens; he only pays attention when she's talking, being Che, the man Che, and her mother comes home and says "you're not coming to the dinner table dressed like that." She takes off her boys' clothes and comes back to the kitchen invisible as herself because then the father stops looking at her. Yes, I explore that, how we respond to each other depending on what mantle we put on. Once again I have to say I'm not naive, I know all about hormones and biology and culture, but in the matter of literature I think culture has a lot to do with how we see the world.

My brother wrote plays for a while, and he wrote using the same material I did. But his protagonists are always male and always doing things that I didn't recognize, not always but. . . . He sets one of his plays in a barracks, with my father in the barracks and my mother waiting, and my mother has just had me. Now if I had told that story, the first thing would have been my mother having just had me with my father in the barracks in the background. And so we went through the same thing but he as a male saw things very differently. And that's not necessarily bad, it's just an acknowledgment that if we all had a little viewing of each other's worlds. . . . What if he had sat through Mamá's stories? Could his stories then open up in a different way? They're wonderful now, but if I had been allowed to go play baseball with him would my world have changed and expanded? I don't know. I can't answer those questions; it's too late for me to go play baseball with my brother, but they're all things I want to explore.

Bartkevicius: In "The Book of Dreams in Spanish," the tree is the father, and both the fruit and the words come from that tree.

Ortiz Cofer: But you're never satisfied; you're always hungry.

Bartkevicius: So there seems such a paradox: the words have so much power, there's the power of story and words over and over again in your work, and yet this lack of satiety.

Ortiz Cofer: Maybe that is the metaphor for the artist, that we're always under that tree waiting for the fruit to come down, and it does, and you eat, but it's not enough, it's not enough. You keep waiting for that which will fill you. Fulfill you maybe. My father was an absence in my life, an absence that I loved, I loved him very much, but he was always gone. And when he was there he was just authority. And so the women filled the void with words and with their physical presence for me. But about that image I have to say that my mother sent me a book of dreams. It has nothing to do with

Freudian psychology, ignores everything that has been learned about the nature of dreams in the last two thousands years, and just says things like, if you dream of a tree it's your father. Next item. . . . Why?

Bartkevicius: It couldn't be the mango tree, an actual tree you sat under.

Ortiz Cofer: Right. There's this whole list, just a series of declarative sentences with no explanation. If you dream of this it's THAT. No explanation, no justification. So I used that book to write some poems because the Freudian symbology had been explored and talked about so much. I kind of like her idea that everyone assigns whatever meaning they want to dreams, and when I dream of my father there's always the sense that he's dead now but we left some thing undone, something unsaid. And maybe that's part of my writing too, to try to find out what it was.

Bartkevicius: A while back you were saying that you're not a romantic.

Ortiz Cofer: I was probably lying.

Bartkevicius: As critics and teachers we like to say "race, class, gender," to look at works in those terms, and I think it's worthwhile to study.

Ortiz Cofer: Yes.

Bartkevicius: But more and more I've been starting to see—oddly enough in Virginia Woolf—and now in your work, something additional, something that I would call nature writing, or a really strong pull towards nature, images of nature.

Ortiz Cofer: Which work?

Bartkevicius: In various pieces, different scenes of nature, different images, like sitting under the mango tree, like the move from Paterson to Georgia.

Ortiz Cofer: In a central story in *The Latin Deli,* "Corazón's Cafe," there are a lot of smells, especially of the vegetation and the cooking. When I said I wasn't a romantic, I meant that I don't believe in the Bohemian lifestyle and I don't believe in a winged creature that comes and inspires you. That's a result of my life; I had to make time to write. I believe that writing is work that you give yourself. You know that it must be done and you do it. So that's what I meant by not being romantic. My students say, "Oh, I only write when I'm depressed." And I say, "Well, for me that would mean every day, for you every other month, right? So you wait around to be depressed and you tell your editor, 'I can't write for the next three months because I'm in an unusually good mood.' " So I'm not romantic in that I don't wait to write. I don't wait for some kind of inspiration, inspiration happens while writing.

But if by romantic you mean an attachment to beauty, as far as I'm concerned the life that I want to lead is an ongoing search for beauty, whether it's in looking at my daughter, or nature or whatever. I don't know enough about nature having grown up in Paterson where we had to travel for miles to see a tree. That is a slight exaggeration. We actually did have to go to Garrett Mountain which was a park outside the city. So I didn't grow up like my southern colleagues or my daughter—we live on a farm and she'll say, "let's go outside and be with nature." And I'll say, "let's just leave nature outside and stay in the air conditioning." But I love the beauty of the world, of course. Nature to me is like food, and I'm not a naturalist and I'm not a cook, but I love what food does to you, to your mind as well as your body, and what nature does to you, to your mind. Even now, though she doesn't live in the country as she used to, my grandmother has *gandules,* and orchids too, so she has coffee, peas, orchids in the same garden. You walk in and there's this invasion of your senses. And then she has something like fifty parakeets, so they're all singing at once. She raises them, they have babies, and so there's all this chirping going on, then the smells, and the last time I went—she's very sick now, perhaps dying—but the last time I went she had ground some coffee that she had grown, and put it in a little bag for me. There's my Mamá, in her life, inextricably bound to these smells and sounds, so that's nature. I can't talk about nature in terms of this leaf is that and that tree is that, but I can talk in terms of this woman that I love and who has become my muse even though I don't believe in the winged one—my muse is an old lady in Puerto Rico, she's surrounded by the sounds of her world.

With my mother it's different. When my mother appears in poems she's got a Mexican Mariachi band in the background, you know, bellowing out this tragic love song with guns, horses, and unfaithful women, and there's Puerto Rican food cooking, but in an American apartment. I just recently wrote a poem, set in the South when I was a teenager. I'm working in a sandwich shop, and I have a turkey club sandwich in it, and a cook who smokes cigarettes in the kitchen and listens to the baseball games with Hank Aaron, and all that. To me writing is all tied up with smells and sounds and nature in that way. I do not set my work in a sterile apartment in every man's America. I am a maximalist if there is such a thing, not a minimalist at all. I want my characters to eat *arroz con pollo* and for their houses to smell like their cooking and like banana leaves or whatever. But neither am I ethnocentric about that. Wherever I am I try to absorb things through my senses. I guess if that makes me a romantic then I am. I certainly do not want to sterilize my work and not put in music and smells and all that. I couldn't live in a world like that; I don't know how anyone can live in a muted world.

Bartkevicius: I keep getting a very strong image of your family sitting beneath the mango tree and the children riding it.

Ortiz Cofer: Well we did you know, and I guess if there's a romantic image of my childhood . . . I recently saw some of my cousins and if we all got on that branch that tree would come down, it would come crashing down. But we were all skinny little brown kids then, as you know from reading the work. There's a road that has split that field now; the tree is still there but it's on the side of the highway. It used to be a field with a steep, grassy incline, and then the tree grew as you have seen trees growing so it actually leaned down over the hill. Three or four of us would get on a thick branch that was still flexible and two or three of us would stay on the ground. Those of us on the ground would move the branch as if it were a ship and those of us out there would just be bouncing up in the leaves. Our mothers would be talking and looking and thinking, which one's going to come down like a mango. But we couldn't really get hurt that badly because it was dirt and grass. We walked around with plenty of scrapes and scratches though. And if I had an ideal sort of equivalent of a Tom Sawyer childhood, it was those months where everything just seemed to be green, you know, you could smell guavas, life on earth.

Moira Crone

Mary Rohrberger

Born in 1952 in North Carolina, Moira Crone is the author of *The Winnebago Mysteries and Other Stories* (1982). During her successful writing career, Crone has been featured in four different anthologies and has published in such renowned magazines as *The Missouri Review, The Washington Review for the Arts, The Southern Review, American Voice, The New Yorker, The Ohio Review,* and *Mademoiselle,* among others. She has also been the recipient of many awards including a National Endowment for the Arts Fellowship in Fiction Writing in 1990 and the Pirate's Alley Faulkner Society Award in 1993. Crone published her first novel, *A Period of Confinement,* which has since been translated into French, in 1986 through Harper and Row Perennial. Her most recent work is her second collection of stories, *Dream State* (1995). She now teaches creative writing in the Department of English at Louisiana State University, where she edits *Numen,* a magazine of contemporary writing.

Rohrberger: When did you know you wanted to be a writer?
Crone: I wrote a story when I was in first grade about a turtle who goes off to see the world. I identified with that turtle. But what I was always praised for in school was my artwork—drawing, painting. I decided somewhere about the third grade—when the only way I could get points in piano was to make little illustrated booklets about the lives of the composers—that I would write and illustrate children's books when I was a grown up. I was painting—in oils—by the time I was in fifth grade. The summer I was ten,

I'd gone on a tour of Europe with my entire family. When I got back I started painting pictures of scenes like St. Mark's in Venice. My mother didn't like me making such a mess, with oils and turpentine in her fancy house. She stuck me in a dark garage that was a scary place—no light, no heat, many spiderwebs—really a tumbledown shed. I was very lonely out there, so you could say I was encouraged and also discouraged from being an artist. Right before I went to college, I had a writing teacher in University of North Carolina summer school—I was going to Smith in the fall, and my mother thought my writing wasn't up to the caliber of the writing of the girls I'd be going to school with, private school girls. I had attended the public high school in a small tobacco town. About fifteen percent of the class was college bound. The second paper I turned in at UNC, my teacher told me the paper was publishable, which was not accurate, but she was young and enthusiastic. So I guess I decided I might enjoy becoming a writer when I was eighteen. I was still hoping to be a painter when I went to college, but by that time everybody was telling me that my writing was good. And I wasn't getting that reaction to my painting. So I wrote, in college. I decided I was a writer when I was studying with V. S. Prichett at Smith. He just told me casually, when we were walking somewhere one day—he was a wonderful man—that I would publish my first book when I was about twenty-eight. So long to wait, I thought. He was right. At that point I pretty much made up my mind. I published my first stories in the *Grecourt Review* at Smith. I would still rather be a painter, truth to tell.

Rohrberger: How and when did you discover short stories? For you, how do short stories and novels differ?

Crone: I first wrote short stories and published them when I was in college, as I said. I didn't really begin to grasp the form until the last ten years or so. I mean consciously, so that I understand what short stories are doing. So my discovery came after I had started writing them. Short stories are about a moment, and novels are about a series of moments. Novels are messy and short stories are very defined. Short stories have a consistent, arguably a universally recognized form, and novels can have any number of forms. There is closure in most short stories. In novels, closure is always a problem. A novel can be made up of a series of short stories, but a short story cannot be made up of novels. You can write a short story in one day or over several years. You cannot write a novel in one day, only over a rather lengthy period of time. Writing a novel is like having a long, lingering illness. Getting a short story right, and being obsessed with it until you do, is more occupying, like having an acute illness, a kind of attack. The whole idea of a novel is that its form is, in every case, novel, new. With every novel you are inventing the wheel. The form of the feature film is now a big influence upon what people think a novel can cover—the scope, the depth, the amount of event, etc.—but there are plenty of purely literary novels that are not influenced by film at all in formal ways. I agree with Susan Sontag that film is a branch of literature, and it is terribly influential, but not entirely determinative by any means. Short stories have not been so influenced by film.

Rohrberger: Many short story writers give up stories because it is obvious that publishers prefer novels, and they make more money, and, as Isabel Allende says in this volume, short stories are infinitely harder to write. Do you see your writing falling into this modality?

Crone: I don't think I will ever give up writing stories because they come upon you, and you have to get them over with. This is going to happen even if you know the markets are not lucrative. If you look at it one way, stories may be going the way of poetry, that is, the only readers of the form will be those who practice it. The good news is there are more practitioners today than there have ever been before. At the same time, it is true that short story anthologies sell better than ever, that little magazines have high standards and publish good work, that many writers who have risen to prominence and become household names in the last fifty years were primarily short story writers. It is also interesting to note that a reputation for short story writing is the imprimatur of seriousness in many cases—it's what makes a writer decidedly literary, and therefore worthy of "critical attention." Short stories still often anchor a literary career—that is, if you write novels that are commercial, that sell, you still haven't "sold out" if your short stories are pristine. (I use quotes here because I don't really buy the difference between commercial and literary as it is usually understood.) So short stories have a place in the literary landscape. This is amusing because short stories, in F. Scott Fitzgerald's day, were something a writer did for a quick dollar. A good short story writer could make a living at that even as late as the fifties—Kurt Vonnegut did, writing stories for the *Saturday Evening Post*. Nowadays a short story writer, if not supported by the university, will starve, unless he can string his stories together and call it a novel. Many very fine writers are doing that. So there is a way that short stories are sneaking into the hands of novel readers, of which there are still a serious number. There are fewer of the casual readers of general interest magazines that used to read short fiction, those people for whom the form was invented in the first place. The good reader of short fiction, indeed, is hard to find. But good short fiction is everywhere.

Rohrberger: What are you writing now?

Crone: I have just, this morning, finished a novel that I have been cracking my head on for the last two and half years, roughly. It is called, tentatively, "Finding Alberta." It is about two women, and a painting they find and the artist the work is attributed to, who is a great woman painter. I am sending it off today. I have also just finished the first draft of a short story, which is about a man who has a wife and a mistress.

Rohrberger: Is there anything a novelist can learn from previous experiences with short stories? Will you be specific with references to your writing?

Crone: Well, let's start with the novella. I have a novella, called "Dream State," which is the lead piece in my recent book of stories. When I say it is a deep short story, I mean that it has a single moment which should be seen as the turning point, and it has a single issue, which is transformed somewhat, and clarified, but which is consistent, which is at stake for several characters. What makes this more than a short story is that a few of the characters are more fully delineated, and their motivations have time and room to change, to show their "other side": a novella is like a short story with a few seemingly round, not flat characters. This is in contrast to the way in most short stories the characters, by virtue of being so rapidly drawn, can only be seen in a single light. Even the setting in this novella, which is also a character, goes through changes. One thing happened.

When you start giving every character in your short story an entire resume and a history, when you start deepening the characterizations so that the reader understands not only how a character is, but why, you have to cut it out or it becomes a novella, at the least. Now if you give some of those characters full stories, literally of their own, and you start to multiply the issues that are at stake then you enter novel territory. What you can learn from the short story is how to get to a single turning point and make sure a certain set of people has a piece of the story, a part of the outcome. If you can write a group of short stories with a similar dramatic conflict, crudely put, if you can come up with several plots with different issues in them that all come to a head in the same momentous event, or short series of events, then you have a convergent novel, which is a group of novellas, in a way, which share the same climax: the outcome has different connotations for characters in each separate story. *Silas Marner* is such a novel, so is *Gathering of Old Men* by Ernest Gaines. So is *All the King's Men*. Many novels are convergent. It's a bundle of threads of different density and types bound together in the same fist—the shared climactic events. Writing short stories with full characters—translate, writing novellas—is a way to make the threads. Nowadays, we have a kind of short story-composed novel that is not convergent—in fact, part of the point is the fact of linked fates, but the lack of shared fates. Louise Erdrich's *Love Medicine* is a sort of exploded convergent novel. It is a real advance, and stunningly done. So it would be possible to write a novel literally out of short stories, although I have never done that. One thing I did when I wrote this present novel was to use the kind of energy I usually use to compose a short story to make the first whole sketch of the book in advance. This was my attempt to prewrite, as they say. It grew out of something Robert Olen Butler said to me. To answer your question, it was like writing a long short story as I usually would, at one sitting, first draft. I think in one day I must have written eighty or a hundred handwritten pages, in notebooks. Doing this caused me to encounter all the difficulties with the story in a way, first hand, before I went to all the trouble of fleshing out every scene. I went crazy trying to figure out the ending, when through some of that crisis I usually go through when I'm writing a short story. It was sort of a rehearsal for writing the novel. A dress rehearsal. Plot, action, the dynamics of the characters are in hand. This was a new way to write a long book for me. It helped the novel to have a governing design, which is what a novel often needs. In a novel so often you can get so bogged down in writing scenes, sort of stitching in a little corner, that you lose the whole fabric, you never see it until it's too late. In short story writing, the whole fabric is with you the minute you have the first draft. Of course, you still have the hundred drafts to go, but you know what you are working with. I think this rehearsal draft helped me work out the novel, and made it possibly more complex than it would have been otherwise. I wasn't worrying so much about what was going to happen. So I could concentrate on other things. This is what is the downfall of a lot of novels: beautifully written, but the plot, pacing, or overall scheme are weak.

Rohrberger: You attended some prestigious schools. Were you involved in creative writing classes? I am assuming you took an English degree?

Crone: I have a B.A. in English from Smith College, and an M.A. from Johns Hopkins. I studied, as I've said, with V. S. Pritchett at Smith. He didn't have much of an idea about creative writing pedagogy—we went in and listened to each other read our stories aloud. In my senior year, he took me as a special student. I also wrote a thesis on D. H. Lawrence and Joyce Carol Oates. The year after I graduated, I knew some people at B.U. and I sort of made myself helpful to the British novelist Penelope Mortimer, author of the *Pumpkin Eater, Long Distance,* many stories in the *New Yorker,* and other books. I moved into her apartment building, actually, and I ended up auditing her classes. I sort of studied her. Like Pritchett, she didn't have much of an idea about creative writing pedagogy. It's not a British thing, not even now. But she was also very encouraging and kind to me. At Hopkins, where I went after my year of following Penelope Mortimer around, I worked with John Barth. He was a remarkable teacher of form in fiction, and I learned everything I know about teaching form from him. Absolutely everything.

Rohrberger: What can/do students learn in creative writing classes? Is it possible to teach a student to write?

Crone: In general, the prevailing wisdom is, you can't do much about language, you can't teach a person to make beautiful sentences, to have an engaging and gorgeous style. And you can't teach a student how to choose interesting settings, characters, anecdotes. They come into the classroom with a facility with language or a lack of it, and they choose to write about what they think makes a good story: you can't teach taste. Some people naturally have interesting subject matter: their lives are interesting. You can't teach a person to have an interesting life. What most creative writing instructors believe, I think, is that you can teach structure, how to shape a story. How to apply what you have learned from the narrative techniques of other writers to your own work, how to read. The prevailing idea is, this is all that can be taught. Some writers who are teachers, a minority, who go against the prevailing wisdom, also try to teach process, which I guess could be translated into methods for generating stories. The trouble is, this only works for those students who know how to use the suggestions, or who want the teacher tinkering with his or her interior process. For the teacher, it's sort of like going inside the students and teaching them how to get the best language out of themselves, or the most interesting anecdotes. Teaching them to enhance their sensibility, to use certain gifts, to remain conscious in a sense, while dreaming, which is what writing is often. Teaching process requires the teacher to get past the critical mind of her students, and for that reason, it can be very dicey. Often the best writers are very resistant to this sort of thing, because they are engaged in the business of working a process out for themselves. And each student has unique gifts and deficits, so that process is quite personal, by nature idiosyncratic. Very often young writers still constructing their egos and their artistic behaviors find this sort of thing extremely intrusive. I do not blame them, really. Process is sort of like Kabbalah, Jewish mystical teachings. The student has to know how to take the teachings, otherwise the ideas will have the opposite of the desired effect. They can be taken in completely the wrong spirit. I have had one very useful encounter with a teacher of process. I have also learned a lot about process from a famous art teacher, a nun who is known by the name Corita, who wrote some wonderful things about teaching art. I have tried to teach some of these methods to my students, and the results have definitely been mixed. I am actually thinking of trying some of these methods with a group of nine year olds this year, at Lusher School in New Orleans. I just talked to them for the first time yesterday, and I observed that their critical minds are not really so critical. They look at you with their eyes and say "come on in." Once I go in there, I cannot be critical at all. But I am never going to have to judge their work, so that's okay.

Rohrberger: What do you find so impelling about New Orleans as a place and setting?

Crone: Well, I am a neo-urbanist. Most of the country is now an automobile suburbia. Efforts to bring people back downtown have basically failed in most cases. Middle class Americans are always in their cars, in clogged arteries, going from one cul-de-sac to another. There is no street life. And there are many kinds of communities—all sorts of new immigrants—but these groups have very little interaction in much of the country, in part because everyone lives in discrete and distant suburbs, segregated ethnically, and according to social class. I often have the feeling in a certain kind of suburban neighborhood—in Baltimore, in Baton Rouge—that I am in a cemetery. New Orleans is not like a cemetery. Indeed, not even its cemeteries are like cemeteries. New Orleans, because it is practically a peninsula, like San Francisco, has retained more of the character of city life than many American cities, and, partly as a result, it is a now mecca for writers and artists and architects. Young musicians and would-be chefs come because it is the place to apprentice, to learn. The culture is here, the action. It's like old-fashioned cities, it's a hub. As the old elites move out to the far suburbs—which takes some doing in New Orleans, such as the building of the longest bridge in the world—these new groups are moving in. There is a perception that there is a higher quality of life, somehow, more ambient beauty than is normal. Members of the old elites say that the city is a "jungle." I'm quoting the present governor of the state. The new people say it is complex and amazing. Of course this preservation of city neighborhoods is not only because New Orleans is nearly surrounded by water. It's also, dangerous as it is, people just won't leave. The city is too alive. In many respects New Orleans, and much of South Louisiana, is not really the South, it is the northern capital of the Caribbean. It has the character of being what America might have been, if certain influences—French, Spanish, African— had conquered, as they did in many of the islands. American influences, Federal influences, were added late to the mix. The character of the city of New Orleans was already well-established before the Louisiana Purchase. South Louisiana is half-in and half-out of the American mainstream. It is a wonderful place from which to observe American progress, such as it is. New Orleans is an extreme, a border, an edge, and it goes against. It is almost-somewhere-else. It is a city with a culture. How rare.

Rohrberger: The first time I heard one of your stories was at one of the International Conferences on the Short Story. It was the one about a man who can't seem to leave Baton Rouge though a hurricane is approaching. I remember thinking that you had a remarkable grasp of certain details seldom matched by one who is not a native. To what do you attribute this "gut reaction"?

Crone: I have spent fifteen years of my life, more than a third of it, in South Louisiana. I have been through two turns of Edwin Edwards as governor, one hurricane, one flood, one sensational manslaughter trial in which I was a reporter and the confidant of many of the principles, more than a dozen Mardi Gras. It has been a learning experience.

Rohrberger: Where does your own hometown appear in your stories? North Carolina cannot be easily forgotten. What are the settings of the Winnebago stories? They seem to me to be entirely different from the stories in *Dream State.*

Crone: I always dream in my hometown. The Southern hometowns in both my volumes of stories—not New Orleans, which has a very distinct placehood, but the small towns—have some combination of attributes of Baton Rouge and Goldsboro, where I grew up. I had never been to Louisiana when I wrote the stories in the *Winnebago Mysteries*—although it is interesting that I made the mother character, who is out of place in the button-down world of the protestant middle South, from New Orleans. That mother is really the energy in the first good story I ever wrote. So maybe even then I knew where I was headed. I had never been to Louisiana in my life until the day I moved here in August of 1981 with my husband and my baby daughter, Anya.

Rohrberger: In fact, in the earlier book, you seem to be reaching for the kind of skewed reality you achieve in the later volume. Did the fantasy world of New Orleans make the difference?

Crone: I think it is interesting to note that magical realism, as a genre, is almost always generated by writers who are very far away from the centers of mainstream Western culture and power—Central and South America are a very great distance from New York and London. I tried to write magical realism set in Baltimore in some of the stories in *Winnebago Mysteries*. I guess, now that I live practically in the Caribbean, I don't have to make so much up, right? If Faulkner had been writing about Connecticut, he couldn't have gotten away with all the "exaggeration." Editors, who live in the Northeast, would have said, "no, that's way out of proportion," with their sense of propriety. But Faulkner just saw that he was telling the truth. His distance from the mainstream gave him range. When Marquez read Faulkner, he felt he had permission to take a complete exit from what is called by critics the "middle range of experience,"—a U-turn right out of the bounds of realism. Which he definitely took, inventing a new genre. I think my stories in *Dream State* are all about things that could have happened to people I actually know. I had no intention to be irreal or irrational in those stories. If they seem like fantasy, which was not something I was aiming for, then it's because truth is stranger—etc. I actually have seen in my life that completely impossible ideas, which are contrary to all notions of rationality and observable reality, are the ones that have the most sway over people. This is true for good or evil. Most religions, the most powerful ideas in the world, are at core, irrational: they do not appeal to common notions of cause and effect; indeed, that is the source of their power. The ideas about race that gave people permission to hold slaves and to fight the Civil War and all of that the White South and African Americans are still dealing with, and the ideas that perpetuated the Cold War, are two examples of very powerful lies, big lies, fictions extraordinaire: what reasonable idea has ever had so much destructive power? In the Big Picture, fiction is way more powerful than truth. Perhaps it is the "middle range of experience" that is the bigger lie. If this is more obvious in stories set in the South Louisiana, it's because we are farther away from those that define the "middle range of experience," which means we can get away with more. Which means we can write actually, with more truth, where the irrational is the overwhelming element, as it actually is in life. So, to certain minds, the work seems more fantastical. The most fantastical idea I can think of is that people act rationally. They almost never do when big things are at stake. To answer your question about New Orleans, there is, as the Cajun writer and anthropologist Barry Ancelet was telling me last spring, more tolerance of contradictions here, so much tolerance for contradictions in South Louisiana as to seem completely un-American. Living here, I have noticed that I have almost lost my ability to perceive whether a piece of news, say, about my life, is good or bad. People in New York almost always know if a piece of news is good or bad to hear them talk. I look at them sometimes and think they are under deep governing illusions. That something new is bound to be better than what is—this is something; it is completely American, I dare say Yankee, to believe, but it is really not borne out by experience. Good news can really do a person in—I have seen it many times.

Rohrberger: *The Winnebago Mysteries and Other Stories* was published by the Fiction Collective. Did you have ties with some of the other writers published by the same group?

Crone: The writer in the Collective that I was closest to was Mark Leyner, who is an hysterically funny writer, who now writes for magazines like *George* and the *New Yorker,* as well as novels. I used to go to Fiction Collective events in New York and walk around with him, laughing all night. I reviewed his first book, *I Smell Esther Williams,* and it was so wild a piece of writing—pure verbal virtuosity, as are all his novels. I am no longer involved in an editorial capacity. In the old days, I used to read manuscripts for them and edit the work now and again. Janice Eidus, whose first novel was *Faithful Rebecca,* was a friend of mine from my Hopkins days, but she went to the Collective about the time I stopped being directly involved. One of my former students, Jaques Servin, a very experimental and interesting writer, has been published by them on two occasions.

Rohrberger: Is the group still in operation?

Crone: Yes, but it has been reorganized several times.

Rohrberger: It may seem odd to you but I keep seeing parallels between the Winnebago story and Barthelme's *The Dead Father.* In Barthelme's story the son survives because in a patriarchal society, sons must, though fathers don't give in without a struggle. In your story both Mother and Daughter survive though not without an epic battle between them. It seems they can not live together or apart; their lives are defined by separation and return;

it's more like Demeter and Persephone, though the male god is still in place and takes charge of the female cluttered Winnebago.

Crone: Well, I have never made this connection but the truth is that the year I wrote the *Winnebago* I read *The Dead Father* and wrote a paper on it for a class at Hopkins with the British critic Tony Tanner. It has never occurred to me that the book had any influence whatsoever on my work. But everything you say is true, so it must have. I will say that I had written about half of it before I read that book, which I found both charming and exasperating. I was consciously thinking of the Persephone and Demeter myth, and of the idea of the Winnebago as a sort of ultimate development: a house that is a car.

Rohrberger: I have been unable to find a copy of your novel *A Period of Confinement* which came between the two volumes of short stories you have published. Were you pleased with the novel?

Crone: In many ways I was, yes. It was published in France, and was in paperback for a few years in this country. It had many very good reviews which I will always cherish. A very good screenplay was written of it. I bought my first computer with the option money for the screenplay.

Rohrberger: I read also that you have another novel in preparation?

Crone: Yes, I've described it already, a little bit.

Rohrberger: I am fascinated by the concept that emptiness defines forms, not so much in physics where it is an elementary concept if a fairly new one, but in so far as emptiness defines form in art. You are clearly not thinking of emptiness in terms of a lack of setting since the New Orleans stories are replete with regional awareness. Are you thinking of silences as, for example, that which surround the epiphany, which is a saying of that which cannot be said?

Crone: Well, this is in reference, I suppose, to my very favorite story in *Dream State,* which is "Desire." Selectivity in art, which is taste, is exercised by leaving things out. To say that something is well done or well made is to say that there was action and there was restraint. Beauty is as much about what is missing as what is there. There is a way in which a short story is the ultimate metonymy, because it is the tiny part that suggests the whole—by its very tininess, it seems to imply a greater and greater world. I think of that moment in which the son, in "Everything That Rises Must Converge," looks up after he realizes his mother has had a stroke: everything after will follow from this. No other word need be said. A novel would be unnecessary, in fact possibly destructive to the universality of that moment. A novel which is monumental in scale, which is comprehensive, let's say, like *Anna Karenina* gives the illusion that everything is contained within, that the world is in the pages, as there are so many of them. In a way it is very definitive, but it manages somehow to shrink-wrap the world. Chekhov implies the whole variety of life by just writing a few pages, giving us a few lines. The world he speaks about is possibly larger than the world Tolstoy speaks about because Chekhov leaves so much out. His very method implies the enormous mystery in things as they are. The idea that emptiness is form and form is emptiness is a Buddhist doctrinal idea. The character in this story I wrote is a photographer struggling with Buddhism in New Orleans, which is a big struggle. He is speaking as a monk, recalling the days when he lived in that gorgeous place. In recollection, when his life has become a studied encounter with emptiness and poverty, the life of a renunciant, he sees his past in New Orleans as very full of every pleasure, as marvelous, delightful. But at the time when he lived that life, it felt completely empty and hollow—the life of the senses, shall we say. The Buddhists have a practice where you try to break down sense impressions so that you realize that these things that seem solid—the day, a meal, an object, another person— are really a discontinuous parade of data which we add up to compose into a "solid whole." It is our own minds that are filling in the gaps, which is a fact we now know from theory of the way the brain operates—we are always filling in the gaps, making little quantum leaps from this instant to the next, on pure hubris and faith. Form is our own invention, to some degree, required by the discontinuity of sense experience. And emptiness is that discontinuity. All the places where you can fall in. A great short story, like "The Lady with the Pet Dog," or "Gooseberries," or "Everything That Rises Must Converge," ends with a discontinuity that the reader feels the urgent need to make a decision about. So we are thrown back upon what came before, and we are looking for the thread, the deep story, the underlying form. So that we can apply that rule to govern the shape of the future—our own future actually, not only the future of the characters—we don't know enough about the characters, we must apply the rules of our own lives. It is the indeterminacy, the reticence, the emptiness, the restraint, of short stories that causes us to feel that they are universal. This is what makes short story writing so hard: if you say too much, you end up with a lesser world. I should follow my own advice.

Ana Maria Del Rio

Maurice Lee

Born in 1948 in Santiago, Chile, Ana Maria Del Rio holds degrees from Rice University in Houston, Texas, and from Pittsburgh. She is the author of numerous short stories and has been anthologized a number of times. Her first book, *Entreparentesis* (*Within Parentheses*), published in 1985, is a collection of thirty short stories which received a number of awards in her home country of Chile. Del Rio has also been successful as a novelist; her first novel, *Oxida de Carmen* (1986) won the Maria Luisa Bombal prize. *Del Golpe, Amalia en el Umbral,* her second prize-winning novel, was published in 1991, as was *Tiempo que ladra,* which received the "Letters of Gold" prize from the University of Miami. Del Rio aims in her fiction to present what concerns people, the things they do not see. Currently, she lives in Arica, Chile, where she is a professor of literature.

Lee: What influenced you to write short stories?
Del Rio: I think that there was a very powerful reason that led me to write short stories, that was the need I had in 1979, more or less. I was just married and my daughter was just born. Then there was a dictatorship. I knew that I needed to begin to feel some kind of freedom, and the only way to feel free of the dictatorship, of all the prejudices and links—societal links—was to begin to write.
Lee: Why do you think it was the written expression that was, for you, some form of liberation? I mean, for example, why was it not politics, or

why was it not some form of social reform? Why was it writing, do you think?

Del Rio: I think it was for two reasons—two main reasons at least. I think that it was because I had written before, but as a hobby. Writing on napkins and, to feel like a writer, working by the street, something very romantic and useless. And the other reason, well, there was a need that I had to give form to all my drafts and intentions of writing. I had something to say. And the other reason was that writing in those times was the only form, artistic form at least, to express some thought, because our theatre or painting was censored.

Lee: Under control?

Del Rio: Under control. Government control. And then it was very difficult to do it.

Lee: Do you know, what was the first story that you wrote?

Del Rio: The first story that I wrote was called "New Year," and it tells the story of a very enslaved housekeeper who goes to a New Year's party with her husband. And then she has an insight, a very aggressive insight, on how enslaved she is. Then she opens the door and goes away, without her hand-bag, without anything. It's a very long story. It's hard to be shortened.

Lee: Was that in anyway reflective, in some respect, of your own feelings and your own . . . life?

Del Rio: In some ways, it was—it was a special time. A dictatorship in those times, in Chile, was not only the government thing. It was the daily things in each one's life. I have a theory about it. I think that under government dictatorship, in each home there is a little dictator at the table giving orders. And sometimes it's the husband. In Chile, as a male-istic country, it is. But, some other times the dictator can be the woman. But there is someone who takes the power in each home, in each particular case. And this happens only under a dictatorship. It's very, very "coups" we say; in a democracy this is not so severe, or so bad.

Lee: You seem to suggest that the households in Chile somehow reflect what the government is doing.

Del Rio: Yes.

Lee: The writing for you enables you to, in some respect, see another way of operating and living. And that is, in a sense, freedom. The first question then is, in relationship to that, was the writing liberating? Did your writing become a kind of liberating process?

Del Rio: Good question. It has been. My writing I think, has been taking more freedom in form. It's going to be difficult to explain, because it's something related with techniques or expression—expression techniques. And in this sense—not in the sense of things, or not in the sense of general theories about life—I think that I have not changed it a lot. But in the sense of technical, technique expressions, I think that I have been liberated of rigid frames and a rigid way of how to say that. And of course, liberated also from the Latin American boom of the sixties.

Lee: You said "the liberation of the form," or "liberated of rigid frames?" So the short story form was for you initially somewhat rigid and now it's more free form?

Del Rio: I don't know if it can be called a more free form, but it's a very different form to express. And you're right in the sense that I am not trying to take care of image and the very special adjective for example, that I have to find it, in writing. No. It doesn't matter. I think that it has to be more important, for example, dialogues and presentation of characters. And I have no landscape in my stories at all—really, I think that it has disappeared completely—and I only have persons acting in the stories trying to find some life, some sense, well, maybe some common goal.

Lee: You said there are no landscapes, and there's a need then to concentrate on individuals. Is it that the land does not matter? Or is it just . . .

Del Rio: Yes, the land matters. But, the interior land. The land we all have, all of us have in our soul.

Lee: I mean, Iquique, as I have seen it from afar, and Arica, as I know from being there, have such a dramatic landscape, in terms of the river and the ocean on one side and this arid dry land, sand, almost no vegetation on the other. It seems to me to be a perfect backdrop for characters. But, you're saying that you don't use that in your works, primarily?

Del Rio: Let me explain. I think that I use it like a stimulus to write and to present the characters, but not to describe it. It has been profusely described by other Northern writers. And not very well. They speak about the dry earth and not having water, and how thirsty the land is, and all of that. But, I think that the landscape is very powerful. I have also said it's difficult too, to create. All the desert characters are strong, although they don't say anything—only with postures or their ways of walking or something.

Lee: What type of characters interest you? And I guess maybe you could talk to that in terms of their class, or in terms of their gender, or in terms of their education. Which characters are of most interest to you?

Del Rio: A strong question. I think that gender is in the back of me. It exists, but it's in the back. And, then, in the first place, I have some family class character. People in our countries are determined by class, not by race. The exception is the north of Chile, because there are two clear phrases. Imardas and Chilean. But, my stories are not of the time in the north of Chile. Mine have to do with a "special jail" of the families. All Latin American families, speaking in a very bad sense, and a critical sense, are a kind of jail.

Lee: A kind of jail?

Del Rio: Jail. Carousel. They close the doors to the young. They have created a lot of dependence, and of course, the man controls the economic dependence. That exists today. My daughter, for example, is a painter. She is 19, but she cannot support herself. And nobody can in these circumstances. This family, any Chilean family, is put in this "jail" of affection, love, and care, but sometimes it is so, so heavy for the young. And this kind of relationship that also has concepts of class and conducts and places where some class they can visit and some class they cannot—all of them I prefer to show in my stories.

Lee: To go back to this point just a little bit, and not to talk about it too much—do you write then to bring about change, as they would say in the States, or just to provide some emotional space for yourself?

Del Rio: I don't know if I understand exactly what you mean.

Lee: In your writing, do you want it to have the effect of changing conditions around you—helping people get out of that "jail"? Or is it just for your own sense of peace and space and a certain kind of internal freedom for yourself? Not necessarily physical freedom. You indicated before that your life had not changed much, but is it a kind of internal freeing?

Del Rio: It's very interesting because at first it was a kind of "catharsis." In my first stories, I am speaking about the seventies and eighties. But after it began to take place, the idea came to me of writing as representing a group, a collectivity. Of course, I knew very well what kind of collectivity I wanted to represent. Not the powerful, but the others that are less so—a great number in Chile. I think that all my recent characters don't represent me; they represent the group.

Lee: Your story "Wash Water" evokes a lot of thought, and I think some sense of fear for this little girl. What inspired you, or what triggered the response for you to write that particular story? Is it because it's representative of a certain type of life in Chile, or is this a sort of isolated situation? What was important to you about writing that particular story?

Del Rio: The story, "Wash Water," was written not to illustrate a particular case at all. It's a very common situation of middle class life. Almost all the people, middle class, in Chile have that.

Lee: Have that experience? [Interviewer's Note: The story, "Wash Water," is about a very young middle class girl (around seven or eight) who is sexually stimulated, excited, and abused by a common laborer working at the house. In this case he uses his fingers and his tongue as the weapons of abuse, and it is clear that such a relationship is abusive. The girl's naive concern is not the abuse, but in not getting her newly starched dress dirty. She "scares" the laborer by asking him if he will come again the next day.]

Del Rio: Yes, in the middle class it's a very, very common situation. And silence—silent situation also. The family, in that case, acts like there is nothing to speak about it. Now there it is—they act as if nothing has happened in all the cases. The girls of a lot of generations of middle class families are raped by the representatives of workers that belong to an inferior class. That class has a lot of anger against the middle class. But I don't want to point in this situation—the situation of the intention of rape. It's a situation of intention to rape any being. What I wanted to do really—was to subvert the intention of rape—to show the other side of the victim. The victim of the dictatorship, the victim of the sexual abuse, of any kind of abuse, can change the situation within two channels. One channel is anger; and the other channel is "innocence." If you don't know you are raped, you are not raped at all. If you enjoy it, for example, in the case of "Wash Water," you are not raped, but you are more powerful than the rapist. The handy man really, in "Wash Water," doesn't represent the lower class. He represents the power of one thing over another. There is some freedom in this short story, because one, if I want, I can change the conditions.

Lee: The fact is that she's not aware of what happens to her, or she's aware, but not aware from a viewer's point of view. In seeing the rape, we know what's happening to her, but she sees it from another point of view.

Del Rio: Yes.

Lee: The girl knows what is happening to her from another point of view, and she is unaware of the rape. For her, it is a combination of pleasure and a little trepidation because she's disobeying—she's getting her dress dirty, and it's not going to be starched. Does that signify, in a larger sense, what you feel happens to people in Chile? That things are happening to them from a dictator point of view that they really don't know about, but they still respond to it? Am I going too far outside of the story in that analysis?

Del Rio: It's a very good reading that you have made, because the sense of guiltiness of the little girl at the end of the story really is related with this general guiltiness that hangs over all the citizens, during any dictatorship from right or from left. It doesn't matter.

Lee: How would you describe yourself as a writer? You know, there are terms that float around such as feminist, or realist, or romanticist, etc. Do those terms apply; do you think about any of that at all as you're writing, or is it just the tale that you want to address? Maybe I'm asking, how do you feel about labels?

Del Rio: Yes. Well, I don't feel fine with labels. I think I can define myself as a rebel writer.

Lee: Rebel writer?

Del Rio: Yes.

Lee: And what does that mean?

Del Rio: That means not to be starched up with forms. Not to be full of frames. And be able to follow freedom conducts that are sometimes very, very difficult to accomplish.

Lee: How important is Chile, the country, in your writing? For example, if you were in the States, do you think that that would impact upon your writing about Chile? How important is your being there in Chile relative to your writing?

Del Rio: Well, to be in Chile, it's important to be able to describe the time. Really, the only way is to live in the time, in the country. If not, you cannot do it. To be a Chilean writer, it's important in the creation of my characters. There are special characters—I don't know if they are called Chilean characters, but there are the determinated reactions, and also they are at the end of stories. It's the same with the reactions, and sometimes the same things that we are expected to write or say. For example, the tendency of the critic to define the very bad of all the national writers, the problem of Isabel Allende.

Lee: The Chileans say what about her?

Del Rio: They say she's very famous, but she writes like García Márquez, and she writes oh, only history, etc. But of course, they buy her books, and would be very happy to have a signed book, of course.

Lee: Did you hear Bharati Mukherjee talk at the conference about how she felt about being typecast? Of only being able to write about Indian characters? Do you feel a similar problem in your writing? Does it bother you if people want you to write all the time about Chile and Chilean characters, and do you want to write about other things, for example, American and American characters? I mean, what are your priorities around that question?

Del Rio: I think that the preference I have to write about Chilean characters is not to make Chile known by the world. The best way I write, my preference is to move easily in between different fashions and affections. This is the best way that I have as a Chilean. I have tried to write American stories. I have a dozen or so stories about America—I was here from '87 to '91, and—well, they are very bad stories. Why? Because I was looking at America from the outside, and then all of what I saw was like magical realism. For example, I have a story about a guy who goes in his car, then he stops, and then begins to cry—to cry about some kind of tree that is there in the highway. Well, this is a very unbelievable situation. But the guy is asking for food in a mechanical way—he is begging.

Lee: So why would that be a bad story, do you feel, in terms of your writing about this young man?

Del Rio: It is a bad story because there exists the situation, the real situation. I am changing it only because I am not understanding it. But it's my problem, not the real problem.

Lee: You mentioned a term that we heard often at the conference: magical realism. How do you define that term, and does it play a part in your writing? What does it mean to you?

Del Rio: Well, I think that the sense of magical realism has changed a lot from García Márquez to 1994. At this moment, magical realism is not representing unbelievable situations, or unbelievable characters. Magical realism means the need to have open eyes to any kind of phenomenon—to any kind of possibilities—to any kind of reality. I think that magical realism represents freedom in our days.

Lee: So it's a way of maybe getting beyond the reality to something that is unreal but is significant?

Del Rio: I think that things are beyond the reality. It's so powerful these things, real things. And sometimes more.

Lee: And do you use this in your writing—magical realism?

Del Rio: A different kind. Not girls flying to the sky and all of that, but it's very difficult for a Latin American writer not to use that kind of magical realism. My bad stories have a García Márquez magical realism. And why is that? Because García Márquez invented that first. Only for that reason. But all of us, with no consciousness, sometimes write these kind of stories.

Lee: Were you influenced by storytelling by parents or grandparents as we heard so many writers say time and time again at the conference, or were there other stimuli for you?

Del Rio: This was something very funny that I saw at the conference. All of the writers had a grandmother who was a storyteller. Really—I didn't! I was a very lonely girl, and I had a very lonely childhood. I think that I was my own storyteller, and, of course, my stories were against the stories that grown-ups tell. And I didn't hear it. It was there, but was of no importance to me.

Lee: Is your experience the more normal one, or are Isabel Allende's and others' who always had this grandmother, or somebody who was telling them stories, the more normal one?

Del Rio: I think it depends on the landscape of Chile. In the rural parts it is very common to have a relative who is a storyteller. But in the cities, of course, not so. I think that Isabella was very lucky to have such "magic" women in her family.

Lee: Do you believe her?

Del Rio: I want to believe it.

Lee: You mentioned America before. Would you ever write another story about America? Or would you ever want to write in English?

Del Rio: No. I have always been writing in Spanish. At this point, I cannot dream to write in English. It may be several decades before I can create a sentence in English.

Lee: The story that you read, "Wash Water," was translated here. How good was the translation?

Del Rio: I don't have confidence in my opinion. I asked professor Jaime Gomez, and he read it very slowly and he told me that it was an excellent, excellent translation.

Lee: You seem to be getting more and more attention in Chile, in terms of your writing. Do you get a sense of how you are received by Chileans? Are you being seen more and more as an important Chilean writer?

Del Rio: The reality is it's very difficult in Chile to be recognized as an important Chilean writer. Well, there is a joke—sometimes we writers get together and laugh about the fact that we will all be dead before we are recognized. Of course, I am exaggerating. The government of Chile has just publicly recognized Allende, and has come to decorate her in a very beautiful ceremony. But, really, it's so difficult because the national prize of literature that exists in Chile is given to writers who are very old. It's difficult.

Lee: Given that situation—is it more difficult for women than for men?

Del Rio: I think not now, but three years or five years ago, yes, it was. There was a tradition that if you are a Chilean woman writer and are participating in a contest, never, never, send the real name; send a pseudonym. But never give a feminine pseudonym. Because you are not going to be read. It's a tradition, and all of us follow it. All female writers have male pseudonyms.

Lee: What is your male pseudonym?

Del Rio: It's a play on words. My name is Ana, and I use the word "Ana-guel." That means Ana and other, but also in Spanish, an *agel* means "shelf of books."

Lee: What do you think has brought about the change that women are now more accepted than before?

Del Rio: I think that world feminism has helped it a lot. During the dictatorship there was severe control. There were very few occasions to publish. With no publishing, a lot of literary workshops were created. The main participants in the workshops were women. They were working each week and reading and criticizing. But men did not have a lot of interest in workshops, because workshops didn't give the occasion to publish. Men needed to publish more than women did. As a result of the workshops, a generation of women writers developed, very strong and very good.

Lee: What things about writing do you not like?

Del Rio: Well, I don't like to correct. I don't have time to correct. I was very jealous of Isabel Allende when she spoke so beautifully about the candles and the space and the time and the magic of the hour, and the time to write. I don't have time to write at all.

Lee: So you certainly don't have time to revise?

Del Rio: I don't ever have time to revise, and I am representative of all women writers who are not famous like Isabel. Really, they don't have the time. Neither do the artists or any of the painters. Anyway, the short story is a very difficult form to correct. Contessa, the Argentinean writer, said that trying to improve a short story is like trying to improve regimes. It's impossible.

Lee: Yes. But is the short story your favorite form of writing, versus poetry, or drama, or the novel?

Del Rio: Unfortunately, yes.

Lee: Why unfortunately?

Del Rio: Because Latin America publishers ask for novels, and novels, and novels. It's very difficult to sell a collection of short stories in Latin America.

Lee: One final question. Have you seen things at the conference that will cause you to change how you write, or how to do different things with the short story form?

Del Rio: Yes. One thing—Sonia Sanchez's reading shows me how far we are from the power of the cry of protest for a situation. We, as Latin American writers, cannot use this powerful voice. But we can use another kind of tool. It is a very urgent task that I have imposed on myself to find the tool for this anger.

Ellen Douglas

Rick Feddersen

Born in Natchez, Mississippi, Ellen Douglas spent much of her childhood in Arkansas and Louisiana but spent the summer with her grandparents in Natchez. She has always maintained close ties with Mississippi, and much of her work is set in fictional locales in that state. After living in New York and Virginia (attending Randolph Macon Women's College), she married Kenneth Haxton in 1945, and they raised three sons in Greenville, Mississippi. Since her first book, *A Family's Affairs* (1962), Douglas has explored conflicts of tradition and values in southern characters who confront racial issues, guilt, and the specter of the past. Douglas's second book, *Black Cloud, White Cloud* (1963), was also her first collection of short fiction. Since then she has published novels. *Where the Dreams Cross* (1968), *Apostles of Light* (1973), *The Rock Cried Out* (1979), *A Lifetime Burning* (1982), and most recently, *Can't Quit You, Baby* (1988). She presently lives in Jackson, Mississippi and is working on another collection of short stories.

Feddersen: I understand that in the forties you worked as a disc jockey in Alexandria, Louisiana, and wrote between spots. Did that experience affect how you began to develop as a writer?

Douglas: I think not . . . except that it gave me the leisure to write while I was also earning a living. But in a way, maybe so. It was in periods of about twenty-seven minutes that I would write, so to begin with, I began to think in twenty-seven-minute thoughts.

Feddersen: When you were working in these regular intervals, did you find yourself working on longer or shorter pieces?

Douglas: I think what happened, which was conveniently pushed into the twenty-seven minutes, was that I had a number of connected stories—stories about the same fictional people, who derived from real people, and I would work on one little piece at a time. Finally, some years later, I realized that those pieces were more closely connected than I had thought; they turned into a novel. *A Family's Affairs* is a loosely constructed novel made up of stories of a number of different characters' lives, originally based on those early stories.

Feddersen: Could any of the segments in *A Family's Affairs* have been called short stories, do you think?

Douglas: Might have been . . . in fact, I did think of a couple of them as short stories. But then when they began to connect with each other, I changed the form and they became novelistic. I work that way a lot, not just in that first novel. I've been interested since the beginning in telling tales and stories, connected stories that eventually find a center that draws them together. In *Black Cloud, White Cloud,* for example, the center is the relationships between black and white people in that particular time and place. The stories remain discrete, so it is a collection of short stories. But in my last book, *Can't Quit You, Baby,* although I originally conceived it as a number of stories to be told by and in the voice of a black woman, I eventually became interested in the relationship between the characters—the black woman and the white woman. Obviously, it seemed to me, this was going to become a novel about the two women, rather than a collection of stories told by a black woman.

Feddersen: It seems that the novel has always enjoyed more commercial success and even more prestige than short fiction.

Douglas: In practical terms, if you're a writer trying to make a little money—and this happened to me early on—it takes me a long time to write a short story. I quit writing short stories after *Black Cloud, White Cloud* because short story collections were so difficult to sell and stories were hard to sell to magazines. So, I turned my attention to the novel. But I think that situation may have changed a little now. You can sell a collection of stories and you can find some limited market for them in magazines. So, I've gone back after twenty-five years of not writing any stories and lately I've begun to do it again.

Feddersen: I believe that one of the stories in *Black Cloud, White Cloud* was actually a much shorter story?

Douglas: No, it was a longer story first, then it was a shorter story. "On the Lake" was the short version which came out in the *New Yorker*. I sent them the whole long piece (which is called "Hold On") but with limitations of space, they didn't want anything that long, so it had to be edited. And then when it came out in the book *Black Cloud, White Cloud,* I went back to the original form because I thought that the life of the rescuer was important to the story I really wanted to tell.

Feddersen: I take it that character development was what was more fully expressed in the longer version?

Douglas: Not only that, but it seemed to me that in the shorter version . . . how do I put it? Well, Estella, who is the black woman, is presented as being rescued by her white employer in a drowning accident. And that's the story in "On the Lake." In the longer original, "Hold On," the white employer's relationship with the young white man gives a kind of reverse story where the young white man tells of having been rescued by an old black woman, which in terms of the society and the time and place, makes a balance which seemed essential to me. It seemed to me to be false to say that black people are rescued by white people; it seemed to me true to say that human beings are rescued by human beings; I had to have the other rescue to balance the first.

Feddersen: I guess I'll go ahead and ask this question now. I don't suppose it's so unusual for a writer to write about characters who have to deal with conflicts like tradition and change—Faulkner did that. But do you see your characters more in terms of individual responsibilities in their struggles than in terms of community or cultural issues? Or is that a ridiculous question?

Douglas: No, of course it isn't ridiculous. I'm not sure how to answer it, though. I think of myself as a political writer in the sense that I'm always concerned with the individual in his society or her society. And certainly, in the South, in the thirties through the seventies, which is what I've mostly written about, the society that those individuals were in was profoundly influential on their lives. But of course, I'm still interested in the *individual* who's in that society rather than sociological questions, or didactics.

Feddersen: Do you object to being called a "Southern" writer, or a "regionalist"?

Douglas: Yes, I do object. I think reviewers sometimes have just a kind of short hand to fill out a paragraph—phrases like "Southern writers" or "women writers" and the like. But I think of myself as being an American writer in the last quarter of the twentieth century.

Feddersen: Maybe because of reawakened interest in voice and identity in writing in general, some people seem almost to suggest that perhaps all writers are in some sense regionalists. Do you think that realistic writers must depend upon a strong sense of place?

Douglas: I don't really believe that a successful story or novel can be written with people in it who are not in a place or places. You can write music without words and you can make sculptures and paintings which are abstractions, but fiction has to have people and places. So I suppose, in that sense, Balzac's a regionalist, Tolstoy's a regionalist, Dostoyevsky's a regionalist, and so on. But place in fiction has to do not only with realistic fiction but also . . . oh, I was just thinking of that strange and wonderful story by a Latin American writer about a man who gets in a boat and goes back and forth across a river for twenty years or so, and can never come ashore.

Feddersen: Was it Márquez?

Douglas: No, I think it was [João] Rosa, "The Third Bank of the River." It's a spooky story—not realism at all—but the river, the boat, the man in it, the floods, the air, the people on the bank wishing he would come ashore—all these become real—just as much as the room where Kafka's cockroach lives and becomes real.

Feddersen: What do you think are the differences between the short story and the longer forms like the novel, or even the novella?

Douglas: I think of the novella as being a form in which you have the concentration and the immediacy and the limitedness of formal structure that is more closely related to the short story. But you can do anything you want to in a novel; it may work, and it may not work. If it works, it's a good novel, if it doesn't work, it's a bad novel. Take for example, . . . well take Tolstoy. He can put lectures in *War and Peace,* and it can be the greatest novel in the world, or Mann's *The Magic Mountain* with those long conversations between Settembrini and the priest. You just stick them in there, and if they don't fall out, it's a good novel. If they do fall out, it's a bad novel.

Feddersen: Could we say that the novella is often simply a very long short story?

Douglas: To me, it seems it usually is. At the outer edges, it goes in each direction. I mean, the *longer* the novella, you think, well, *maybe* it's a novel, but there's always an indefinite line.

Feddersen: Something like Tolstoy's *The Death of Ivan Ilyich* would be . . .

Douglas: A very long short story. But then, something like *The Great Gatsby* is almost a novella, you know—it's so concentrated and so structured, but somehow it has crossed the line and become a novel.

Feddersen: Of course, *Gatsby* is told from one limited point of view. Do you think that the structural difference between the short story and the novel sometimes has to do more with point of view than it does with just narrative? I guess what I'm trying to ask is this: Is something about the process of narration different for shorter forms and longer forms?

Douglas: I don't know whether I can give a sensible answer to that. What pops into mind is something Eudora Welty said one time about the short story: a short story has to *seem* to have been written at one sitting. Maybe it took you twenty years to write it, but it's like the drawing of a deep, long breath. It's as if you had written all the way through it at one sitting. And of course, that has to do with just a deep unity—of subjects and tone and style and everything else that goes into it.

Feddersen: Is Eudora Welty one of the writers who influenced you?

Douglas: Mm . . . Not so much influenced. More I think, I admired her, when I began to read her work. I guess I was in my early twenties and I had already read Faulkner and had begun to read Dostoyevsky and Conrad and others. So Welty, well, Welty's only ten or twelve years older than I am, so I almost think of her as being in my generation. But I admire her work greatly. Katherine Anne Porter influenced me. And of course, she would have been ten or twelve years older than Welty. I think when I first began to write stories there may have been some influence just in similarities—the tone, the subjects, the South, or in Porter's case the Southwest—she was a writer in whom I was very much interested when I was young.

Feddersen: You mentioned Faulkner. Did his work influence you?

Douglas: I don't think any writer of my generation in the South could possibly not have been influenced by Faulkner, by his vision of the world, if not his style. When we came to Faulkner, it was for me anyway, in the middle-to-late thirties when I was fifteen, sixteen, seventeen, eighteen years old. It was like, "Hey, this is the world I live in. I can't believe it! Somebody's put it into a book." So, it was very influential—like an explosion. The other thing about it is, I remember reading *Light in August* when I was sixteen. What in the world did I think of *Light in August* when I was sixteen, you know? I couldn't have understood what was going on. I was sheltered and naive—a southern girl-child. But somehow, I think that all penetrated, you know.

Feddersen: Do you remember when you first decided to become a writer?

Douglas: Well, I was writing bad little poems by the time I was ten or twelve years old. Fortunately for me and everyone else, I abandoned that in middle adolescence. I didn't have any conception of people being able to do that, to make a living writing, particularly, I guess, women. I planned to get married and have children and have somebody else make a living for me, as most women of my generation did. But I looked around for a man who would think it was fine if I wanted to write, and I found one. I was lucky in being supported in my work by my husband, who was also interested in writing. I edited some of his stories when I was coming along. He is not a published writer, but he's a composer and musician, and he's done a lot of writing.

Feddersen: Getting back to Katherine Anne Porter, she utilized a highly developed sense of place.

Douglas: Right, she did. And she also used that same thing I'm talking about: when a number of stories have a deep thematic and subjective connection, they sometimes waiver between being a collection of stories and a novel.

Feddersen: I can remember reading Porter's *The Old Order.* Some critics call this type of work a short story cycle, or story sequence. It's somewhat like a novel in that themes are related throughout, but individual portions can stand alone as short stories.

Douglas: Right. And of course, Welty uses that same technique in *The Golden Apples.*

Feddersen: Do you think you have done something like that with *Black Could, White Cloud*?

Douglas: To a degree. *Black Cloud, White Cloud* is unified mainly by the preoccupation with black/white relationships in that period.

Feddersen: So, unity of theme?

Douglas: Yes, theme. But in *Can't Quit You, Baby,* Tweet's stories—the black woman's stories about her life—as the novel moves along, you learn about Tweet's life because she tells the stories, but those stories really are discrete. Several of them could be read as stories, because she tells them as stories.

Feddersen: I think it's especially interesting the way Tweet tells her stories about her past with such a strong sense of voice. Of course, her white friend just doesn't seem to be catching on to what Tweet is saying.

Douglas: Yes—Cornelia's deafness is metaphorical as well as physical.

Feddersen: Do you think that story cycles—tightly unified collections—are sometimes promoted as novels?

Douglas: Yes, I was thinking of William Maxwell and *Billy Dyer and Other Stories* which is a collection of very intimately connected stories, but it is really marketed as a novel.

Feddersen: Do you think that short fiction can achieve the same level of excellence and importance as the novel?

Douglas: Oh Gosh . . . anybody who could write stories like "Araby" would never have to write anything else as long as he lived—not to mention a few others in *Dubliners*.

Feddersen: You have a collection called *The Magic Carpet and Other Tales* which I have not been able to find. How did you come to do this collection and why isn't it available?

Douglas: The man who did those marvelous linoleum cuts for the illustrations was a Mississippi artist who had died by the time I wrote those versions of the stories, all of them being classic and ancient folk tales, myths, and fairy tales. The University Press of Mississippi asked me to do them—to give a stylistically consistent text; they wanted to publish a book with those illustrations done by Walter Anderson years earlier. So I really didn't pick the stories—Walter Anderson just chose to illustrate those. When I was asked by the University Press to write those versions of the stories, I thought, Oh this'll be a breeze; it'll be so simple. But when I began to do it, I did lots of reading of alternative versions and thought a lot about what I was doing before I actually did it. It turned out to be, I think, a beautiful book. Unfortunately, it's out of print now, but they are talking about doing another printing. [*The Magic Carpet and Other Tales* was reprinted in 1997 by University Press of Mississippi.]

Feddersen: Do you always know when a narrative is going to be a short story or a novel?

Douglas: No . . . I trust in the Lord [laugh]. Well, to illustrate, again I'll go back to *Can't Quit You, Baby,* or even to the one before that, *A Lifetime Burning*—I knew when I began to work on that book that it was a novel. It never crossed my mind that any part of it would stand alone as a short story. So, yes, sometimes you can know very early. But in my last book, *Can't Quit You, Baby* I started out thinking that what I would have would be a collection of stories, but I had not gotten very far before I realized that was not the case. And I guess with *The Rock Cried Out,* which LSU Press has recently republished, I knew from the beginning that although it would incorporate several tales that I had heard over the years which seemed to be connected, I knew that it was going to be a novel about a young man trying to find himself.

Feddersen: Have you ever had a single story that turned into a novel?

Douglas: Not yet.

Feddersen: How do you think you have changed as a writer over the last decade or so? Or have you?

Douglas: I think after *Apostles of Light,* when I began writing *The Rock Cried Out,* I got more interested in . . . I'm not sure how to say it, but the subjects I chose required a different sort of treatment, I guess. My writing changed radically. First, in *The Rock Cried Out,* dealing with one first-person voice, then having to fiddle around—in a big novel—with presenting the other major characters without filtering them through the first-person narrator's mind. Then in *A Lifetime Burning,* I got really interested in lies and truth and obsession—how obsession affects people. Then again in *Can't Quit You, Baby,* I was very interested in lies and truth. Those are the major changes I think—and then what one does formally is always influenced by what one's been reading. And I've been reading for forty or fifty years now.

Feddersen: You mentioned your return to the short story. Is that what you are working on now?

Douglas: Yes, I've written a couple—one is almost a novella—it's about fifty pages. And that's hard to sell, you know, getting back to livelihood, the profession. Nobody wants to publish a fifty-page story. Or even a twenty-five page story. People want things a little shorter. But I am writing stories and I hope eventually to have a collection.

Feddersen: Do you draw for characters on people you have known?

Douglas: Absolutely—a lot. And I just hope they don't sue me.

Feddersen: Has there ever been any danger of that?

Douglas: No. I don't think so. One of my books, *Where the Dreams Cross,* the main character was based on a friend of my mine, but I asked her ahead of time if she minded, and she said, no—as long as she didn't have to read it.

Feddersen: The narrator in *Can't Quit You, Baby* appears to become highly dramatized and begins to take on an identity with almost as much presence as the major characters. The narrator even claims in one passage that there is something at stake—what is at stake for this narrator?

Douglas: Yes, the narrator actually warns the reader—as much as says, I am writing this book and you have to take into account who I am and what my slant might be. No matter how hard I may try to be honest, I am a narrator. So what you have in this book is a fictional novelist. Although she doesn't have any physical presence, I think just her voice on the page lets you know that she's a woman. She says, well I tried to choose this or that narrative identity, maybe that of a black Ph.D., but even if I had done that "I" would still be here behind the narrator. The value of that to me in writing that book was the dramatic tension of the effort to tell the truth, knowing that one is always tempted to lie.

Feddersen: Such narrative self-reflexiveness is reminiscent of what post-modernists like Nabokov or Barth have done . . .

Douglas: Or, Kundera, another writer whose work interested me at that time.

Feddersen: How close is the narrator—or the fictional novelist—to the real author? Is it something which just takes place in the fiction?

Douglas: I think that's just what happens in the work. I hope it's subsumed in the work. It's not me, Josephine Haxton, who does all sorts of things, nor is it me, Ellen Douglas, the writer—it's a fictional novelist.

Feddersen: When did you take your pen name and why?

Douglas: Oh Lord, that's a long, complicated story, but I'll be as brief as possible. I sold my first book by accident. I didn't send it to anybody, I gave it to a friend who was a poet and novelist—Charles Bell—to read. He was in Annapolis teaching at St. John's College. He, in turn, gave it to his editor at Houghton-Mifflin who was looking for manuscripts for their fellowship competition. And the first thing I knew about it was when the editor at Houghton-Mifflin called me and asked if I would enter my manuscript in the competition. Being very young and naive—stupid might be a better word than naive—I had not really thought about the consequences of having put to use the lives of members of my family, my two aunts, in particular; I had really invaded their privacy. I felt I had to ask them if they would mind, and of course, what that amounted to was blackmail. They were decent ladies and they wouldn't say no, particularly after I won the competition. So when I went down to ask my aunts if it would be all right to publish it, they said (again) it was okay so long as they didn't have to read it and if I would use a pen name and not tell anybody who I was. So, my first books had no mention of my actual identity on the dust jackets or in any of the reviews. But after that, it was so well known in Mississippi that it really ceased to have any significance. By that time my publisher would not have wanted me to change back, so I just went ahead and left it as it was.

Feddersen: Have they all forgiven you?

Douglas: My two aunts forgave me immediately, although they felt uneasy about it. My uncle, who was also involved, I don't think ever really forgave me. I was surprised; I didn't think it would bother him. Of course, they're all dead now, so I can talk about it. But there's an example—those are lives that I used, transformed into a novel. Maybe, in a sense, they were dull lives, but there was heroism and character and place and time. To me, it was fascinating.

Feddersen: I remember hearing W. P. Kinsella say that fiction is a work of the imagination; you make it up; most peoples lives are too dull simply to transcribe into fiction. I take it that you find "real life" to be interesting enough to start with.

Douglas: I've heard some wonderful stories about things in other peoples' lives and I've put these to use even more than what's happened in my own life. In either case, it's what happens to the material. It gets completely transformed and becomes something else. It becomes fiction and one hopes that it doesn't stay dull.

Feddersen: You have begun to write stories again after twenty-five years. Do you still find yourself more inclined toward the novel?

Douglas: I know I have been in the past; maybe my attention span is getting shorter, but I have returned to writing short stories.

Feddersen: Are you working on anything longer?

Douglas: No, just stories.

Richard Ford

Ned Stuckey-French

Richard Ford has written four novels and a collection of short stories, as well as a screenplay and several essays, articles, and reviews. His first novel, *A Piece of My Heart* (1976), helped its author win both a Guggenheim Fellowship (1977–78) and a National Endowment for the Arts Fellowship (1979–80). It was followed by *The Ultimate Good Luck* (1981), a bruising, cinematic portrayal of Harry Quinn's attempt to get his brother out of a Oaxaca jail. In *The Sportswriter* (1986), Ford chronicled an Easter weekend of crisis in the life of Frank Bascombe, a funny and reflective New Jersey sportswriter who is recovering from a divorce precipitated by, among other things, the death of his son Ralph. *The Sportswriter* was in many ways Ford's breakthrough book of realism. Recently, he has published a novella, *Wildlife* (1990), and edited and introduced *The Grant Book of the American Short Story* (1992). In 1996 he was awarded the Pulitzer Prize for his novel *Independence Day.* Richard Ford was born in Jackson, Mississippi, in 1944 and has taught at The University of Michigan, Williams College, Princeton, and Harvard.

Stuckey-French: A few years back in your introduction to the *Pushcart Anthology,* you said that when you were first starting out you wrote many short stories and sent them out, but had to face the rejection time after time and decided to heck with this, I'm going to start a longer project so I can get some more sustained time to write.

Ford: That's right. That's exactly right. I began writing *A Piece of My Heart.*

Stuckey-French: What finally led you back to short stories and when did you start writing them again?

Ford: I started writing short stories again in 1979. I was teaching at Williams College, and Ray Carver and I were great friends. He and I were kicking around and went to the dog track down on the Vermont-Massachusetts line, with Kristina. I had been thinking the dog track was sort of intriguing; but Ray really loved to gamble. He'd gamble on most anything—in a kind of sporting way. Nothing serious. I remember the three of us in the stands at the dog track, and Ray was continually going off to make a bet. And of course he knew nothing about dogs. We'd bought these little tout books they sold you when you came in.

Stuckey-French: Which don't tell you much anyway.

Ford: They don't tell you *very* much. They tell you about the history of an individual dog, and its weight and age and where it was from. But that was all the inside dope he needed. And I'll never forget; he went down and made his bet, and he won. Then he went back down to get his money. This was in 1978, I guess, '78, '79. But when he came back up those concrete stairs, I saw a look in his eye of, sort of, wonderful, low-grade fury and frenzy. He had not been long from drinking at that time, and he still had a sort of wildness about him. But seeing that look made me think I'd like to write a story where somebody had that look. It was so vivid. I didn't really have an idea for a story, because I was at the time working on *The Ultimate Good Luck* and had pretty much put story-writing out of my mind, thinking that what I was was a novelist and not a story writer. But here was some little spark to seeing that look in Ray's eyes. God knows what its components were: avarice, pleasure, surprise, a glimpse at a life in which you were routinely a big winner. He liked thoughts of being a big winner—and he was one. But I went home to this big converted barn I was living in, and I thought to myself that I hadn't written a short story now in probably five or six years, or even tried. But I thought I'd try to write one, my first, all in a day. And so I sat down and I wrote it all in a day. It's a pretty short little story called "Going to the Dogs." It's about a man and it's not really about Ray, but a man who hatches a petty scheme to make a lot of money, and then doesn't. Ray's look, I guess, inclined me to that man.

Stuckey-French: So what was his anger about?

Ford: Oh, it wasn't anger. It was an ecstasy. He'd been having a few years of losses then, and this was different, and he liked it very, very much. It was sweet, really, and also funny. He pissed all the money away eventually that night.

Stuckey-French: By the sixth race it was gone.

Ford: By the sixth race, right. But anyway, I wrote that story and then didn't write another story till 1981. The stories all came one at a time. All the stories in *Rock Springs,* except for maybe the last two, were written one and two years apart. I wrote several of them during the time I was writing *The Sportswriter,* when I'd come to a patch of time when I wanted to stop and didn't know what else to do but wanted to keep writing. Kristina and I were living in Montana by then. And I would write one more story. And over time I began to think, as the stories accumulated, well maybe I can do this, whereas before I didn't think I could. And I thought it was natural in the life of a writer: that you at some point can do some things and at some other point you can't. Now, since 1987, I've written two stories, one of which is a novella-length piece and the other is a long story called "Jealous." And I thought in each instance that those were going to be short stories, of some short story length. But they weren't. They were longer. So, short stories weren't available to me at first, and then they came, and then they went away again. It's not mystical, at all. But I don't really want to belabor the point. Maybe they'll become available again. Who knows?

Stuckey-French: So the most recent stories outgrew themselves?

Ford: Well, I'd like to write stories again. At the tag end of a long novel, novels seem like such a long thing to do. I'd like to do something that is somewhat less hard. And stories—for me—are less hard.

Stuckey-French: A novel is such a long project, such a big commitment of yourself and your time that it seems you must believe in it, believe that it's really going to hit, that this one's really going to work. But, with a short story, is it easier to believe that you have a little more leeway?

Ford: Well, if stories fail, then they don't make a short story. It's like bread. Either it's a loaf of bread or it's doughy goo. And you can put it away and not think to yourself you've just pissed away two years of your life, or lost your whole purchase on your vocation. I've never written a story I didn't finish though.

Stuckey-French: They always feel like a loaf of bread?

Ford: Yeah. I haven't written many, though.

Stuckey-French: Each one at the end, it feels like it's a winner?

Ford: Well, it's a finished story, anyway. I've really only written twelve short or slightly longer stories in my life—that is since I decided I might could write them at all. And what I do, which in a sense addresses what you just said, is try to compensate for the lesser status of a short story by over-preparing, by considering it at the time I write it as the most important thing in the world. I don't think other people are like that necessarily. Some probably are. But some can write stories perfectly well from one side of their desk, or one side of their mind. But I've found it most expeditious to really clear my decks completely and concentrate only on the story at hand, which makes it as important as I can make it.

Stuckey-French: That sounds in a way like what I've read about the way Ray Carver worked too. I remember reading about his desk one time and that he kept a very neat desk and that each story was in a folder and that he only had the one folder on the desk at a time.

Ford: Maybe. I don't know. I saw Ray's desk a few times. It didn't make a big impression on me. It was just where he wrote.

Stuckey-French: Not that neat?

Ford: I don't remember. That's the side of a writer's life that doesn't much interest me. This business of how you go about writing—your desk, etc.—doesn't seem to reveal anything very interesting. And when it does seem to reveal something interesting, I finally think it's trivial. It's the stories that are interesting. The other, I suppose, is an amateur fascination whose implication is that the "magic" of literature can somehow be penetrated by examining the rather inert artifacts of its making. Of course, maybe I'm wrong. That's always possible. Maybe you can get at something that way.

Stuckey-French: So in the generation of a short story you say you really prepare. Yet, you say that first one, the first one when you started again, "Going to the Dogs," came in a day. Do you usually feel that they just come in a rush now, once you're ready to write?

Ford: No. It took me about five days to write "Rock Springs." It took me thirty days to write "Empire." One of my continual wrestling matches with myself is to work harder, longer, have more concentration—the Protestant virtues of selflessness. And I'd like to get back to the point that in writing stories I *could* write them in a day, or write them, you know, in four days—some succinct time. But, I probably overprepare, which makes writing them a longer proposition. I habitually want to ward off a day when in the course of writing a story or a novel, I suddenly don't have anything else to write about and I'm only two-thirds through. That's more concern to me than writing a story quickly. It's hard completely to explain but I think it's me trying to be better, me trying to take my work more seriously, to prepare more, to get more into stories. But it's possible, I suppose, to reach a point of diminishing returns where your preparation and your wish to be serious begin to turn on you slightly.

Stuckey-French: I remember talking to Scott Russell Sanders—I don't know if you know his work, but he's written both stories and essays—and he said that the difference for him between an essay and a story is that for an essay he takes a lot of notes. He's an ex-scientist so he even numbers the notes; whereas for a story, it is more likely to grow out of an image, like the image you mentioned of Ray Carver coming back with the money from the window. Sanders said that for him a story almost writes itself, it comes in a rush, it comes at once, whereas an essay is more assembled. Is that some of what you're talking about when you say you want to guard against over-preparing? Do you want to move your stories away from being assembled and back toward the image?

Ford: The idea of an assemblage is not foreign to the way I write essays, or to the way I write anything—stories included. I think of stories as constructions, and their logical, sequential nature is an achieved quality: the process of first putting one thing next to one thing, then putting the next; all of which creates, if you're lucky, the illusion of a cohesive story. You create the illusion of a told tale, and you create the illusion of naturally occurring linearness. I think I know what he means by things coming in a rush, as though they came to him and found their existence on the page in an already cohesive shape. That might be good if the story was full enough. My way at least lets me put whatever I want into a story and work at making it fit; instead of becoming, early on, submissive to a wholly formed, "naturally occurring" story whose structure is difficult to fiddle with.

Stuckey-French: Another couple of this phenomenon is that Faulkner said that when he sat down to start *The Sound and the Fury,* all he had was the image of a little girl crawling out of a window and he could see her drawers . . .

Ford: If that's true. I guess he said that. Who knows if it was true. Why would he tell the truth?

Stuckey-French: Isn't it pretty to think so?

Ford: Well, to fit myself into that idea, it's possible that my recollection of what provoked "Going to the Dogs" is just a convenience of my memory. I'm sure I had other things circulating in my notebook, or so to speak, in my thinking, and I'm sure I wanted to work them into the story. That's certainly typical of me, and it's truthfully and fundamentally the way stories come into being for me. There all these things that are accumulating in my head or my notebook, things I like or am interested in, and what I want to do is get them into stories. That's my use for them, and that's my understanding of what literary art is. I want to find or make a context in language and logic into which this detail, this line of dialogue, this concept will fit, and which context will, by making them contiguous and interactive, develop in all into something unforeseen, something that is actually new, larger than the sum of parts, and useful and perhaps pretty. And so, for me, it does slightly belie how stories occur when I say they originate in an image. Beyond that, stories originate in my life because of the inherited form of the short story into which I fit my practices. If that makes any sense.

Stuckey-French: Sure.

Ford: So that first there was a thing called the short story, and I work, and I find a way to inhabit it.

Stuckey-French: It makes lots of sense, and I guess, thinking about that, in looking for that linearity that the short story as a form has or is supposed to have, or does have.

Ford: Sometimes.

Stuckey-French: Right. It seems to me that in your stories often one of the things that kickstarts that line is an allusion to violence, or the threat of violence. That is often there and then the story unfolds.

Ford: I suppose.

Stuckey-French: Claude's father yanking him by the hair out of the car, that kind of thing. And then we wonder how bad can this get? Or how do we keep this from getting so bad it's just too awful?

Ford: My notion about what I guess you could call the ontogeny of fiction is that fiction is about (it is, anyway, when I write it) what we do as a consequence to dramatic acts. Much of our lives is spent dealing with the consequences of our own and others' important acts; trying to make virtues out of vices, trying to make normal things that have happened against our will and against all logic, seem normal, survivable. And so, for me, at least up to now, it has seemed that what stories can be about is how people put their lives in order after rather dramatic, sometimes violent, percussive events. And because I know those things happen to all of us—or if they don't happen to us literally, they happen to us in our ambient life—I know we're curious about them as determinants. We're natively curious about events that change even small personal histories. So, insofar as a story of mine might be instructive, it's that it is about what people do when bad things happen. For me, what's mostly threatened in the stories I've written is the fabric of affection that holds people close enough together to survive.

Stuckey-French: And that there might at least be the hope then at the end that that fabric of affection can be regained somehow?

Ford: In some fashion. At least it can be glimpsed by the reader, if not always the characters.

Stuckey-French: Or at least we can see some understanding of how it was lost?

Ford: That's right, and in that understanding, achieve some kind of reconnection. I mean I know you can't ever put things back how they were. But maybe you can put them together in some way that they could never have been otherwise. There's a little moment at the end of "Optimists" when a man whose family has gone completely kaflooey sees his mother in a convenience store. She goes over to him and kisses him on the cheek and basically, implicitly, tells him that she loves him. And people have said to me, "God that's such a bleak view of the world. That's such a small grain of solace to have." But I think, well no it's not, because if in the midst of your hectic life you can unexpectedly see your mother, and she comes over and says, "You know, I loved your father and by extension loved you" well, gee, that's a lot to me.

Stuckey-French: Right, and if that's all there is, then that has to be enough. Certainly, it's a memory you could hold onto, that could help carry you through life from then on.

Ford: I'll tell you one part of the origin of that story too. I was once in a convenience store in Billings, and I was in getting some Cokes for Kristina and me. We were, as usual, driving somewhere, I don't know where, and I saw a woman, who was clearly an Indian woman. But, she was quite done up in the way that you sometimes see Indian women. That is to say, she had on very tight jeans, and she had on very shiny boots, and she had on a lovely Western belt and brocaded white shirt. She had her hair done very slick and pulled way back strictly off of her forehead, and she looked very, very sleek. But she was also pretty drunk, because she was reeling a bit in the aisles. I looked at her and it was only a couple, three years after my mother had died, and I thought to myself as I looked at her—she was a woman of about sixty—I thought, that's somebody's mother, even though she seemed utterly independent of anybody around.

Stuckey-French: The outfit had served to make her not a mother?

Ford: That's right, but maybe she was. At any rate, I went back and I sat down in the car and wrote out some notes on that story just sitting there in the car.

Stuckey-French: You talk about the preparation you do for your stories. In that case it seems like maybe you had been preparing for that story, but you needed that image of her to bring those things together. The convenience store gave you something.

Ford: Yeah, you gotta pay attention.

Stuckey-French: I wanted to ask you about the end of another story, "Rock Springs," and how its final moment of understanding is arrived at. It seems to me to be the same kind of moment of understanding and recognition, but it also seems to work a little differently because of the move into direct address at the very end. I guess direct address is always implicit in a first person narrator. I mean, there is always a "you," but . . .

Ford: Yes, but it had only been implicit up to then.

Stuckey-French: Right, and there it becomes explicit, and it's a way to summarize those understandings such as they are at that moment. They are there in a list of questions.

Ford: I think it comes less into that story as a rhetorical strategy than as a gesture of sympathy; the story trying to find a way to connect itself with whomever might be reading. It's saying, "we're alike."

Stuckey-French: Exactly, and that's the way I read it from the get-go. I just think it's a wonderful ending and that it really works that way.

Ford: It was just an act of God, with me doing God's bidding. I wrote that story sitting in a little loft in New York in February of 1981, with no heat and with construction going on. Kristina and I were living in this illegal loft on Greene Street, and the Streets People came and said, "You're using PVC to conduct gas into your apartment and we're going to cut you off." And they did. They cut us off. We had rented this apartment, and we had no place to go, and I had to sit with a little space heater in just the most remote place you could be from Rock Springs and I wrote that story then. In some ways, I think, if that story has any intensity in it at all, it has the intensity of wanting very much not to be where I was. In a way, empathizing with myself for being in a really bad situation which I didn't see anyway of getting out of, and then writing about a situation in which a guy was in a bad situation which he doesn't see any way of getting out of.

Stuckey-French: My wife has taught that story and occasionally, she'll run into a student who just . . .

Ford: . . . hates him.

Stuckey-French: . . . just doesn't like the . . .

Ford: I know.

Stuckey-French: . . . who says, "Don't say 'you.' I'm not like you."

Ford: "I don't steal cars."

Stuckey-French: Exactly. I don't know the source of such a mis-reading. Well, I hate to call it a mis-reading . . .

Ford: Well, they're youngsters for one thing, and that is definitely not a youngsters' story. You know, I remember when I read *The Moviegoer* by Walker Percy I was living in New Orleans, on leave from the University of Michigan, and I couldn't wait to get back to Michigan and get other people to read it. Joe Blotner and I taught it, and the graduate students at Michigan could not understand why anybody in the world would be the way Binx was in that novel. They were just too young.

Stuckey-French: It's a wonderful book.

Ford: Oh, one of the great American books, I think. But, here is a guy turning thirty at Mardi Gras, and these graduate kids were smart, but they were not thirty and they weren't melancholy and it wasn't the '50s, and they had no purchase on that story whatsoever and it doesn't denigrate it in any way as a story. And I think that in "Rock Springs" you may have to have a few miles on you for that story to have the resonance that it could conceivably have.

Stuckey-French: And I wonder too if you have to have, in some way, stepped into that class, or have been in that class. Not that you have to have stolen cars, you know, but that you somehow need to have felt that desperation, that need to get out. In that story, it seems to me, a lot of it is not just getting out of that place, but getting out of that . . .

Ford: . . . mentality . . .

Stuckey-French: Right, or that economic situation.

Ford: Well, the story would, if it could, establish a sympathy for a person like that. And I've had that same sentiment expressed to me about my stories: "I don't like these people. These people are marginal and they're crooks and they're sort of lowlifes." And I think to myself . . .

Stuckey-French: Try to have some heart?

Ford: Yeah. This story says you have to have some sympathy for these people, and maybe it strains the point to say that you have to have some sympathy because you are like them. But, basically it says you have to have sympathy because they are on the earth here beside you. And if you don't have that sympathy, in my view . . . you ought to.

Stuckey-French: I agree. Somewhere, perhaps it was in your introduction to the Grant collection of American short stories, you mentioned that there could be such a thing as a Republican story . . .

Ford: (laughter)

Stuckey-French: . . . a story that tells you what it's like to be a Republican and why one should be a Republican, and thankfully, I think, you shuddered at such a thought, but do you write democratic short stories with a small *d*?

Ford: Yeah, I do. I think my playing field is broad and level. Though not everybody agrees with me about that. I don't think that's the only way to write stories. People have said to me, "Well, you didn't grow up lower middle class. You didn't grow up in those circumstances." Though I did grow up in circumstances of life in which my family had grappled themselves up out of that other stratum into one where there was some clear air to breathe. And I think one of the things that I grew up realizing was that they were terrifically fearful that something was going to happen that was going to drop them back down into worse circumstances. That's dramatic, I think.

Stuckey-French: I remember reading somewhere the adage that in our society every woman is just one man away from welfare.

Ford: And I believe that, and I think it about myself, about being a writer. Nothing's promised. I know my father felt that way. Maybe I inherited it from him.

Stuckey-French: He was a salesman. I thought of that in *A Piece of My Heart* where I guess it's Hewes who is talking about what that work can do to you, which I think a lot of people aren't aware of. Even those who've read *Death of a Salesman*, maybe they don't think about the hemorrhoids and . . .

Ford: . . . closing your hand up in the door and all those nights alone in motels and years and years of that. The thing I couldn't figure out was why he loved his work so much. He just loved it. I would think about all the particulars—loneliness, drive, drive, drive, hot, hot, hot. It was before the days of air-conditioning. I couldn't figure that out. Still, really, in a way can't. It's a fit subject for art, I think; to investigate that unknown.

Stuckey-French: So what did he love about it, do you think? The independence?

Ford: I don't know. He loved my mother desperately, and they had had this wonderful life together for years before I was born . . . fifteen years . . . and my mother was a really interesting person and compelling in a way, and I can't imagine what it would have been like to have had all those years together with her and then suddenly for me to have come along and for his life then to start out in a slightly different tack, which is being mostly alone. Maybe it is just that he wasn't a very sophisticated man, or maybe he just liked new beginnings every week, and the end of the week was the beginning of the weekend, and the beginning of the following week was the beginning of another week in which he didn't know exactly how things would go. And maybe, it was on that low level of satisfaction. Or maybe it was something entirely unknown to me. But really, when in a piece of fiction a writer says he "investigates" something, he is really just inventing possible answers—obvious ones and less obvious, fanciful ones.

Stuckey-French: And I guess part of those new beginnings is that you are just constantly meeting new people and you have that opportunity to talk.

Ford: That's right, and he did. A kind of endless, almost unhierarchical diversity. Once again, you go along this flat plain and you're constantly like a pinball being baffled back and forth among people, and maybe he just liked that. I don't know. I'm going to write an essay about him next year.

Stuckey-French: Are you?

Ford: I wrote a long essay about my mother. And I'd like to write something about my father. But the problem is that he wasn't around after I was sixteen, because he died, and I don't want to write the absent father essay. I'll have to figure out something different.

Stuckey-French: I noticed that *Wildlife* and "Great Falls" and, I don't know, a couple of other things that you've written are all about 1960–61 and a seventeen-year-old narrator. Is it important for you in some way to return to that moment when your father died?

Ford: Probably, but not I think in an autobiographical way. One of the things writers often do is contend that their life is just like everybody else's life, and if something happened to me when I was sixteen that changed my life forever. . . .

Stuckey-French: . . . everybody had something that did?

Ford: At least it is possible they did. Women and men too. Obviously there are limits to that contention, but I think it is true that when boys, and girls too, reach that age, they're beginning to leave adolescence or childhood and heading into adulthood, and all kinds of important things happen. And I thought for me it was crucial, and I thought all kinds of other things happened to kids all over the country that were crucial. So it was just the natural kind of writerly participation in the lives of others, which originates in my participation in my own life. But I didn't write anything in those stories there about fathers dying, because I didn't want to write about that.

Stuckey-French: Right, they're not about that.

Ford: I was interested, as I said before, in what happens beyond some crucial event, which even though it changes life it also lets it come back together, maybe in a more interesting way. I wished to have as many participants survive the event as can be. So death of the father didn't figure in.

Stuckey-French: Those stories, it seems to me, are more about the relationship between the boy and the mother, and how they're both at some turning point and have to get to what's next.

Ford: That's right. I guess I'm just interested in the whole configuration; from one permutation to the next at a particular age, or at least I was. I don't know if I'll write about it anymore.

Stuckey-French: The whole country turned at that moment too, I guess.

Ford: Well, the fifties officially ended. But I'm not sure the fifties ended until Kennedy was killed, really. But at least if you set something on the cusp of '59–'60, the reader now can look back at that time, and, through the focus of a story, history can be made to seem more intelligible, or at least seem to have implications that weren't immediately apparent then.

Stuckey-French: So, do you feel a responsibility or a desire not only to try to understand what happened on a personal level, but also . . .

Ford: In an historical way? No, I don't think so. I think history for me is a convenience, which is of the same kind of convenience as time-setting *The Sportswriter* on Easter was or time-setting other stories of mine: that is, they're set on days or years that are recognizable by the reader—on holidays or Halloween or Thanksgiving, or precise years. I like to set events at a time that the reader has some memory of. The reader then is more easily convinced to participate in the story's illusion, and the story then begins to inform that time for the reader through the agency of his memory. But I don't myself pretend to have any particular purchase on that time. I'm using it just as a mnemonic. Somebody asked me when I was in France a couple of weeks ago, what I took to be a theoretical question . . .

Stuckey-French: Well, you were in France.

Ford: . . . which had to do with my sense of history, and my view of it. And if I hadn't been respectful of the guy, I would have laughed, because I have almost no sense of history. But, in a way that the French might appreciate,

I have a kind of existential freedom regarding history. I convert it. Traduce it. Change it. Maybe that means I have a sense, after all.

Stuckey-French: A sense of moment?

Ford: Yeah, or a willingness to change it, a willingness to say, "History's like this. For me, history's like this. I'll bet it was like that for you." And all I have to do is get you to agree that it was, because that's basically the nature of literary truth. If you and I can posit an important possibility and agree to it and live in accordance to it, I'm afraid it's on the way to becoming truth.

Stuckey-French: So, for instance, it can be Thanksgiving [in the story "Going to the Dogs"], but also on this other vector coming in it's the time I had to move out and stiff this guy on his lease?

Ford: That's right.

Stuckey-French: By bringing those two things together it's that much more memorable or believable?

Ford: You get a whole package of memories and a whole package of responses, which you otherwise weren't going to get if you had it be the 5th of November. We story writers need all the help we can get. And yet, when people say about *The Sportswriter* "You set it on Easter because it's a story about redemption, isn't it?" I think to myself, yeah, maybe that's right, maybe that's right. But the *real* reason I set it on Easter was that's the day I began writing it. Easter Day in 1982. And I think I began it then because Easter just struck me as a very memorable holiday—one anybody in America had some vivid associations with. Plus, I was looking for a short period of time in which a novel could take place and I thought "Well, Good Friday to Easter. That's a nice short little course that you can set a novel in." So that's what it was. That it became interested in redemptive issues was really after the fact.

Stuckey-French: So, it wasn't a question of trying to resurrect Ralph?

Ford: No, but I'll tell you, as I've said before, if you start monkeying around with these Judeo-Christian myths, you're in over your boot tops in a hurry. You better be up to it. They have remarkable potency, whether you're acquainted with them or just are a novice, as I was.

Stuckey-French: You better be ready for some readers who know it better than you?

Ford: R. Z. Sheppard in *Time,* when that book was reviewed (and he liked it), said he thought I had made it have fourteen chapters because there are fourteen stations to the Cross. But that was the first time I'd heard there were fourteen stations to the Cross.

Stuckey-French: I remember reading an interview where Bill Gass talking about how his story "In the Heart of the Heart of the Country," which opens with the allusion to "Sailing to Byzantium," "And so I have sailed the seas and come . . . / to B . . . / a small town fastened to a field in Indiana." Then it's written in those sections, you know "People," "Weather," whatever, and some critic counted the sections and said, "Ah ha, 32 and 32 lines in 'Sailing to Byzantium." And he [Gass] said the same thing you just said, "I'd never thought of that."

Ford: On the other hand, it's sometimes nice to think that you plugged your finger into a hot current, even if by accident. Only a fool would argue much.

Stuckey-French: What about some things that I wondered if you do put in a little more consciously? For instance, humor. It seems like you really enjoy writing something funny.

Ford: I'm actually quite bereft if I write a story which doesn't have any humor in it; and for various reasons: one, that humor finds its way into any piece of literature as a relief, and also because I think often people actually say important, serious things under the guise of not being serious about it. One of the purposes of any story is to ask the reader to pay attention to this which she or he might not have paid attention before, and, indeed, pay attention to it in this degree of particularity, whereas in ordinary life things flow by and we don't pay much attention to them. So, I want stories to draw the reader's attention to something and say, "This is important." And humans always make jokes when they aren't joking at all. So, it has at least two sides to it and maybe it has other sides too—one of which is that writing something funny pleases *me*. Nothing makes me happier than when I can be writing a story and make myself laugh. I call that a triumph, even if I later throw it out, and I often do throw it out.

Stuckey-French: So what are some of the funniest moments for you?

Ford: I can't remember.

Stuckey-French: Well, I was thinking when you were saying that humor can instruct . . . that in "Winterkill" when the woman . . . ah, is it Nola?

Ford: Yeah, Nola, who just came out of the song, you know, "walking along a thoroughfare." Do you know that song, "Nola"? That's the only reason I used the name. I have a friend in Chicago who can play "Nola"—the song—*on his head,* by hitting the top of his head with his knuckles and moving his open mouth in and out. Possibly you'd have to see it to think it was funny. In fact, I'm sure you would. But I thought it was very funny.

Stuckey-French: I would love to see and hear that. In the story, Nola's talking about when her husband knew he was going to die and he spontaneously decided that he wanted flank steak, and Troy connects right with it. He says, "I know. I thought of lobster when I was lying there dying." And I laughed there.

Ford: I wanted you to. I thought Troy was a comic character. But, in that story anyway, Troy seems comic in spite of being wrecked physically. Ultimately, too, of course, he isn't comic, but rather noble.

Stuckey-French: He's sad, and yet he's such a wonderful audience to her.

Ford: He's so thrilled to get to talk to a woman, whereas ordinarily he might've just been cast aside. I remember when I wrote *The Ultimate Good Luck* and Walter Clemons, who I'm sorry to say just died this summer, reviewed it in *Newsweek*. One of the things he said about it was that he liked the book, but he said I'd managed to write a book that short-circuited something I could do—which was to be funny. He'd liked another book of mine, *A Piece of My Heart,* which had comic parts. And that made an impression on me, and I just thought that I wasn't going to write anything else that short-circuited humor. (I've since broken that promise a time or two). But one of the things that you want to do as a writer is to get everything you know and are capable of as a writer onto the page so that you can exceed it in the act of writing; gain access to something you couldn't otherwise ever have gotten access to. That's a problem for many young writers; they tap into only part of their abilities. It's something you can overcome with hard work, of course.

Stuckey-French: I'm thinking a little more about the humor in your stories. It seems like one of the agents for bringing the humor into your stories is children.

Ford: Oh, yeah, because I sometimes see them as such malevolent little creatures who rule (and often not benignly) the lives of adults.

Stuckey-French: Yeah, like Cherry imitating Paul Harvey. There's something wicked about that.

Ford: Yeah, well I think kids can be wicked by not knowing wicked.

Stuckey-French: They're not expected yet to have a conscience, or manners, or something.

Ford: That's a very Victorian idea. If you read Hardy and you read kids in Hardy. Or, if you remember in *Wuthering Heights,* there's a scene which occurs in a kitchen, and the children hanging puppies by a string off the back of a chair. And Father Time in *Jude the Obscure* comes into the book as a child but ages unnaturally fast and speaks only as an adult, speaks runically, speaks rivetingly to Jude. I think that's where I determined how to use children. You use them as extremely potent characters, rather than as bothersome non-entities (which they mostly are in life); little oracles who speak as adults or who affect events in large ways yet remain deceptively "innocent." You know, if you have to have children speak as children, they won't say anything very interesting. They don't know anything.

Stuckey-French: It's when they're imitating adults or trying to horn in on the adults' conversation that they get spooky, because there are these adult voices coming out of their mouths.

Ford: Truthfully, though, I'm only interested in adults. I think that's the only time when life begins to make any difference; when you can take responsibility for your actions and your actions can have a consequence which you can oversee. So, children are, for me, little condiments in stories. You know, you shake them in to spice it up, but the real events take place in the lives of people who are responsible, who bear the consequences of action as fully as it can be borne. I think that would probably get me in trouble with the Pope. [laughter] But he probably doesn't read my stories in Italian—or, really, know much about real life. I mean, he's a priest.

Stuckey-French: I don't know. He's laid up now with that broken leg. Maybe he has the time to read some fiction.

Ford: I want to know how he broke his hip. I want to know how he got down on the floor in that bathroom. That's what I want to know.

Robert Franklin Gish

Chesney Baker

Robert F. Gish began writing short fiction in mid-career. A University of Northern Iowa English professor of twenty-six years who managed also to teach some ethnic studies courses, Gish began writing short fiction during his work on *Frontier's End: The Life and Literature of Harvey Fergusson,* published in 1988 by the University of Nebraska Press. His short fiction was not published, however, until five years later, after he had become Director of Ethnic Studies and English professor at California Polytechnic State University, San Luis Obispo, and after he had completed two other works: a critical work, *William Carlos Williams: The Short Fiction* (Macmillan, 1989), and a memoir, *Songs of My Hunter Heart: A Western Kinship* (Iowa State University Press, 1992; University of New Mexico Press, paperback, 1994). In 1993 Gish made his fictional debut with *First Horses: Stories of the New West* (University of Nevada Press), a collection of short stories set in the American Southwest of the 1950's. Gish's latest work is *When Coyote Howls: A Lavaland Fable* (University of New Mexico Press, 1994).

Baker: Your many years as an English professor, as well as your published literary biographies and literary criticism, attest to the fact that you have spent much of your life studying the lives and works of other writers. You are an expert, then, on what elements should be present in a great work of literature. How did this expertise affect your writing process? Did it daunt or inspire you?

Gish: Well, I think both. It's good to know literature from a critical point of view, but that can also be hampering sometimes. My own evolution as an imaginative writer has been veering away from a conscious analytical utilization of some of the theory that I know to just sort of letting it come through me, in the same sense that you can study very hard about how to ride a bike, but there comes a point when you just ride the bike. So in my writing I tried to say the things that I really want to say without worrying too much about technique. When I go back to read a story I've written, however, I'll see technique from a critical perspective that intuitively I was working with when I was writing it. There's always an antipathy between a critic and a writer; there's that alleged antagonism between the critic and the author. I think that's a needless antagonism.

Baker: Do you schedule appointments with the muse, or do you wait for her to call you?

Gish: I think that it's very important to listen to the muse when the muse calls, and I've tried to develop that capability so that I can recognize it and translate it. I do try to write daily, but sometimes when the general concept comes to me as to what the next book should be, what I should be writing about, I try to write on that as much as I possibly can, which may necessitate that I put other projects on the back burner for a while.

Baker: Do you organize your collections of short stories with a particular idea in mind, then, around a certain theme or subject?

Gish: Yes, I have been. *First Horses,* for example, is a cycle of short stories centered around a theme of social and physical stigma: one character has port wine stain, one has a club foot, one stutters. There are various kinds of ethnicities at work in these stories as well as gender issues where social stigma of one kind or another come into play. My next book of short stories, in which the characters are outlaws, will also be a thematic grouping.

Baker: Were you inspired to write the short story by a particular writer or writers? Do you consider your style similar to that of another writer?

Gish: I've been influenced as a critic by William Carlos Williams. I wrote a book on William Carlos Williams' short stories. He's generally thought of by the mass readership as a great American poet, but he did write a lot of fine short stories. I think the most immediate influence on me, turning from literary biography to memoir to short stories and then to allegory and fable and then back again two books down the road to short story, would be William Carlos Williams. I researched his papers for a couple of weeks at Buffalo and got some interesting insights into his creative process—how he was able to juggle the medical profession to which he was devoted and the artistic process. I owe a lot, then, to William Carlos Williams. There are, of course, many contemporary writers who have influenced me: John Keeble, the author of *Broken Ground* and *Yellow Fish,* and Russell Banks, the author of *Continental Drift.* I have an affinity with those writers.

Baker: Was there a particular event that inspired you to begin writing short fiction?

Gish: Yes, I was writing a literary biography, *The Life and Literature of Harvey Fergusson,* which required a lot of research. I became very impatient with myself then because I was devoting so much of my life to writing about someone else's life. I began thinking about how my life paralleled his, how we both grew up in the same part of New Mexico. That triggered *Songs of My Hunter Heart,* a memoir which had what many people would call "fictional techniques" in it. The memoir is a series of narratives or narrative essays and personal essays which aren't entirely true. They're basically true, but some of the truth is a fictionalized truth colored over with the imagination and with distortions of memory. After going from literary biography to memoir and autobiography, I went to the short story. I found myself working pretty comfortably within the short story. So, writing that literary biography was a turning point for me. It kicked off a lot of things.

Baker: Why did you choose the short story as your means of expression instead of poetry or the novel?

Gish: I think it's because of the comfort I felt in making the transition from the narrative forms within expository writing to the narrative forms within memoir, a transition which developed my sense for the rhythms and patterns within narrative structures. The short story, then, was a natural evolution for me. I had set a goal of building up to the novel, and I probably will write a novel one day, but right now I'm really satisfied with exploring some of the potential of the short story.

Baker: Before your debut as a short fiction writer, you wrote a literary biography of Harvey Fergusson, another New Mexico writer. In the preface to that work, you describe literary biography as "part fact, part fiction, as much associated with the narrative techniques of the novel as with history" (x). While writing the literary biography of Fergusson, you wrote autobiographical narratives which you compiled in *Songs of My Hunter Heart.* How would you distinguish literary biography, autobiographical narrative, and the short story as you have written them?

Gish: There's a lot of things in common between those three. The literary biography has to retain a closer allegiance to at least a modicum of what we think factuality is, though I'm coming more and more to assume that absolute categorical truth is a very difficult thing to pin down, that what we all have are really just perceptions of the truth, though it may be our truth. Not withstanding any of that, the literary biographer has a deeper and more abiding obligation to staying as close as possible to the verifiable materials and to reining in his or her predilections or biases or even sensibilities. It's not always possible to rein them in, however, and ultimately the biographer shines through the biography, as we know from comparing four or five different biographies of the same person.

Although there is some leeway in biography, there is more freedom in autobiography because the only allegiance the autobiographer really has is to his or her own remembered perceptions, perceptions that are easily recognized as distorted if, for example, one asks people who knew the autobiographer about their perceptions of him or her. We all remember different things: siblings will remember different things about their parents; parents will remember different things about their children. That phenomenon is related to the fallibility of memory and to the natural disposition within autobiography to aggrandize and even to romanticize one's past, to block out the negative things and to dwell on the positive things. In *Songs of My Hunter Heart,* for example, I celebrate my family and pay tribute to them and to the region where I grew up and to the people who influenced me. So the basis of the writer's allegiance to fact changes as well as to his or her identity as he or she perceives that fact.

In short story, of course, the writer is freer with fact. Fact, the truth of what the short story is, becomes more transcendent and more idealized. When I write a short story, however, I do research certain topics so that the credibility is there. For example, when I write about a historical outlaw in my forthcoming cycle of stories about outlaws, I feel compelled to stay within general boundaries of the myth or perception of that outlaw. I'm freer to distort it, however, than if I were writing a literary biography about that historical person. In fiction, then, a writer can approach in a strangely more oblique but also a more direct way the mythic and archetypal aspects of the narrative. It's a very fascinating process to try to figure out how these narrative boundaries bleed into each other, cross over, distort each other, transcend each other. That process is one of the reasons why I try to write in different forms, different genres. It's exciting to see how I can push the envelope.

Baker: Many of your short stories involve characters experiencing identity crises, and in many cases, it seems that characters find their true selves through embracing their hidden talents, their pasts, or both. Do you feel that you have come closer to understanding yourself, your identity, through embracing your past and your until now hidden talent of writing short fiction?

Gish: I do think of writing as a discovery process, for everyone, regardless of genre or even of the occasion. It's a discovery process in which you find out all kinds of things about yourself and about what the story is that you're writing. I don't really plot out my stories or heavily outline them, so the process of the story is a discovery process, and in the process of that process, I've discovered a lot about myself. Of course, I didn't write anything at all other than essays when I was a young adult. I started writing in a narrative vein and writing short stories once I hit middle age. So it's been an interesting rediscovery of aspects of my life, particularly my younger years, in middle age.

Baker: Will you continue writing short story collections?

Gish: Well, *When Coyote Howls* is a fable and a novel. It's a long fable or allegory of the West and of the creative process in which a coyote wakes up one morning and can't howl. So he goes in quest of his lost howl. He talks to all of his animal friends and listens to how they talk, what their sounds are and what their messages are, what their advice is. He rediscovers his voice, his lost voice, through empathizing with his buddies.

Baker: Is the novel a more difficult form for you?

Gish: Yes.

Baker: Would you consider it a higher form?

Gish: I don't consider it a higher form. It's just more sustained. I need a longer period of time to write a novel. I'm able to write short stories by writing maybe two hours a day over a shorter period of time, like six months or maybe even nine months. But the ideas I have for novels, particularly the novels for which *When Coyote Howls* would be a prelude, would take probably eighteen months to two years each to complete. I need a sustained, focused time to complete a novel.

Baker: Is the process of writing a novel like that of writing a short story in that you don't have a pre-established plot?

Gish: The novel cycle that I'm projecting, insofar as I have completed it in my mind, is going to be, at least the outlines of it, more knowable. Now, what I find once I get into the details of it will be that total discovery process again, but I think I have pretty good mapping of where I want to go with the novel.

Baker: Most of your short stories, "Kimo," "First Horses," and especially "Salvation," provide traditional plot lines in that they flow through exposition, complication, climax, and resolution. Some have shown a more modern character: "Blessed," for example, is a cluster of remembered events, placing the reader in the middle of those events to sort out their meaning. None of your short stories, however, follow the contemporary mode of distorting or abandoning plot. None of them merge into the fantastic or the surreal. How do you feel about this form of writing?

Gish: Part of it is identifying myself with or having been imprinted or identified by the West, because I think of myself as a Western writer or a writer about the American West or, even more specifically, a writer about the Southwest or, now that I'm in California, about the California West. In *When Coyote Howls,* however, I'm getting further and further into the surreal, particularly in terms of some of the reveries and some of the very lyrical epiphanies that come through in that narrative. Also, in the next cycle of short stories that I'm writing about outlaws, there are several stories which are an interesting blend of genres—gothic Western, for example. I'm moving away, then, from a basic kind of realism into different narrative techniques such as stream of consciousness and even more fantasized imaginings like personifying the animals in the fables. I don't know how far that will go in terms of ever writing fantasy, pure fantasy, if there is such a thing.

Baker: Is that type of writing something that just developed in your evolution as a writer, or did you make a conscious effort . . . ?

Gish: Just developed. I never have read much fantasy. I never read much science fiction, and I never read romance, medieval type romance stories. So I'm more grounded in realism.

Baker: You have shown incredible versatility in your use of various points of view. One point of view, however, that I have not found in your short stories is a multiple point of view in which one story employs more than one narrator. Do you think that this is a point of view better suited to the novel?

Gish: No, not necessarily. I just finished a short story, a triptych, involving a series of three different narrators. It was a fun form to work with. It was perhaps a little too formalized, but it was fun to alternate those narrators and to decide whether I'd want to keep the original sequence of one, two, three, one, two, three or whether I'd want to alternate one, three, two, for example, or two, one, three. So the short story can employ multiple narrators and voices, both large and small, choral voicings, individual voicings, voices that bounce off one another.

Baker: You have been praised for your ability to write from various perspectives including the perspectives of both male and female. What do you feel are some of the differences between your male and female narrators' perspectives, and do you feel as comfortable writing from the female perspective as from the male perspective?

Gish: That's a daunting question. I've often wondered whether a man can write like a woman or whether a man should try, whether a woman can write like a man, whether a woman should try. I've reconciled that by saying, "Sure," and leaving it to the critics to decide whether or not it's convincing or true or appropriate. A writer subjects himself or herself to all kinds of criticism by presuming too much. Following that kind of *reductio ad absurdum,* however, an Anglo would never try to empathize with people of color, for example, or a woman would never try to empathize with men, or a child would never try to empathize with the aged. . . . That all seems very contradictory. Criticisms of presumption or political incorrectness are stifling. The creative artist has to be daring enough to try to cross all of those gender and ethnic borders and to grow in the process. Perhaps the readership can grow that way, too. I'm a little frightened of people who talk about misappropriation of either gender or ethnicity because I think that the true obligation is really to the growth of the artist and to the growth of the reader outside of themselves through a certain empathetic transcendence.

Baker: One of the characters in the title story of *First Horses* is a Mexican-American history teacher, Mr. Marez, who blends fact with personal historical perspective. This is a situation which you seem to warn against in the preface to the collection, explaining that the West, old and new, should be understood as a complex and varied web of people, places, and perspectives, none of which encompasses all the others. Do you consider yourself something of a New Historicist, then, believing that one's historical perspective prevents one from fully comprehending past reality, perhaps even somewhat of a relativist, believing that there is no one reality to grasp?

Gish: I'm more of a relativist and a New Historian than I realized I was. I don't think that history has to be seen in either/or terms. One accounting of history doesn't necessarily negate another accounting of history. What is important is to see history more fully—top side, bottom side, lateral side, or the full mosaic rather than just seeing the single dimensionality. That kind of historical relativism could invite intra- and inter-ethnic and inter- and intra-gender perspectives, which represent one of the exciting outcomes of the process of reperceiving or restructuring our old paradigms about culture and about how we interact with each other and about what civilizations are. It's fun writing at this particular period. If we were writing earlier, we wouldn't have had the benefit of so many people talking about the possibilities of these different perceptions. We're coming more and more to know how little we know about what reality is.

Baker: Do you consider short stories like yours, especially like "First Horses," a means through which to discount a monolithic view of history and of the West? A better means than a history lecture and a history textbook?

Gish: I don't know that literature is a better means, but I think it's an important means because it encourages empathy with cultures and with the environment. Literature also provides emotional interaction. It has a powerful immediacy to it that a history lecture doesn't. I don't mean to suggest that a history lecture would be lacking. It's a different experience, but an important one. I don't mean to suggest either that literature should be used for propagandistic purposes, for distortion and confusion, but literature does have healing, didactic, and resourceful qualities, so that there is a lot to be said for literature as equipment for living, to refer to an old Kenneth Burke phrase. Literature is also great equipment for living with others, because it allows us to empathize, not only to travel vicariously but psychologically and culturally, to experience different people's experiences. I just don't see a monocultural experience in America.

Baker: In the Preface to *First Horses,* you disparage the language of present-day "political correctness" as too limited to describe the variety of experience in the Southwest you first knew. Will you give an example of that language?

Gish: In a simple instance, in the Southwest of the '50s, which is the setting of the stories in *First Horses,* most people of Latin descent referred to themselves as Spanish-American rather than Chicano because Chicano hadn't really been coined even as a movement in the '50s. So it would be a distortion if, because of either a sense of political correctness or a political agenda, we were to ban the word "Spanish-American" from our vocabularies when that was the current name certain groups of people accepted for themselves. That's a very small example but it deals with making judgments retrospectively, imposing certain values. Another example is the effort to censor a book like *Huckleberry Finn* because by certain current standards, however short-sighted, the book is politically incorrect because of certain language.

Baker: In a 1993 interview with Jan Greene, you say that you are "interested in how fiction can be used for artistic propaganda," and in the Preface to *First Horses* you state that you intend "not to instruct but to entertain." What do you think the connection is between instruction and entertainment in fiction, especially in the short story?

Gish: I don't set out to write short stories which will change the social milieu or to change injustices or to change biases or narrow-mindedness or prejudice, but I'm working through a lot of change in my own attitudes, so that some people may interpret much of what I come up with in my short stories as an agenda. To be more tolerant, for example, to see the greater variety of experiences, is the kind of thing that is just opening up to me. My stories express where I am personally rather than what I'm trying to impose on someone else. My stories have reflected some of my own struggles, then, particularly over the past four or five years in which I have been developing an ethnic studies program. Instruction and entertainment in fiction do intersect, however, and they intersect in different ways. Sometimes instruction in fiction is heavy-handed, and sometimes it's light-handed. I try to make it light-handed because I don't like stories that are so heavily didactic that they become more of a lesson or a homily in a very obvious way. Narratives, the short story as well as larger fictions, do lend themselves to instruction, however.

Baker: Do you think that the title story to your *First Horses* collection is more didactic than the others?

Gish: Maybe so because it deals with a rearranging of historical perceptions. The interpretation would depend, however, on the reader. I've had different readers read that story with different perspectives. The heroine in that story is an American Indian young woman. The savior is an Anglo cowboy, however, and the saving comes in a paternalistic way. Certain Hispanic or Chicano readers of that story may wonder why an Anglo cowboy and an Indian pair up at the expense of a Hispanic or a Chicano. I don't mean to suggest that this was my intention, but in the instance of that narrative, that's the way those characters may reveal themselves. Another reader could read "First Horses" as an unfair story from another political perspective.

Baker: But your intention was not to make it a didactic story?

Gish: No, my intention wasn't to make it so predominantly a didactic story. But, you know, you should always trust the tale, not the teller.

Baker: Do you believe that fiction should entertain before it instructs? Do you think that instruction can be absent from good fiction?

Gish: Well, I'm generally leery of either/or kinds of propositions. I don't go to short stories to derive moral lessons; I go to short stories to be entertained. And I think I write them because I enjoy writing them, not because I feel that I am making people better people or I'm a better person for having written them. I write and read more for enjoyment than I do for moral purpose. Remember the debate of a few years back when people were talking about moral fiction as opposed to fabulation or fiction in and of itself for its own terms, as a word display without any moral center or even a moral edge to it? Given my temperament, which was shaped by a strongly Protestant background, I think that that religiosity works itself out in me nevertheless, even though I work against it. That background was a very formative thing to me, making it important to me to make my time count and to take advantage of my opportunities. Puritanism and middle class values converged for me. That convergence may influence my writing. It may account for the fact that I am so diligent about trying to write every day. Although I avoid either/or dichotomies, I vacillate between freedom and discipline and delight and didacticism. In some instances one holds sway over the other, in other instances, it's the reverse.

Baker: What do you predict for the future of the short story? Will it continue to be a viable form of entertainment / instruction?

Gish: Yes. At least for me, the short story is becoming more and more important and relevant rather than less and less. We're seeing the short story undergoing another regeneration. And not only the short story but the long short story and the short short story and all the different variations including the three-minute short story and the fifteen-minute short story. It's becoming more and more difficult for me to determine where a short story stops being a short story and becomes a chapter in a longer narrative. You can cut this pie in all kinds of interesting, different ways, then, but I think that the short story is really being vitalized, revitalized, reperceived, and that there's going to be all kinds of new things happening. I recently attended The American Booksellers Association Convention in Los Angeles, the whole thrust of which was electronic books that are interactive, a possibility also open to the short story.

Wilson Harris

Maurice Lee

Wilson Harris has written *The Carnival Trilogy: Carnival, The Infinite Rehearsal & The Four Banks of the River of Space* (1994), *The Guyana Quartet* (1985), *The Womb of Space: The Cross-Cultural Imagination* (1983), and *History, Fable and Myth in the Caribbean & Guianas* (1994). Harris was born in 1921 in New Amsterdam, British Guiana (now Guyana). A land surveyor for a number of years, he began his writing career as a poet. His first published work was a book of poetry entitled *Fetish* (1951). Another edition of poetry entitled *Eternity to Season* followed in 1954, and his first novel, *Palace of the Peacock,* was published in 1960. His other novels include *The Eye of the Scarecrow* (1965), *Tamatumari* (1968), and *Da Silva da Silva's Cultivated Wilderness* (1977). For his contributions to the literary world, Harris has received numerous honors and awards, including Guggenheim Fellow and the Commonwealth Fellow at University of Leeds. Not only a novelist and poet, Harris has authored and edited numerous works of criticism, the most well known being *Tradition, the Writer and Society* (1967). Two collections of short stories round off his literary accomplishments: *The Sleepers of Roraima* (1970) and *The Age of the Rainmakers* (1971).

Lee: You have written many texts—a lot of works; you have also written criticisms—essays, etc. At the conference, we had both critics and writers, and there was a sense at times that they were at odds with each other in terms of almost ownership, in a strange way, of the text. What is your response to that in terms of the problems associated with that ownership and then within your own writing; are there two forces that are calling upon you as your write—one the critic and the other one the writer?

Harris: Well, I think that I wouldn't see a conflict, but nevertheless the antagonism, if that is the word, between critics and writers—I think that is inevitable at this stage—mind you antagonism may be too strong a word, but differences, then. I think that that comes largely from the fact that we live in a civilization which has been conditioned by a certain mindset. I would say, a Cartesian mindset, "I think; therefore, I am." Now, the break from that requires a very careful and close scrutiny of fictions of the text, of the living text, and critics may not always be willing to do this, partly because they are pursuing their own theories, understandably, and they may have read a body of fiction already, and they may not want to move into other areas—new fictions that are arising. And this is understandable, because they are pursuing a certain line.

Lee: So do you think that critics actually come to a text with preconceived notions about how to examine it and what to look for as opposed to just looking at the text freshly?

Harris: I think so, yes, I do. This is understandable in my view, but a problem that is arising. If one is to break the mindset, then we have, in my view, to look at the Cartesian dictum, "I think, therefore, I am;" I would revise that in this way—I would say, "I think, because creation is." Now if one starts to do that, one begins to move away from the human-centered world, which the Cartesian dictum seems to me to uphold, and which for small-minded theorists upholds well, because they believe the discourse which they employ is a discourse that has to be centered on the human utterance. Now, if one is sensitive to other voices which are not human voices, but which are out there in the extra-human world, then one is aware of the necessity to read new fictions with great care to see whether those voices are coming through because of peculiar necessities within the imaginative writer. I mean, it seems to me that there are rhythms in nature, there are rhythms in rivers—rocks, which seem fixed and static, but which are not as fixed and static as they appear. They possess rhythms. One can disclose those rhythms on things when one examines the shapes and rocks in rapids and waterfalls. There is a coincidence between rocks and tides. The tide appears to be fluid; the rock appears to be solid and fixed. But in fact, these are interchangeable masks, upon dimensionalities that address us from the world outside of human discourse. Now, there are various strategies, it seems to me, through which a writer may imagine what this discourse is outside of human logic.

Lee: Let's get back to that for a moment. When you say outside of human logic, one of the things I know is that writers, in terms of coming to grips with how they are going to depict a character, in many respects see that character and locate that character in the center of what you would call the human condition. Are you saying that that causes a certain kind of limitation and, that in effect, both the writer in depicting the character and the character that is depicted must go beyond the human condition?

Harris: Yes, that's my feeling. And I am not being dogmatic, but this is a deep-seated feeling I have because of my travels in the rain-forests—I worked as a hydrographer on a land survey. I had to keep my ear very close to the ground (to speak metaphorically) with regard to certain rhythms which I had to bring into play when I was studying the discharges of rivers. And the peculiar thing with rivers is that each river is unique. The rivers that correspond. It would be quite wrong to think that you could work out some kind of blueprint from one river and apply it, you know, to other rivers, without considering peculiar, subtle divergences in other rivers. Rivers can't be taken for granted, and this applies to the primordial landscape which I was traversing. A primordial landscape has a very peculiar life to it. And then one begins to respond to this. As an imaginative writer, one begins to ask oneself, "How can I bring this language which lies outside of human discourse into active play within the fiction one is writing?"

Lee: What you seem to be saying then is that because one cannot accept the primordial landscape, one cannot also, in mere respect, accept the human condition as constant.

Harris: I will accept the primordial landscape as a ceaseless resource which brings its gifts to us and, therefore, human discourse has to see itself as partial. It is not as absolute as some critics declare, or, as some writers declare, because there are many writers who are convinced that the only discourse they have lies within the human condition.

Lee: Yes. If I can change the focus for just a moment, because we at this conference discussed the short story, and when I first looked at your *Guyana Quartet* in some respect because they put them all in one volume, you could see those as four novellas, or do you see those as short stories?

Harris: I see *Guyana Quartet* as typically, in my estimation as four novels. But beyond that, they relate to each other, because one discovers what I call a revisionary momentum running through the fabric of the four novels. In other words, precisely because of what I was saying earlier, an image may appear in a certain context, and then one discovers that that image comes up again, but revises itself subtly—there is a sudden change, and then you go on again and you discover that another image appears which has a series; and this series has a backwards play in the sense that one thing revises something else, and then you go forward as well. But the future sometimes seems to be arriving. One seems to be going to meet the future. At another level, the future is coming to meet us. Therefore, one has to be equipped in certain ways to cope with the future, because the future seems to bring with it elements that one could never foresee.

Lee: It seems to me that's the case with your characters, particularly in terms of how they do time and place and space. Your characters would have to have what I think Husserl calls an "internal time consciousness" in which there is a sense of the future unknown. There is a knowledge of the past which has gone before, but there is a sort of continuing present?

Harris: Well, let me be very careful about this. The past for me can never be taken for granted. Traditions in the past in my estimation have within them what I would call gestating resources.

Lee: So you see the past as constantly changing, too.

Harris: It is changing in the sense that if time possesses a womb, then time conceals what is gestating in itself. We tend to see the past as constant—as changeless. I mean, many people look at traditions of the past as absolute tokens of the past, whereas, it seems to me, the traditions in the past are half-gestating resources, and when we begin to tap those gestating resources, in a curious way we begin to equip ourselves to face the unknown future.

Lee: So, is that another way of saying that one rethinks what went on before?

Harris: It is deeper than rethinking. It is a deep intuitive process that seems to me to arise in a mysterious way. I have no formula for it. C. G. Jung would have called this the collective unconscious. C. G. Jung, however, confined his collective unconscious to the human psyche. It does seem to me that collective unconscious extends into nature as well, into rocks, trees, stars; and this is somehow in parallel with quantum physics and quantum mechanics, which claim that we should have contact with everything. But because of a biological flaw in ourselves, we do not have that contact. In fact, in this very conference, I quoted a passage from an American physicist in which he advanced a notion that he might be able to design parallel universes if he could invent a quantum microscope. And I said that I think that in addition to that, if we could tap into the collective unconscious and sense that it extends out every year, we would be able to pull into fiction realities that have to do with parallel worlds and parallel universes. One universe is the extra-human; the other is the human—those are running in parallel. You won't be able to pick up, you know, connections and bridges. But those bridges are never absolute; they can break again, and they have to be reshaped again. So this is what creativity is about. If we had a formula for absolutes, then what need would there be for creativity? But we live in a very peculiar and enigmatic world and universe, and we have to discover, or get into strategies that allow us to bridge chasms within ourselves and within the universe, and within too many activities that we pursue as if these activities were fixed, remorseless, unswerving. This fashions then which we very often pursue. Do our fashions merely involve us in a kind of game? I am not concerned simply with the game. I am saying that there is something much deeper which we have to sense and relate to within creativity that alters our vision of reality.

Lee: Let me see if I can nail down a little bit clearer the sense of what you mean by extra-human. Because as we have talked, it seems to me as though there are three possibilities which emerge: one, that it is outside of human existence, and that is maybe physical landscapes.

Harris: Yes.

Lee: Another possibility, and correct me if I am wrong, is that part of a "supernatural," and in some respect maybe what some of the Latin American writers talk about in terms of "magical realism." Then a third seems to be some kind of superstructure which we might even refer to as creation—a creativity. Are those the kinds of realities that you are talking about when you say extra-human?

Harris: It has to do with creation. What extra-human means outside of the human, beyond the human. But my sensation is that what lies beyond the human is also in dialogue with the human. It brings gifts; it discloses dimensions, and our tendency is to either bypass this or to turn away from it because our human-centered world tends to take everything around it for granted in a sense. The landscape is manipulated as if it is a piece of furniture to be moved around; rivers are turned in different directions without any close dialogue or scrutiny with the rhythms of the landscape. We have seen the pollution of the globe; we have seen centuries of conquest in which the conquistador invariably believes his command over the so-called subject peoples that he has captured, if you want to use that word, is absolute in a sense.

Lee: So there is this sense then in your characters: you use them to depict this philosophy, therefore, i.e., characters, writers, societies who see the human condition as central. The human condition as absolute is at risk and in some respect guilty of a heinous crime against humanity because it does not take into consideration things outside of itself. It does not take into consideration, as you indicated, the landscapes; it does not take into consideration the sense that it is just a part of the universe and not in some respect the whole universe.

Harris: Yes, I intend that once we live in a system in which the human discourse is regarded as absolute, not only do we lose the rhythm of landscapes, but we may lose other voices which we cannot understand absolutely. And that is why, for example, in the resurrection story I use the term ventriloquism, or "spirit," suggesting the voices that come to us through nature, you see, are voices that you cannot get an exact idea of what those voices say. I describe this in the fiction as numinous inexactitudes. Spiritual inexactitudes. The spirit is addressing us, but it is warning us of the same thing, not to become too fanatical about what we think we hear. So we are driven all the time, rather than sealing up what we hear in absolute commandments and then believing that is the total and absolute truth. We tend to project upon others our deficiencies, our evil, our malaise, and to regard ourselves as having the absolute truth, and thus you get these conflicts between religions that we have seen around the world. I mean at least now after long travail, you know, the Islamic people are coming into conversation with the Jewish people. And yet the Islamic and the Jewish people spring from the same father, Abraham, and so do the Christians.

Lee: Yes.

Harris: But look how long, how each group believes it has the total truth, that they have—the most they do is tolerate the other side. So there is no genuine cross-culturality, there may be multi-culturality in the sense that what they would seek to do is to have an umbrella of tolerance over these groups. But really, there is no radical, creative, new discourse. I'm saying that radical, creative, new discourse has to pay attention to other voices, mysterious as these voices are, which do exist in the universe, and that these voices require us to begin to examine the kind of language we have formulated for a long time which sends us totally and absolutely on human discourse, and which, therefore, defeats the enterprise of profundus creativity.

Therefore, you have to examine texts which may have a kind of density. This density signifies that the so-called transparency or clarities which we enshrine may be fallacious, they may be another kind of transparency within densities, and you may discover these as you look at the layers of the text and the way the text revises itself so that the writer himself or herself is in the text—as if the fiction is creating the writer as well as the characters which the writer appears to create.

Lee: That brings me to another question, and I am focusing on the nature of characters in *Palace of the Peacock* and *The Secret Ladder*. As I read and begin to discover some of the kinds of things that you are talking about, what strikes me is that in many respects, the characters do not have the capacity to understand some of those philosophies themselves. They are part of it, but often they may be a laborer, could be maybe a surveyor, could be a workman, simply a girl, someone's girlfriend, and I've often wondered when those concepts of density and in terms of a trans-human, and so forth, come forward, do they come more from you, the writer who is sort of in that text, or do they come more from the characters themselves? There is one other part about that. It seems to me somewhat peculiar that many of the characters really do not have the facility of language, even the sort of intelligence, if I can use that word, to enunciate this philosophy, though they still enunciate it. I would like you to talk about that.

Harris: Well, you know, I will give you a surprising answer to that. Those characters enter into this kind of philosophy, if philosophy is the word, because of the density within them. Now this may be a surprising reply, but it is what I have discovered, and it has always been there in the work, but I had never seen it as I see it now. When I completed *Resurrection at Sorrow Hill,* I only saw it when the published book was in my hand and I was reading it, you know. Density means for me—I'll give you a for instance. You see, when one travels in the real forest, you come up against very peculiar densities, because you have to deal, first of all, with the top history of the rainforest—the rocks. You don't have electricity in the rainforest, and the stars come right down on most of the tops of the trees. So you have to deal with—what I call a transitive corridor running through the densities. In other words, what seems to be fixed and solid is much stranger than we think. It has a fluidity in it; it has various things in it, and it has a kind of rhythm in it, a kind of music in it, you know; and this transitive cord, when you begin to tap it, something happens on the other side. Let me give you an illustration: Carrol, the singer in *Palace,* who dives in the waterfall, and then reappears at the end of the novel, singing through—whistling within a window—which we could describe as a window in Eldorado—when he whistles through this window, the window is a density, and when he whistles through this window the whistle changes and becomes majestic music erupting in the text. But coincident to that is an incandescent—something incandescent which is to give to the actual symbol, concrete symbol in the text which has to do with the lightning bark of a tree. A storm seems to sweep through the tree, and the tree becomes like lightning. So you have this incandescence, very close to the musical phenomenon. When that happens, you have a key in the landscape that you thought was passive. The landscape appears now to erupt with this fire, and the voice, the music as well. Now, this could not have happened if you were not dealing with densities. The agnostics call these densities "wills," that divide us from the creator, and there is no end to these wills. Each time you have to face the will, or the density differently, there is no uniform formula. So these so-called ordinary people are much more mysterious than we think, and that was one of the things I discovered in the crews that I used to take into the interior. See, I had a lot of time to talk to men sometimes who could hardly read or write, and if I had met them in Georgetown, I would have passed them on the street. I would have just, oh, you know, nodded—he would have seemed so ordinary. We had to live together. I was the surveyor, the officer in charge. I had to live with these men. I mean, one of my colleagues was shot to death by one of these men. One had to have a dialogue with them, and then you would grant the sense that these men are not as ordinary as you think. They may have more in them perhaps than any men, you know, who function with complacency in the world outside. These men are trouble. They are living under very difficult conditions. Their economic circumstances are hazardous, and the extraordinary thing is this: they knew that I was writing poems and songs, so I kept it secret that they knew, because one or two poems would appear in magazines. What they wanted me to do was to deepen their thick society. They felt that it was useless describing them as newspeople describe them—that these newspapers were not taping their resources. They saw a writer like myself, who seemed complex, as more attuned to resources which they could not articulate; so their density became a phenomenon, because through their density I began to learn things about the human condition which alerted me to the extra-human world, which seemed to suggest as being necessary for their ultimate survival. Now that is a paradox; that is a curious thing. These are ordinary people with ordinary names like Vishrop. Vishrop, that is a natural name. All the names in *Palace* are actual names, except Don. Carrol was actually a man in the crew who used to sing and play his guitar. Vishrop was the climber. Jennings was the engineer. Vigilance, a fast moving chap who was the eye. He would stand in the bow of the boat and scan the river and read the rocks lurking under the surface of the stream. He could read a ripple. That ripple addressed his mind, his mind's ear. And he could see it and hear it, so that the faculties these men were bringing into play were faculties which lay outside of convention.

Lee: Is there another paradox? Is the paradox that these men had incredible awareness of an environment, but could not articulate it?

Harris: That's right.

Lee: And that you had the skills of articulation, and that you had to learn the densities?

Harris: I had to learn that the density must not be bypassed, that there are transparencies within density which can be written, but only in terms of creativity in which one begins for the first time to see how limited one absolute human discourse is. Then one looks for transparencies through which these other voices come into play; in part they are there in these men; they are there in me as well. They are there in the world outside, but I mean it is curious that men whom you would regard as ordinary men, and indeed in some respects they were ordinary men, I mean, they could collapse back in the world where they were drinking, you know, whoring, or whatever, like ordinary men. But then you get them in a special context within the primordial rainforest and you suddenly discover that they are crying out for something which the civilization is not giving them—it is not just that they want money, they want to live, but they want something else, some other sustenance.

Lee: How much has that experience, in terms of being the surveyor, impacted upon your writing and how much has the sense of the densities—you've often mentioned, for example, science and music and literature, almost synonymously in terms of impact—impacted upon the form that you choose to write, for example, novels as opposed to short stories or as opposed to poetry?

Harris: Oh, it has impacted enormously. Right through the whole grain of the fiction I have written novels in various ways coming right through up to in *Resurrection,* for example, one discovers that Butterfly is just an ordinary naive girl. And I say that in the text; I say she is like that, and you would not think that she would have, therefore, any deep-seated philosophy. And yet, she becomes extremely important, because she is a personification of the spouse of humanity which is trapped today in so many death-dealing regimes. I mean you look around the world, whether in Africa, Bosnia or wherever, Rwanda is a recent case; masses of people are moving there; they are married to the tyrants who rule them. They live within a sovereign territory, which it is not easy to move into, you know. They could say that this is our place, our land, our territory, why are you coming here to interfere with us? Now what has happened here, as I may have mentioned in my talk, is that the Orpheus-Euripides legend in which Euripides is the wife of Orpheus and Euripides is threatened by Lord Death, conquistador death, I would say, and deep into the underworld. The reverse happens in *Resurrection.* Butterfly is the wife of Lord Death and "Hope" is having a surreptitious series of affairs with her and is in dread, after all, of his great sovereign lord who could extinguish him, it appears. He takes that risk and then he discovers that there is some subtle change in Lord Death himself. Lord Death seems involuntary, in some latent way to reach out at times and encourage him to take Butterfly out of his grasp (I describe that as the Christ faculty—Christ wrestling with death). So Christ seems to reach out at times, and then suddenly Death asserts himself, and fires. This is the ground of Hope. Hope is a victim and it comes from the sensation he has that he is being killed all the time—shot, and yet, coming up again. And when he comes up he continues his surreptitious affair with the Death wife, and he discovers that Death is a little split—that Death has a side which seems to be helping him, even as it is hindering him and killing him again. Without taking that risk, he would not discover resources running through nature, which may suggest to us that we can deal with death-dealing regimes. We have to take the risk first of all.

Lee: Yes.

Harris: Of somehow identifying ourselves with this spouse of humanity, first.

Lee: You are talking about taking the spouse of humanity out of the grips of death.

Harris: Out of the grips of death, and we live in a world like that. We have tyrants around the globe who seem to me to be agents of death, because of the way they are treating their subjects, whether in terms of ethnic cleansing, or whether in terms of monstrous things that are being done very often to helpless people. At some level we have to discover that even with that tyrant, we may be able to take a certain kind of creative risk; we may be able to discover that that tyrant has a latent good in himself or herself.

Lee: Your work *Angel at the Gate* seems to be a little bit different than, say, *Palace of the Peacock,* and *Resurrection at Sorrow Hill.* What is the history of that text, and can you elaborate on that?

Harris: *Angel at the Gate* is set largely in London. It has to do with drug addiction; it is not totally engaged with that, but one man is involved in drugs. We have here a series of images, some of which engage with music like that of Louis Armstrong. Even though that seems to be removed from what I have been doing, it is still involved with what I have been doing, because you have a series of encounters where people begin to discover, for example, that they have resources which they have long bypassed. I actually quote scenes from slave auction rooms in the novel, and I think in one instance I refer to some slave, African slave, who was sold in an auction room. Well, a woman in the novel remembers this, while listening to Armstrong's music, and the funny thing is the way she remembers. You get certain animal figures that seem to erupt from her unconscious—birds, other creatures.

Lee: It becomes almost clairvoyant, in a way.

Harris: Yes, and these animal creatures have a bearing upon her understanding of the past. I can't go into detail, because I haven't got the text here, but you see how the extra-human dimension comes in if you look closely at it.

Lee: One of the interests I had in this is that it was set in London. As you mentioned earlier, you came to London in 1959. And you were in your mid-thirties. What has been the impact of London on your writing? And I ask that question as I have of many writers who have left their homelands, and gone to other places to live in terms of writing. As an example, Baldwin, who went to France and lived there for a while, eventually had to come back because he said he was too far away from the impulse of his writing. Is that something that occurs with you, or does it matter if you're in London, as opposed to Guyana, in terms of writing?

Harris: It does not occur with me for this reason: I didn't go to London until I was 38 years old. Even older than you suggest. So the answer is, I lived a pretty full, and in some degree, tormented life in Guyana. But I had learned a great deal from my journeys and the fears I've indicated to you. So I won't go over that. I arrived there, and I wrote *Palace of the Peacock* when I got to London. The basic experiences lie in my fourth major expedition in 1942. When these figures like Carrol, Vishrop, and so on and so forth, come into play, it—I had written three or four novels which I had discarded because I hadn't formed the rhythms and sort of orchestration of images that you find in *Palace*. What I discovered living in England? First of all, there is almost an inevitability that Caribbean writers in this century would move. Not all of them moved there, but the majority of them did. I think that is almost an historical inevitability, because of the circumstances of colonialism and so on. Maybe in the next century it won't happen.

Lee: Due to economic situations?

Harris: Yes. Everything. Everything. But, perhaps I've been fortunate in a sense. I have never really desired to be at the center of things. I have no desire to be called an English novelist, you know. I mean, I—in this conference, you have the strong desire by people to be called American novelists. This has never been of my concern. My concern, really, is to write at a level which is profoundly true to pressures within myself that are tormenting, but pressures which are always disclosing something else. Therefore, I could live in England in a strange way, on the margins of things. I had a little dialogue with the establishment. Sometimes I would be invited to this or that, but really and truly, I was not writing in the new Kinsian frame, the neo frame. Not that I don't admire such novels. You know, I like such novels. Living there gave me an opportunity to get deeply into sensibilities that I may have otherwise bypassed if I had remained on the coasts of Guyana, because that is where most of the people live. And the political shadows there, the political realities there, the political situation there, could be distracting. I had experienced it. I was not like some friends of mine who left at 19, who hungered to go back. I had had an experience of that. So that living in Europe gave me—I don't want to use the word distance—but it gave me an opportunity to sense that.

Lee: Maybe objectivity?

Harris: Mine—yes! My marginality—let me put it this way—my marginality in Europe is very close to the marginality of countries like Guyana which are regarded as marginal. I think I don't regard Guyana as a third world country. I regard Guyana as on the extremities of western civilization. I see Brazil like that as well, yes, also Venezuela, Argentina. They're all on the extremities of western civilization. They build on western civilization, you see. I pretend to lock them away, and lock them out, and think of them so that my marginality personified that marginality. I don't know I'd have seen it like that if I had remained. So . . .

Lee: So you have no desire to be a British writer, but clearly in terms of all of your works, putting forth the concept in terms of more—in terms of being a Caribbean writer—is that how you view yourself?

Harris: I see myself, if I had to put any label, it would have to be half soul-American, half Caribbean. I mean, if there are critics who describe me in bibliographies as a British writer, fair enough. But I have no obsession about it. I don't think Herman Melville had an obsession about being called an American writer. He was deeply and profoundly concerned with issues that went far beyond the situation, united, you see; that's why you get all these different characters on a ship. They come from different cultures.

Lee: I don't know if you know it or not, but your work is often compared with that of Conrad and Melville. Did those writers have any influence at all in terms of your writing?

Harris: Yes. In this sense, that Conrad for me has always been—or appears to me to be a novelist who came to the frontiers of change. He employed the European convention, you know. But one always senses that he was looking for something beyond the European convention. To me these writers are grit because they moved onto a frontier, which they never crossed. It's up to writers like myself, if I may put it like that, to cross that frontier. They came to this frontier, and it is as if . . . they knew instinctively, intuitively, that the novel form they brought with them was dying. And that's because it was so human-centered. I mean, Conrad has this error, so that those cries in the forest were distressing. You see, I see Conrad differently from Achebe. He thinks of Conrad as racist. I don't think Conrad was a racist. I think Conrad was listening to these songs that were arising from the African forest in his *Heart of Darkness*. He was listening to these songs, and of course, they were distressing. But they threw him back to contemplate a time and the times may have been like that—like the river he was following. So he was hearing voices that seemed to come from another world. Suddenly you would hear enough frequent cry, or something, you know. And a voice. And you get a kind of peculiar music. But he never really and truly crossed—because in the end you have crossing the horror—"The horror." So that in the end, you know something . . . a closure occurred, and the breaching of this closure becomes vitally important to the acts of the imagination. Conrad informs us of this at the deep level. Amasa Delano in Melville's *Benito Cereno*, curiously enough, has no utterance after a certain moment in Melville's novel. I think Melville had a deep intuitive sensation, therefore, that some utterance was required which he could not encompass in his fiction. Another writer who didn't listen as carefully as Melville was listening to the sea, to the various songs, you know. . . . I thought that Melville could have done more with this. I've actually said it in an essay—that there could have been more to this opera—it's like an opera. But, come to think of it, whatever one may say about it, and that comes from my own compulsion, but whatever one may say about it, Melville was aware that the novel form which he was employing needed to pull into it qualities of experience that were excluded by the norm. There was a norm, which one obeyed and followed, but there were qualities of experience outside of the norm which needed to be drawn in, And, at a certain point, he knew he could not do it, and he stopped there. But there's an eloquence that comes out of the silence. Out of Babo's silence. Babo has nothing more to say. No other utterance to make. The novel has to find ways of, I've said before, bringing that utterance in. And that is where you come into the density; there's a density in Babo—that's it—put it like that, which remains formidable to the end.

Lee: Because he doesn't speak.

Harris: Yes. You see. So as—in this sense, I regard those novelists as very important novelists because they bring us onto a frontier where we perceive what the challenges ahead are. Alas, most novelists, most novelists have disregarded that entirely.

Lee: Do you see, then, your work as extending the form of the novel?

Harris: I would like to think that the work that I am doing is bringing into play resources which have largely been negated and bypassed in the conventional European novel. The comedy of man as novel. The social realism of the protest novel. I would like to think that what I am doing at the time is tapping these resources. I am not the only one doing it. There was a question that was raised by someone when we were discussing these matters. A woman spoke up and said that Australian novelists are excluded. I remember replying to her and saying that, when I was teaching in Austin, Texas, one of the texts that I employed was Randolph Stow's *Tourmaline*. I think she misunderstood me. She went on to rattle off a whole list of relevant names and that seemed to move entirely from what I was saying. I'm simply saying that it is possible to employ a text by an Australian writer that does better on important matters. *Tourmaline* is a landscape that is virtually on fire. It's as if the landscape is seeking revenge on the community. So, water cannot be found. He begins, therefore, to address issues to do with resources that you don't find in the conventional novel. For example, the

Law. There's a character called Law, but Law seems to be becoming more and more—more invalid. That novel can be read in parallel with *Heart of Darkness*. There is the poet who is burning because the landscape is on fire. And there is the Australian dream thing, Aboriginal dream thing, which seems to hover over the novel. So the novel is tapping different resources. Stow has not pursued this as actively as I would like to see it pursued. But I, my life has been, I don't know what word to use, positioned in that direction—pursuing these resources.

Lee: Well you know, a very simplistic reading of *Palace* is your input in terms of the densities and of the rhythms. As the characters go deeper and deeper into the forest, and then as they slowly begin to climb up and out, it's almost as though there is a great understanding—a clarity for them, though still unarticulated, about the importance of the density.

Harris: Yes. That's right.

Lee: And it's almost as though, when Carrol is at the top and sort of falls into the river, in some respect I don't see it—any of the deaths as suicidal, so much as in terms of the fact that they've given up symbolically—he's given up on the meaning of that density. There is a realization that there are some things which impact upon their lives significantly, but yet they cannot understand them.

Harris: Well, when Carrol falls, that's an important point you raised. When Carrol falls, remember, that this is a moment when something very peculiar beings to happen. Because of the wretched Arawak old woman they have in the vessel whom they conscripted to be their guide, suddenly something happens. This woman appears to be majestic, and to become young again. She becomes therefore, a kind of gateway into the past, because then there's a sense that these people have come all the way from the Straits. For thousands of years they have been voyaging from the Bering Straits, along the Americas into Central and South America. She becomes majestic—and when this happens, they seem to hear a music that virtually tears into their ears and unseals their deaf ears. Their eyes begin to see differently. So you get this acute terror, sight by sight with an understanding that is transfigurative. When they stand on the precipice, it's as if they're slipping into the maelstrom. That is when Carrol falls and you get what is called this baptismal lamentation. His head becomes like a rock in the waterfall, for a moment, as it utilizes him. He doesn't throw himself in the river; he falls. But they do come through, and when they come through they're enriched by this understanding. So at the end when Carrol plays his music, in a way he is involved in that enrichment. And remember that this woman's gender is transfigured because the men can see through something which is no longer absolute in female terms, or absolute in male terms, you know. There's a transfiguration of gender too. You know, one has to remember when these ancient peoples traveled along that long road, the things they saw had an animate aspect to them. They might see a tree, and this tree could shape itself up as if the flesh of the tree was in them. There were voices that would come to them, as in an ancient epic when the masterful ship addressed Jason, the vessel, the Argot, making its way for the golden fleece. The master of the ship spoke, you know. They came all the way, 12,000 years. What is the womb? I read a passage from *The Infinite Rehearsal* when Robin is described as having been born from the ships—ships that have been voyaging for a long time since the circumnavigation of the globe, either in the early 16th century or the end of the 15th century. Since then, vessels have been mothering, and vessels have been terrifying. Well, there's the middle passage. The people who came through the middle passage came within the womb of the vessel. The vessel became their mother. So you had what appeared to be an inanimate object which became the womb. They were coming into a new world. It was a terrifying womb, you know, but they were coming into the Americas, and there, they were—whether they liked it or not—pushed out of the womb. They had to face new terrors, but at the same time secrete a liberation within their activities. And it is in this sense that that passage articulates gender in a different way. That is why this woman could suddenly come up like that. The vessel that is going into the mighty storm seems to become the mother, a terrifying mother; she becomes their terrifying mother. That is why Carrol, who falls in, can come up at the end again, as if he comes out of the womb.

Lee: What you do, then, is what I would call the fusion of these times, for example. Clearly there's a sense of which there's a continuing past. In other words, it's not absolute. There's a continuing present. I like the idea, as a matter of fact, it's really interesting in terms of not a going to the future, but the future coming towards you.

Harris: Yes.

Lee: Which means, then, in capsulation of that, that you destroy the absolutes.

Harris: Yes. That's right.

Lee: So that the finite is the infinite. So that the old is also the young. So that the inanimate is also the animate. So that, in some respect fiction is moving into the reality.

Harris: That's right! That is a haunting term. Fiction moving into reality.

Lee: So the form changes because the form is never absolute.

Harris: The form is not absolute. The form is always partial. And for that reason, the form sometimes has to die.

Lee: Postmodernists and deconstructionists would like that comment.

Harris: I don't trust them.

Lee: I don't trust them either, but can you say a few sentences about your thoughts on postmodernism and deconstructionism, and what you think it's doing, or its significance for the literature today?

Harris: Well, what I don't like about postmodernism is that it—from the theories I have read, they all seem to suggest there is no depth. That's number one. That the surface is all, that's number two. And also, that the discourse is absolute, without any awareness of the things we've been discussing. Now if I'm wrong about them, I apologize.

Lee: My students who read you religiously speak of the fact that your writing seems metaphorical to them, and often they don't understand metaphors, so they can't deal with that. They often don't understand symbolism. But also, there's a sense to which they want things to be rather didactic, and that is the past is the past, and the present the present, and the future the future.

Harris: That's right.

Lee: You mentioned earlier that writers want themselves to be American writers; writers want themselves—to have a voice in terms of dictating in some respects to the public about what to do and how to think about their works, writers who want somehow to be seen the way they want it to be seen. Is there something that fiction should do? Often the role of fiction has been defined in terms of conveying the human condition. But you've already said, from your point of view, it's not absolute. How would you elaborate on the relationship between the writer and literature?

Harris: Well, I think it's quite understandable, every writer would like the public to see his or her work as he would like it to be seen, or as she would like it to be seen. This is very human. The point, however, that you raised when you said fiction moves into reality, is that a writer has to bear the torment of a reality which is not necessarily the real world. That reality, therefore, when it breaks out of the real world, can bring different voices in. And some of these voices will address his or her fiction in terms of which he or she may find, I mean, the writer may find extremes, or a reader discussing his fiction, in a way in which perhaps he may not like. On the other hand, there are times when readers can discover things in fictions that are true of those fictions, and they do not necessarily diminish truth fictions. I mean, enlarge those fictions and deepen those fictions. So that the writer is a reader too. And the reader sometimes is a writer, and not necessarily writing fiction, but he's writing something else. If we could get this—if we could understand this dissonance, it's a kind of dissonance—it may be very meaningful. Because the fiction that is moving into reality, is not within the writer's grasp, therefore the writer should not be a tyrant, but open himself to many voices. Some of these voices may be ignorant voices. Fair enough. And the writer has to carry the burden of that antagonism and that ignorance. But on the other hand, there are voices that have something peculiar to say. And one mustn't turn away from this peculiarity. We have to learn by degrees. That this dissonance could be meaningful, and could be—it could enlarge the comprehension of things. And that is what I understand you to imply by reality—fiction moving into reality. Reality breaks through the real world. I suggest that reality is not simply the real world. Therefore, you must have a kind of dissonance. Because the real world is never abolished. What did calm the real world, the so-called real world in which people have to move and earn their living and so on and so forth, is never who you abolished, but it can be fractured in a meaningful way, because reality then seeps in, and creates a kind of dissonance. The music that reality brings is not in harmony with the real world. It fractures the real world in some degree. But that fracture brings up an orchestration, an orchestration of mind and heart and judgment, and sensibility. And that is what I understand you to mean by reality. When you say fiction moves into reality.

Lee: Yes. What I'm saying also is that once it is read, or once it is perceived, or once even the characters on the page emerge—maybe even not read—there's a certain kind of reality that exists of that situation and even for both the reader, as well as the writer.

Harris: Yes.

Lee: Such that all of a sudden there is an appearance on the page toward the end of the book, or maybe again at the beginning of the book after it's over, of reality—of a lot of things that began with fiction, which are now permanent.

Harris: Yes.

Lee: Not absolute, but permanent.

Harris: Delightful fiction, therefore, is immensely important because of the imaginative truths that reside in fiction.

Lee: Yes. Which means, that in some respect imaginative truth and imaginative writing might be more important than biographies, for example, because the biography is the end, the beginning and the middle and the end.

Harris: That is why some writers have requested in their wills that no biography should be written. But, of course, people can't follow the rules.

Shirley Geok-lin Lim

Jennie Wang

Shirley Geok-lin Lim is a short story writer, poet, novelist, leading Asian American critic, professor of English and Women's Studies at UC, Santa Barbara. She has published a book of short stories, *Another Country and Other Stories* (1982); four volumes of poetry, *Crossing the Peninsula and Other Poems* (1980), which won the Commonwealth Poetry Prize, *No Man's Grove and Other Poems* (1985), *Modern Secrets* (1989), and *Monsoon History* (1994). Her autobiographical *Among the White Moon Faces: An Asian-American Memoir of Homelands* received the American Book Award for 1997. She is currently working on her novel tentatively titled "Circling." Lim is also the editor of *The Forbidden Stitch: An Asian American Women's Anthology* (1989), which won the American Book Award, 1989, and the MLA publication *Approaches to Teaching Kingston's "The Woman Warrior"* (1991). She is coeditor of *Reading the Literatures of Asian America* (1992) and *One-World of Literatures* (1992). In addition, she has published articles, stories, poems, and reviews in *New Literary History, Journal of Commonwealth Literature, Commentary, MELUS,* and *Feminist Studies.* She is the author of *Nationalism and Literature: English-Language Writers from the Philippines and Singapore* (1993).

Wang: How have you managed to be so successful in your career both as a writer and an academic critic? I suppose this is what many of us in this profession would like to do, but not everyone can manage to do it, I mean, to write stories, novels, and poems while doing research and academic writing.

Lim: Thank you, Jennie, I am flattered you think my work is good. I began first as a creative writer, at the age of ten, as someone who wanted to write. My desire to write came from two motivations. One was that I loved to read. I was a reader. I was an unhappy child. One way to deal with my unhappy childhood was to withdraw into reading. But as a reader, at a certain point, I began to tell myself: "You can do this too. You don't have to write this about this strange country called 'England' that you'll never visit. You can write about your family, your country, and these secrets, and all these wonderful things around you that you've never seen between the covers of a book. You can put them in between the covers of a book." So from a very early age I was moved to do this kind of "insertion," the insertion of my own space, my own country, and my own reality.

Wang: What did you read as a child in your home country?

Lim: I grew up in Malaysia, which was a British colony, where the medium of education was English. Until I was an adult I was a British-colonized subject. I read all the usual canonical English writers—Shakespeare, D. H. Lawrence, Conrad, T. S. Eliot. . . . You name them and I read them. I did a traditional B.A. We had what we called the "Oxbridge" teachers, that is, the professors from Oxford and Cambridge, who came to read our exams. The British Empire was extensive. One of the ways in which the British Empire maintained its power was to institute this global educational system, and I was a little cog in that global education system.

Wang: Did you choose your career to be a writer or a professor?

Lim: Well, the common notion is that one cannot support oneself through poetry. Most poets would have starved to death if they had to live on their earnings from writing poetry. This was much more so in a country like Malaysia where I was writing poetry in English. From early on it occurred to me that I couldn't support myself through my writing. Having been a convinced feminist from the moment of my birth, I was persuaded that I had to earn a living. This was the kind of problem that faced the characters in Henry James's *The Portrait of a Lady* and George Eliot's *Middlemarch,* except that those women were from middle class or upper middle class, and they had their own resources. What to do with your life? A woman is faced with that question as much as a man is, except that until very recently the answer to that question was given to women. She was to get married. But I knew from a very early age that I didn't trust marriage; instead I had to trust myself, and I had to earn a living. So getting into scholarship, getting into academia was really in some ways a bread and butter issue for me. What does a woman do who loves to read and write and especially who knows how to do it, but get into academia. I guess your question was: Why I get to do both?

Wang: Yes, because you strike me as more than just making a living. I know you are a very dedicated professional to the field of your interest, Asian American literature, multiculturalism, and now global education and post-colonialism. You also have a strong commitment to your ethnic community. I want to know what gave you this sense of commitment? Or let me put it this way, I know you were schooled in British Literature, read Shakespeare and mainstream English literature, but how did you become interested in Asian American literature?

Lim: That is very true. I am tenured at this point. I can teach what I want. I think, essentially, having been a colonial subject, I have to self-reflexively question my commitment to Anglophone writing, and question my love of English literature as a colonial subject, at a time of decolonization when this literature and language come under sharp attack by nationalists. I have to ponder certain strong identity questions, as to who is the self that I think is my self. How have I benefited from or how I have lived off the backs of certain colonial systems of oppression? How am I in place in these global economies? There are always these paradoxically and deeply implicated embedded systems where I am myself, not only an oppressed person, but perhaps an oppressor, caught within the system. These very difficult questions that have to do with identity and integrity.

Coming to the U.S. I made a commitment to stay in the U.S. I came to the United States to do a Ph.D. at Brandeis University, but I decided to stay in the U.S., because there were a number of difficult political issues in Malaysia, where, as an Malaysian of Chinese descent I felt I was disempowered and disenfranchised. The month I left Malaysia there were enormous riots and massacres of Malaysian Chinese. At that point I realized I could never go back, because to go back was to become a marginalized citizen. But then, of course, the irony was that to stay in the U.S. I was already marginalizing myself. I was going to be a transnational dislocated person. These are difficult and crucial questions that continue to haunt me. When I decided to study Asian American literature, it wasn't a matter of career choice, it was a matter of attempting to resolve fundamental problems of being and belonging. What you see as dedication and commitment is an entire self project in some ways; and a self project can serve as a community project. Many people do not see that what an author does for himself or herself can also be community involved. Working in Asian American literature and Asian American culture, I feel fortunate that what I write and teach also involves evolutions in community issues in the United States.

Wang: In the United States, as I know, there are at least two different groups among Asian Americans, those who are born here and those who came abroad in recent years, many through the gate of the universities. These two groups belong to separate communities, often alienated from each other. But you seem to be able to relate to both of the two groups well. How do you relate yourself to these two groups? How do you identify yourself as a postcolonial writer, as you called yourself, "a British subject," and as an Asian American writer as now you are an American citizen?

Lim: When you talk about "two identities," I don't see that kind of paradigm. Identity is just a word, a figment of the imagination, a term, a sense of self that is continuously evolving. The moment a child is born, she begins to construct or have constructed for her a sense of identity. This identity is always in evolution, in conflict, in crisis. People who do not live the life of the mind and who do not question would seem to have settled into an identity that is given to them. For someone like me the situation is entirely impossible. I would go so far as to say that in American mainstream culture, it is impossible for any American to settle into two identities. American identity itself has always been in evolution and in crisis, at every point, in the sixties in terms of civil rights, during Great Depression in terms of class, and in the seventies in terms of gender conflicts, so American identity is always in evolution. I am quite comfortable with American culture, since my identity, too, is in evolution. But the ways I deal with these identities, the historically situated identity from my country of origin and this new country, this "promised land" to which I have entered, is through my writing. I am completing a book of memoirs for Feminist Press, called *Among the White Moon Faces: An Asian-American Memoir of Homelands*. It's a book of memoirs, looking backwards. It does not just look back to my life, but also to my father and my mother, my grandmother's life in Malaysia. It looks back from the present, the moment of transition. I have just finished a chapter titled "Resident Alien," a technical term that you will find with the Immigrant Bureau. The "Resident Alien" is not a citizen. She comes from abroad, but is not an immigrant. She has the papers to reside in the United States as an "alien." I have another chapter which will talk about assimilation and becoming an American. I hope to end my memoir with this chapter.

Wang: This fluid sense of identity is really a significant perspective that the marginal, migrating writers, "resident aliens," bring to the mainstream of American literature and American culture. But beyond self identity there is still ethnic identity. Do you see any common identity among Asian Americans as a group, as an internally colonized group in the U.S. by the dominant culture, the same kind of colonial identity under the British Empire as you just talked about?

Lim: When we use the term "Asian Americans" we are already dealing with a construct. I teach Asian American Literature, and I write Asian American literature. I teach to a very diverse population. Over 50% of the students sitting in my lecture are white Americans and the other half are not what we might think of as a homogeneously Asian American group. We have "yansei," who are fourth generation Japanese Americans, immigrant Chinese students, and visiting students from Japan. Some of my Korean American students cannot bring home a Japanese boyfriend, because their Korean American parents still dislike the Japanese with their memories of the Second World War, of Japanese Imperialism, of colonialism in Korea in the 20th century. When I deal with my Asian American students, I am constantly aware that they don't form a clump; they themselves are in the process of discovering what it means to be "Asian American," a term that was produced by the U.S. Census Bureau.

I have asked for that kind of identification. "Asian American" was only produced in the late 1960s. Prior to the 1960s, "Asian Americans" did not exist. There were Japanese Americans and Chinese Americans; there were Koreans and Filipinos; there wasn't such a group as "the Asian Americans." After the Immigration Laws changed in the 1960s, a radical shift took place in immigrant population both in numbers and in status, so that the Asian American population grew from zero point three to three per cent of the population. Also the status between the American-born and foreign-born Asian Americans.

Until the 1960s the majority of Americans of Asian descendent were mostly second or third or fourth generation of Asian American immigrants. Now over 60% of Asian Americans are either first generation immigrants or the children of immigrants. There is a shift in the ways that the Asian Americans have to be dealt with in this country. This is a very exciting moment for the Asian American communities. It is a moment that is defining, because we are in the process of defining our issues and who we are. It is also an exciting moment for the United States in general, because many Americans are looking around and saying: "Asian Americans are also us." So there is one interconnection between what is happening within the ethnic community and what's happening outside the ethnic community. They are not separate, but inter-related issues. I myself am an Asian American in transition; I think I have a lot in common with my students.

Wang: So as a writer how do you place yourself within the tradition of Asian American writing? When you described your forthcoming book, you used the word "Memoir," the very word Kingston used in her first book *The Woman Warrior: Memoirs of a Girlhood Among Ghosts.* The word has misled some critics to read it as "autobiography." Whereas, Kingston has written the kind of memoir as Proust did in *Remembrance of Things Past.* Are you using the word in the same sense as Kingston did?

Lim: Oh, no. Kingston is a writer I admire tremendously. She has a great deal of integrity. She is my model. Although she is not much older than I, she has achieved more, in a much more profound way in terms of writing. I have also committed myself to the life of teaching and the life of research. She is a writer whom I deeply appreciate and admire. But my "memoir," perhaps deliberately, has not sought to model on *The Woman Warrior* or *China Men.* The book is pretty much historicized. It has a pretty straightforward historical narrative, there is a great deal of straightforward storytelling, psychologizing. I see a different way of myth-making. It is not that I cannot do or "imitate" these experimental forms, but that I don't want to be a second-rate Kingston. I want to be myself. My memoir is not much influenced at all by Kingston, much as I admire her work.

Wang: Being a professor and a literary critic, inevitably you have a theoretical perspective. How does that theoretical perspective come into play in your creative writing?

Lim: Yes, that is both a problem and an advantage. It's an advantage in writing the memoir, because I am theoretically informed, and I make a lot of decisions that come out of that kind of very broad reading and intensive thinking of theoretical issues. The placement of the point of view, for example, the need to do historical research and be accurate—that kind of thinking is theoretically informed obviously. Actually I am much better known as a poet than as an academician or as a fictionist, because I have three books of poetry and my first book won the Commonwealth Poetry Prize, which got me a lot of international attention outside of the United States. I think that being a poet has a disadvantage—a different sense of language, which almost has to be prior to intellectualization and to theory. When I write poetry, I am continuously disturbed by this intellectual sense that I have to leave behind me. I have to strip to get down to another level, where in fact the voice is not heard until it appears. So it is difficult for me as a poet.

Wang: I would imagine the most difficult thing in writing poetry is translating two languages and two cultures in one's mind. For me, I value the rich tradition of classic Chinese poetry and hate to lose it. But it is almost impossible for me to translate Chinese feelings and Chinese material when it comes to rhyme and rhythm. I wonder if you have that kind of problem. When you write poems, how these two languages work in your mind?

Lim: That's a good question. Actually there are three languages in my mind. Until the age of five, I spoke Malay. I speak Hokkien, which is a dialect of Chinese. But I am illiterate in Chinese; I don't read Mandarin. From the moment I became a reader, I was an Anglophone reader. That is, when I think of myself as a language person—the language of literacy—I am only an English reader, although I don't agree with the political movement in California for "English Only," which is a way to protect the English speakers against the Spanish speakers coming from the South. I have really strongly identified myself with an Anglophone tradition, and by Anglophone I mean a tradition that is just not British literature.

There is a publication called *World Englishes*. That may be a very awkward term "Englishes," but that is exactly what I am thinking of. English has become a global language. There is the pidgin English of the West Indies. In Singapore people speak Singalish, a highly idiomatic and rhythmic English, different from British English. Someone just told me that she grew up with Chinglish, speaking a mixture of Cantonese and English in the United States. There are various forms of English, that we call "World Englishes." I see myself as a member of that species of Anglophone writers. When I write poetry, that's the language I hear in my head, though occasionally I have these lapses into my Hokkien or Malay childhood. But then even English speakers and English writers have these lapses into a nursery English.

Wang: What is "nursery English"?

Lim: You know, when mothers speak to their children, they do not really speak to them in straightforward English. They say "Oh, Oh, you sweetie pie, what are you doing now. Let your mommy kiss your thumb." We grow up with that kind of nursery or mamma or home English. I would think that Jewish children from immigrant parents' homes hear a kind of Yiddish English; we could call it Yidglish maybe. Italian American parents probably raise their children with a certain kind of Italian inflected English. Many Americans grow up with a kind of English which is inflected and different from what we hear on CNN.

Wang: In your poetry, do you write Malaysian English or in California, we have Asian American English? Is there a regional boundary in your poetry?

Lim: Well, this is a question that someone else should answer for me. A critic just published a essay about my work, entitled "On Whose Canons and on Whose Margins." It asks the question which canon do I belong and which margin am I at. I thought it a pretty insightful essay on my work. Regional boundary is not a question I ask myself, yet I am moved to write on certain thematic issues. But the question is timely. I have just written a series of poems on California. I may call them "Learning to Love America." It may be hilariously "politically incorrect" to have a poem titled "Learning to Love America" by a Chinese American.

Wang: Well, I can understand that with this series of poems you have arrived at a different stage in your transformation of identity, from a Malaysian writer to an Asian American writer in California.

Lim: Yes, you are right. It is an evolution.

Wang: Evolution? Can you talk about the themes of your two books, *Among the White Moon Faces* and "That Farther Country: Circling, Crossing, Landing" [tentative title]. I am particularly interested in the latter. What a fascinating title!

Lim: *Among the White Moon Faces* is a book of memoir, that will come out next year. "That Farther Country" started some seventeen years ago. This is a confession of an academic woman. The novel is in three books, but they are small books, a little over a hundred pages each. So far I have written the first two books. The first one was written about some seventeen years ago, maybe not that long ago, maybe some fourteen or fifteen years ago; and the second book was written when I had a fellowship as a Writer-in-Residence at the East West Center some six years ago, and I wrote that in three weeks. I haven't had any time to do the third one. I hope I will have time to do it next summer. When my students procrastinate, they come to me and say: "Professor, I cannot finish my paper because I have other papers to write." I always forgive them. I have no choice, as I have this novel I have not written because I always have other papers to write.

Basically the geography of the novel is set half in the United States and half in Malaysia. So already this is a novel in transition. You can tell from the titles of the three books, "Circling," "Crossing," and "Landing," that I had in mind the tropes of motion, of moving and flying.

There is something about motion in the 20th century, which is very different from that in the 19th century. Human societies have always been in motion. When the anthropologists study the Native American groups, they talk about "the Bering Straits" and the crossing of the peoples from Asia across "the Bering Straits" into North and South America, the people now we know as the indigenous populations in the Americas. With the 20th century the airplane was invented. Today people not only move, but also they can move back. One not only moves to a different country, but one can also always return to one's original country. So the sense of the self, which used to be a painful loss and dislocation, and eventual immigration, settling in the formation of a different identity, is now in some ways, one can say, in reversal, as one can also return. David Mura's book *Turning Japanese,* which is his one year experience in Japan, is a manifestation of that kind of exploration, of what happens to identity when one retraces one's forebears' steps back. What would happen to a Native American Indian were he to go back across the Bering Strait to Asia, and do that voyage that his forebears had taken ten thousand years ago? That was impossible in the past, when the Bering Strait froze over, and then water came in, and they could never come back to Asia. But many first generation of Chinese from Hong Kong can go back to Hong Kong and pick up a job there. This is a new problematic, if you want to use the term, or maybe it's a new opportunity.

What the human species has to come up with is a questioning of national identity, maybe a sense of multi-nationality if not bi-nationality, and perhaps a different way of trying to solve those ancient tensions that we see in its most brutal form in Rwanda and in Yugoslavia, I mean a vision of the world, as humans brutally massacring one another because of some construction of atavistic ties. We look the same, we speak the same, but for some reason we are not the same, and therefore, we have the right to massacre you. I hope that we can break down this atavistic distinction; and that perhaps we can work positively to sense that we are all one global species. We all began at some point and from some original place as a global species.

Wang: This is wonderful theory that you have developed, that is, one can reverse, retrace, and perhaps as I understand it, renew one's sense of origin and identity. How often are you going back to Asia?

Lim: Oh, I try to go back every three years. Sometimes I return for six months. In 1985 and 1986 I went back for a year; I am going back this summer for two weeks. The problem is that I have an American husband and a son, and maybe, here is where I displace my anxieties of my assimilation onto my American son. I want him to be an American son. I don't want him to be someone who feels torn in his identity. I want him to discover identity as rich and empowering rather than disempowering and conflictual. That is, I wish him to have those gifts that I had to fight for myself. I don't want him to go through those struggles, I want him just to have the joys, if you know what I mean. Maybe as usual I am being an overprotective mother. But it is hard for me to return frequently to Asia because I have an American son and an American husband. But my son will go to university in four years, and at that point I think I will be able to return to Asia more frequently and for longer stays.

Wang: So far, how have your trips and visits to Asia influenced your writing? Is there anything special that you have brought back from Asia—new materials and perspectives?

Lim: Of course, it always provides new material. What it does for me is to tell me, very sharply, how wonderfully those countries have been doing. I don't have this nostalgia as if I had left behind a country frozen in time. Every time I go back I see these societies are advancing by leaps and bounds. In Malaysia and Singapore the economy has been growing much more rapidly and in better ways than in the United States. Those societies are making certain cultural changes and decisions that are right for them. I don't feel that I should return to intervene making those proclamations about what's wrong with them. Because others have stayed, it's up to them where they want their societies to go. I am now an outsider. What I write is about that moment of my existence when I was there and then. But I do not speak for them, nor do I want to, except when they invite me to speak as a visitor of what I observe. In that case I am always very careful that I make my positionality very clear.

Wang: So you are saying that even memory can be renewed. I remember you said that from the day you were born you were a feminist. How does the change of women's status in Asia now change your memory and your position?

Lim: The whole issue of the changes of women's status is as complicated as the issue of any kind of cultural change. For a long time, I was the only daughter in my family, a large family. I have two brothers before me and then I have six brothers after me. I was in a family of boys. In a family of boys either you disappear or you fight back. I was a fighter as I still am. I am not sure what happened or is happening in Euro-American feminist movements is the right route for what should happen with women in Asia, because the societies and cultures are different. But at the same time, I think there is a lot to learn from each other.

Wang: This is really a nice way of putting it. I have just read your publication "Hegemony and 'Anglo-American Feminism': Living in the Funny House," in which you speak of the problematics of representation in feminist studies. I know you have a rich three dimensional perspective of the feminist movement in this country and how it relates to women's liberation in third world countries. Can you give us your perspective from the viewpoint of an Asian American postcolonial woman writer?

Lim: You know, injustice is injustice. People keep talking about the great universals of great literature, the emotions and the value of human lives. Then there are other universals. The universals of injustice. Injustice is found in any society. In many societies, many of the injustices are afflicted upon women. Being born with a vagina immediately makes you open to these injustices. There is, for example, a documentary film called "A Small Happiness," which is about the traditional roles of women in China. Before there was contraception, women were continuously child-bearing. When you go to New England, you see these graves, these cemeteries. It is amazing how many of those headstones are of women who died in childbirth after having had five children, or four children; and how frequently the men died at the age of seventy, having gone through three wives. I would not say that these men were bad men, that they must have mistreated their wives. But I can assume that the men didn't go through the trauma of continuous childbirth; and that continuous childbirth is a real physical trauma. So now with the inception of voluntary choice, that is my choice. It is important for women to have that political position. If women cannot control their bodies they cannot control their lives; it is as simple as that.

When I think about feminism, I think about family control and the control over women's bodies, contraceptive, and AIDS in these countries. Controlling one's life is also controlling what one can choose to do with one's life, including if one wants to be a tennis-player, a banker, a doctor, a fireperson, or a postperson. These were the jobs women were always excluded from. When I was a child I was told as a woman, "Well you don't want these jobs. It's so much better to be taken care of." But I don't see men clamoring to stay at home and be taken care of. If it were so wonderful, how come men are not clamoring to do that too? What we know as the public and domestic spheres is what has been constructed as men's and women's spheres, and we are led to believe that we are innately and naturally constructed to enter these spheres.

These positions need to be questioned. But they cannot be answered as if the answers were the same for every culture, every society, and in every history. Obviously in India, where women still do not have the tools for economic empowerment, that is, they are still dependent upon men because the state has not created education opportunities and job opportunities for them, then obviously economic sufficiency would depend on having children to take care of them in their old age. To tell these women you cannot have more than two children is in essence to take away their economic sufficiency, whereas, as we find in Calcutta, where the women are given the opportunities for education and jobs, they voluntarily choose to limit their families, because they have these other economic forms of self-sufficiency.

We need to give women those opportunities and choices rather than impose on them certain answers that would work in U.S. society, but might not work for them. I do believe that the control of reproduction is essential. I do believe in giving women educational opportunities and economic opportunities so that they can make their own decisions of self empowerment. These are the two major positions I would go along.

Wang: How are they reflected in your creative writing?

Lim: I don't know if they are reflected so much in my creative writing, although I have written some poems about women's experience. I have a poem "Phantom for Chinese Women." In it I have a scene where a woman has a baby girl, and her family commits female infanticide. The poem tells about the woman's deep loss and pain. It begins: "A child with two mouths is no good." The two mouths is the girl-child, and if the girl-child is seen as dependent, and if the family cannot afford that dependency, the child would be destroyed; but if a girl-child is seen as also economically to be independent and empowered someday, families would not destroy their daughter. Humans are constructed to love their children. Female infanticide is only a manifestation of women's economic disempowerment.

Wang: I see your point. Since you mentioned "infanticide," I have to ask you this last question in regard to the misreading of Kingston's *The Woman Warrior*. Maybe it was the story of "No Name Woman" that created the stereotype of "infanticide" in popular fantasy as though it were a typical Chinese practice. Since you are the editor of the MLA publication of *Ap-*

proaches to Teaching Kingston's "The Woman Warrior," also a Chinese American woman as well as a feminist critic, may I ask you to comment on the misuse of Kingston's *The Woman Warrior* by white feminist critics?

Lim: Before I answer your question, Jennie, I want to point out that Kingston also wrote *China Men* and *Tripmaster Monkey,* two wonderful books as well. To look at *The Woman Warrior* alone, which is the tendency in the United States, is to reduce her achievement. *The Woman Warrior* is a remarkable book, because it breaks so many things. It breaks one's notions of propriety and genre. It is not an autobiography, it is not a series of short stories, although Kingston herself has called it a series of short stories. It's not fiction, but it's not fact either. Its breaking of genre propriety is really very exciting and liberating, perhaps it reminds us that literature is an active imagination; or all literature, all writing, even when it is presented to us as history or autobiography, is ultimately an active imagination.

The imagination in *The Woman Warrior* is very fierce on many levels. Some white feminists, I don't want to reduce this, because many other white feminists have seen this work in its full complexity, but a number of white feminists have gone to it to take from it what they needed. What they have needed is but a sense of representation of Asian American women, and what they have taken from it is the idea that Asian societies are patriarchal, and Asian American women have to rebel against that patriarchy.

When I teach that book, I use, for example, that story of Fa Mu Lan. The story of Fa Mu Lan gives the title to the book. A number of critics have picked it up as showing how women have to rebel against their family. But I would point out that if you look at the conclusion of Fa Mu Lan, where the Woman Warrior returns home, she's married, she's got a baby son, she gives up her soldier's uniform, her general's uniform, puts on her own clothes, even kneels down in front of her in-laws, and swears to filial duty and to take care of them. This is how the myth of Fa Mu Lan ends in *The Woman Warrior.* Kingston's *The Woman Warrior* also constructs the myth of Chinese filial piety as much as it deconstructs and critiques the myth. So the book is much more complicated than how some white feminists might want to read it.

Wang: Thank you very much. It has been a wonderful experience listening to you, very inspiring, very instructive. I am looking forward to reading your novel *Among the White Moon Faces,* as well as your book *Nationalism and Literature.*

Susan Lohafer

Hilary Siebert

S usan Lohafer is a professor of English at The University of Iowa. For most of her career there, she has worked in the area of short fiction theory. Her books in this field include *Coming to Terms with the Short Story* (1983) and the co-edited collection, *Short Story Theory at a Crossroads* (1989). Her articles have appeared in places like *Short Story, Style,* and *Visions Critiques,* and she has published short stories in *The Southern Review, The Antioch Review, Story Quarterly,* and *South Carolina Review.* She continues to be active in planning international short story conferences, and was the first elected president of the Society for the Study of the Short Story.

Siebert: Given your extensive study of short story theory and your regular teaching of courses in the short story, I'm curious to know how you feel about the current emphasis on discussion of social issues. My recent experience with students has been that the text—or student response to the text— seems to require that we address social issues from the start. Otherwise, students seem to come in with conflicting ways of reading that create confusion among class members.

Lohafer: That's part of what I was getting at in my talk for the "pedagogy" panel at this conference. I described my experience teaching Katherine Mansfield's "Life of Ma Parker," a brief tale about a London charwoman whose suffering is clearly a function of her class and gender. The text seems almost made-to-order for the discussion of social issues. And that, for me, was the problem. Students, I knew, would come to class with ready-made responses to the way Ma Parker's employer treats her, to the way she accepts the emotional burdens of her entire family. Here's a woman who seeks—but never finds—a place to be *by* herself, *for* herself. My students would know exactly how to label a society that denies her any "personal space," a society that forces her to "construct her identity" in terms of compliance, decorum, and loss.

And, of course, I don't mean to say the interest, the concern with social injustice, isn't real or important. What bothers me, though, is the *pre-packaging* of the story's "message." Nowadays, nobody would think of forcing the meaning of a story into a didactic moral; but we do, routinely, channel its impact into well-worn grooves of cultural criticism. There's a difference, of course, but also a similarity. No matter how strong your passion is, if you talk about it over and over again in the same terms, the language ossifies, petrifies, codifies into jargon.

Now, as a literature teacher and as a writing teacher, I want to break up these pieces of language, these pre-formulated responses. My question to the audience the other day was this: when you have a story that begs for translation into class and gender issues, how do you prevent students from leaping straight over the story to what they perceive as the end-products of literary discussion—issues and concerns formulated in other classes, for other texts? First of all, why should you *want* to prevent this, and second of all, how do you do it?

I am still enough of a text-based critic and reader-response advocate to want my students to travel through the story and to feel the road, so to speak. I've said as much in everything I've ever written about short stories: How do we "go through" story? How do we undergo the experience of moving through the text—in a way that doesn't ignore the *text*ure? What strategy can you use to get students to do it in a way that then becomes useful for a *later* discussion of gender and class, or other social issues? Clearly, I don't want to avoid these issues. I simply want to make sure students approach them by a route through the text, not through dogma about the issues. I want to make sure they have a fresh experience of what the issue means *in a particular story*.

Siebert: And that the issue is really present in the text.

Lohafer: And that it's really present in the text, right. Because there may be cases where it's not so obviously in the text. And yet the teacher will—given the title of the course or the teacher's agenda—get the students to see it.

And when you have topics as general as gender and probably class, and maybe less often, race, you're going to be able to find these ideas constructed in the text. Gender, certainly, if it's a story about more than one gender, or if it has any relation to the gendered world we know. That's just it—these issues *are* there for the using. I think every short story critic in the 20th century—or at least since Charles May's first *Short Story Theories* in 1976—has tried to deal with the fact that stories are too disposable, too easily dismissed precisely because they are so adaptable to any discussion. In the past, their very usefulness in the introductory literature classroom has contributed to their lower status. My fear that a story like "Life of Ma Parker" might be pre-empted by, let's say, a perfectly legitimate feminist indignation, is just another way of saying that stories are compliant material. They're easily exploited by a dominant agenda, whether it's formalist or *anti*-formalist.

Siebert: Let's talk about your broader perspective on the short story. You're a theorist of the story and a writer of stories yourself. But you've also been a gatherer of the stories that other critics have told, trying to define what the story is or what the story does. Where do you see short story theory having gone in the past ten years or so since the appearance of your book *Coming to Terms with the Short Story*? Where was story theory at that point when you entered into the discussion? And how has your own thinking evolved in relation to the field?

Lohafer: My first book on short fiction was published in 1983, but I started working on it in the middle seventies. I'd been interested in short stories because I had a master's degree in fiction writing and had published a few, a very few, stories myself. As a critic, I was looking for a systematic and focused treatment of narrative theory applied to the short story. Of course, there was Poe, and other writers who had talked about their own work. In other words, there were scattered bits of what I came to call "practitioner criticism." These writings tend to be intuitive, impressionistic, and therefore a little hard for critics to use as is. Narrative theory in general was much in vogue, but most of it had to do with the novel, or used the short story merely for illustrative purposes. In talking with a prosody expert in my department, I became interested in the question of whether short stories have a special kind of prose rhythm. Perhaps privately, in a very modest way, I thought of myself as a practitioner critic, but I wanted to reach out to a more systematic, theoretically-informed aesthetics of the short story. At the time, that search seemed to lead through stylistics to reader-response criticism, and toward certain aspects of text-grammar, as developed by Teun van Dijk and the Amsterdam School.

Once I began talking about short stories as distinct from any other genre, I realized there were others who had tried to do the same thing. Mary Rohrberger, in the sixties, had historicized the modern short story as an outgrowth of Hawthorne's Romanticism. And I learned about Frank O'Connor, a famous practitioner critic, whose approach was largely impressionistic, but whose notion of the short story as the voice of a "submerged [now we'd say 'marginalized'] population" has been endlessly suggestive.

His, however, wasn't really a literary theory; it was more a characterization. And I guess what I was trying to do was to move beyond characterizations (which appeal to me as a writer) to something I could call a branch of narrative theory (which appeals to me as a critic). I was looking for my own way of getting at what others were calling a text grammar, but I was trying to build it up from something observable in increments, on the sentence level, something *experienced* as a progress-through-the-text.

Siebert: That's different from story-grammar, say.

Lohafer: Yes. Text-grammar, as I'm referring to it here, follows a linguistic model, transforming sentences into progressively higher levels of macro-propositions until the story becomes, in effect, one sentence. *Story*-grammars, which I became interested in later, tend to be top-down models of narrative structure, from which individual stories can be generated, and by which individual texts are processed *as* stories. But at the time I was writing *Coming to Terms,* I was interested in the hands-on, "low-tech" process of entering, moving through, and exiting a story. This process took its distinctive qualities from the salient and unique feature of short fiction—the imminence of the end. The anticipation of closure. That, in the most summary form, is what that book was about.

Siebert: Right.

Lohafer: Then, from 1983 up until the 1989 collection (*Short Story Theory at a Crossroads),* I became more interested in what other disciplines had been doing with the idea of storyness, and particularly what cognitive scientists were finding out about the way the mind processes texts that are stories as opposed to texts that are not. That's what I was up to myself. However, the 1989 book is a collection of essays by a variety of critics. It was an attempt to map the field of short fiction studies as it had evolved to that point. Obviously, others could come up with different maps and might see the field differently, but that book does declare how I—and my co-editor,

Jo Ellyn Clarey—saw the array of interests and approaches available at the time.

What's on that map? Certainly a continuing interest in narratology, in taxonomies, in the old question, "What is a short story?" Then there is the move beyond the short story, looking at the story in relation to other genres, particularly a kind of intermediate thing called "the story volume." Oddly enough, short fiction theory got a little boost from the effort to distinguish a series of connected short stories from the standard form of long fiction, the novel. A minor explosion of activity focused on that question.

In our book, we acknowledged the ongoing influence of practitioner criticism, and although we did not include any work presented in that light, we did note that several of our contributors had published short fiction themselves. I still believe critics in our field have an unusual willingness to listen to writers, and that's why, in introducing Isabel Allende before her talk the other day, I quoted some of her own comments about the short story. Finally, of course, I know there is an incipient—and hope there is a growing—interest in interdisciplinary work, especially between cognitive scientists and narrative theorists. And so we included some work on frame theory and on discourse analysis.

Our book did not include work labeled as feminist or new historicist, for example, and so we have been glad to see the mapping of new territories in the Fall 1993 special issue of *Style* and Charles May's updated collection (*The New Short Story Theories,* 1994). Thinking of developments in the field over the last ten years, I have to add the appearance of a new journal, Mary Rohrberger's *Short Story,* and the change in the editorship of *Short Fiction Studies,* where Michael O'Shea now presides. These editors aren't just publishing material about short stories; they're helping to define and develop a field of study.

It was probably inevitable that something like the Society for the Study of the Short Story would emerge, in tandem with a series of international conferences. So there's an effort not only to map where we've been and where we're going, but to organize our movement as a joint venture. Yet, the more established we become as a field, the more we begin to lose some of the very characteristics which drew some of us—certainly me—to this study in the first place. I mean a certain quirkiness, a maverick quality, a resistance to any ideology. I did not have to be a devotee of Foucault or Lacan, I did not have to subscribe to any fashion of criticism. The consequences were a certain freedom, a certain obscurity, a certain license, a certain danger of self-absorption.

And so, in the last couple of years—to go a step beyond the *Crossroads* book—I've been doing two things at once. I've been applauding the growth of a field that didn't really exist before the eighties, a field that is taking many important and useful steps to define and perpetuate itself. At the same time, I've been holding out for the mavericks, for the people who follow where stories, not "societies," lead.

Siebert: Right, and it seems there's a real paradox there.

Lohafer: Yes, there is.

Siebert: At the end of The Second International Conference on the Short Story in English, in the closing remarks you gave, you were calling for the "mainstreaming" of short story theory—and yet it seems as soon as you start mainstreaming, then "the short story" disappears.

Lohafer: I'm so glad you reminded me of that, because I think what I meant to say was that we should do what is necessary to be taken seriously, to be heard by the larger community of scholars. As I said then, what we need to do is find a place within short fiction studies for people who are practicing the full array of contemporary approaches: feminism, new historicism, ethnicity and gender studies, cultural criticism of any and all stripes. Short fiction studies should be an inviting place for these scholars to work without sacrificing their commitments or trivializing their interests for the sake of narrowly-conceived "genre" focus.

Siebert: I suppose the question I have there is, at what point does discussion of genre become dispensable?

Lohafer: Well, again, of course, discussion of genre used to mean, "What is a short story?" From now on, I think, that question will be passé—at least for the next hundred years. Out-moded, too, are attempts to say what's allowable in this genre. But there are other questions we can ask that localize study in a particular genre without essentializing its status. Instead of asking what the genre is (as Poe's descendants have done) or what the genre "is like" to read (as I have spend many years investigating), we can ask how, for example, female identity is constructed in texts historically known as short stories.

Of course, we're still predicating the significance of the genre label, even if we qualify it as an historical term. And I, for one, am not ready to throw out a distinction based in part, yes, on editorial convention or expedience; in part, yes, on culturally-mediated practices of oral and written delivery;

but in part, also, on a cognitive difference in processing strategies. I admit I have a vested interest here. I feel there's a lot more to be learned about the unique behavior of texts we agree to call "short stories."

Siebert: Even there I've seen trouble, in the sense that people these days are so interested in breaking down boundaries and denying categories that they may not want to agree on distinctions between short story, autobiography, essay, and novel. People don't necessarily want to agree to or acknowledge, say, what Austin Wright calls a group of tendencies for the short story rather than an absolute. And yet, if you agree with what Allende said at this conference, there's a particular experience to story, not one experience and not one that's an essential thing, THE short story—but kinds of short story. And I'd like to say that even within these variations, story is different from poem and different from novel and different from other forms.

Lohafer: Yes—and while our intuitive sense of these differences may be merely the effect of cultural habit, that seems to me as good a reason for examining the precedent as for throwing it out. But you're right that there is a strong tendency, influenced by Foucault, to see all such categories as artificial and logocentric.

Siebert: Right, because they precondition what we see and what we value.

Lohafer: Exactly. Well, of course, the glib answer to that charge is to turn it around, to say that the boundary-breakers, the genre-busters, are simply setting up their own structure, applying their own labels, in place of the old ones. The value of the enterprise is in the initial motivation, the initial "fresh look." Soon enough, if the reform is successful, it becomes as hide-bound as the system it replaced. There's the question, too, of venue. You read a text in private, you talk about it with your friends, you talk about it with people who share your political views. "The story," you might say, or "this particular thing I have read, regardless of what I am calling it, speaks to me on this particular point." Any response to the text is fine in its venue. The question is, what should happen in the classroom?

The classroom, too, is a construct, or, more aptly, a schema. In the sixties, in particular, some people tried to revise or discard the conventional script for classroom behavior, looking for an "alterative," something more "open." My own view is going to sound conservative. In most cases I see my responsibility as managing, preserving, and passing along certain kinds of information, well aware that the categories in which I've placed it, by which I've even *recognized* it, are provisional and functional or expedient, and not somehow carved in stone forever. One of my missions in life is to get people to read and think about those texts which have been conventionally labeled short stories, so I see that label as a means to an end, a pointer on the map of reading experience. It's a way of getting your eyes on the same page I'm looking at. There will be different pointers, no doubt, when we're all chasing each other through the cybernetic fields of hypertext.

I think I'm saying you always need to have some modality of discourse, and if you're not using one set of critical constructs, you're using another. There *are* others out there, that don't make use of genre labels as we know them. My classroom script allows me to acknowledge these other paradigms, but I'm not the best person to ask about them.

Siebert: Could I take a try?

Lohafer: Yes, indeed.

Siebert: Well, I'm afraid I'd have the same difficulties you would, but I just wanted to point to a particular teaching problem that might get at it. I was asking Austin Wright at lunch to talk about his attitudes toward Formalism and neo-Aristotelian approaches to teaching literature in the first place. I mentioned a problem I saw in a graduate course I taught on the short story when I gave my students your article called "A Cognitive Approach to Storyness," from *Short Story*. This was toward the very end of the course, and the reason I gave it to them is I thought it would bring together the students' very passionate interest in cultural questions and my own concern that they be able to work closely with texts in presenting cultural readings. I wanted them to develop awareness of linguistic features of narrative so they would have a language to discuss their reading experience. But I found that for my students, given the education they've received, the only critical vocabulary they know is from "critical theory." They don't have any idea what paratactic or hypotactic syntax is, for instance, and so I'm afraid that when there's an article like yours that's written very much with an aim toward understanding how a particular story or kind of story in an era functions culturally, students don't have the materials to grasp it.

Lohafer: Right, and I think the teacher makes a certain kind of decision. I mean, it takes a little soul-searching and intellectual self-definition to stand in front of a classroom. You can't just walk in and teach "Young Goodman Brown" and ask, "Was he dreaming or not?" and then add, in meaningful tones, *"Does it really matter whether he was dreaming or not?"* You can't just say, "Wow, look at all the imagery of *half-lights!*" Or, "Gee, isn't it interesting he gets all these anxieties right after his initiation into marital sex." Nor, I think, can you simply tack and weave between Brown's Puritan society and

Hawthorne's own culture two centuries later. You need to figure out what you can offer your students, and whether, to do that, you have to teach them about Freud, or about legal codes in the 17th century, or about parataxis.

For a long time, faculty in universities have scratched their heads, saying, "Oh, I wish the students had been taught to write, I wish the students had had more grammar in high school, or more this, or more that. . . ." The only thing you can do is decide what you want the students to have gained from having had you as a teacher. If someone studies the short story with me, I want him or her to take certain things away from that experience. Of course, I can't give you a list here, but in light of your very specific question about grammar, I'll say this: I don't teach the litany of terms for stylistic and rhetorical analysis, but I do teach a recognition for the basic strategies for managing language: serialization, parallelism, and periodicity. What I'm teaching is a feel for the fundamental styles of cognitive arrangement. My objective, of course, is to help students appreciate the workings of whole texts called short stories, where periodicity, for example, can be a feature of closure.

Many of my students naturally do have a strong resistance to what they perceive as formal analysis. If nothing else, they don't have the equipment for it, as you said. So I try to maneuver them into the recognition of something happening in the text, something that surprises and intrigues them. I position them to recognize a formal feature before they know how to identify it, and then I work from that starting point. For me, critical theory and social commentary *both* begin with a hands-on experience of language and its resources.

Siebert: Experientially?

Lohafer: Uh-huh. I'm not just talking about teaching certain skills. I think it has to do with winning people over. Sometimes students come into the classroom with very set notions that are going to interfere with their experience of your course. It's a matter of interesting, amusing, and enticing them intellectually. And that's why I use certain kinds of little exercises, little strategies, little things that are manageable and engaging, that don't telegraph up front their ultimate purpose. All I'm interested in doing, at first, is shifting and focusing attention, and so it's always a test of my imagination: what do I need to do to get the attention of this particular group of students?

Siebert: What you're describing is very hard to do, I find. You're modest about your "exercises" because you do this so well.

Lohafer: It *is* hard, very very hard, and I often feel I don't succeed. But what

I'm trying to do is re-enact the old cycle: from particulars to generalities and back again—over and over. I said I wanted to avoid leapfrogging over the text, but it's just as important not to bury your nose in the lily pad. Anyone who teaches writing (which I also do) knows how to ask for the evidence, the concrete particulars, and how to push for the insight, the idea, that links them meaningfully. You're constantly going up and down that ladder, and you avoid perching too long at either end. Close reading is, for me, always at the bottom of the ladder; theories, "issues," social concerns, at the top. I will admit, however, that I feel professionally qualified to climb certain ladders and not others. I am not, for example, a social historian or a political activist or, for that matter, a cognitive scientist, so, for the most part, I let others climb those ladders. Maybe I should say my approach is "formally attentive" rather than formalist. Perhaps because I have done a little fiction-writing myself, I feel a great passion for the effort to put imagined experience into words, into the English language. I think every writer has undergone a great effort to make those words—as they used to say—the "right" ones. I think of myself as honoring that effort, and it's hard for me to believe that even the most politically active writer sees his or her work purely in terms of its social efficacy. It's hard to imagine the writer has not struggled with the form, if only to break with known forms. In some cases, of course, a writer might feel abused by the kind of attentiveness I teach, but only, I think, if we linger there and never look up.

Siebert: That sense of wanting to honor the writer's investment makes sense to me when I see what you do with reader response because, in a way, that's a second kind of investment, one that the reader has in the text. And you're honoring that, too, by asking readers to acknowledge where they see the sense of story or how they feel the story and how the story takes shape with them.

Lohafer: You put that very well—and give me the perfect opening to talk about my work with preclosure. Theoretically, of course, it's connected to my discussion of closure in *Coming to Terms,* but it developed, typically enough, out of those little classroom exercises, those attempts to maneuver my students into recognizing what they already knew about storyness.

I wanted to find a way to have students record, as unobtrusively as possible, a certain aspect of their reading experience. I wanted this record to be empirical and quantifiable, but only initially, since its real value would emerge only in the later, interpretive contexts I'd supply.

Siebert: How would you even set it up in the first place? In other words, how could you take a story and work with a class so that they could give you the information?

Lohafer: Okay, that's a basic procedural question, and I've done this kind of exercise many times now. The mechanism is a very simple one. I take a story that is short enough to be read in less than an hour—i.e., within the normal fifty-minute class period—and I make sure it's a story that has some relevance to the course, but probably hasn't been read by most of the students. Then I transcribe it, leaving out all paragraph marks and, ideally, all section breaks. However, instead of transcribing the story in its original format, I break it up into a list of sentences, numbered consecutively. In other words, the story has been deformed from its usual textual appearance, but can still be read easily enough as a continuous text.

I ask the students to read the deformed text, and whenever they come to a sentence that could possibly end the story, to mark that sentence. What's generated, of course, is a list of preclosure points—places in the text where the reader's sense of whole-storyness was triggered by some signal the author provided, though not so obviously or incontrovertibly as at the actual ending of the story. These selections are very revealing, especially when collated with other information, such as gender, or the educational level of the reader, or whether he or she has tried to write fiction, and other sorts of contextualizing data. What's most exciting, of course, is seeing which sentences strike the greatest number of readers as preclosural.

I've usually found that about five or six sentences capture most of the responses. It has also turned out that no one sentence gets more than about 20% agreement—a near-constant that perhaps my colleagues in psychology can explain to me someday. By looking at the concentration-pattern of the responses, I'm able to plot a sort of normative experience for the way readers perceive the "staging" of closure throughout the text. Who is it who actually *has* this normative experience? Perhaps some one reader will have had it. Certainly no idealized reader ("*the* reader") has had it. I don't want to say a composite reader has had it, because the value of the exercise is that it tracks what really happens to real readers. So, for now, I refer to "the distributed reader." "He/she" is clearly a construct, but very literally a data-based one.

It's easy for me to re-characterize *that* reader—to look, for example, at the preclosure choices of all the male readers in the group. That, for example, is exactly what I did with the results of a preclosure exercise on "Life of Ma Parker." I was able to surprise the students with their own record of gender-differentiated responses, to focus attention on certain target sentences where this difference was most marked, and to develop a discussion of gender-coding that was not imported from other classes, but which originated in a fresh encounter with Mansfield's fictional world in a particular story.

Well, as you can see, you can do all sorts of things with the data generated by this kind of exercise. Behind it all is the assumption that storying is a very primal experience. How many short story critics and theorists have made that point—Charles May, in particular! People have something we might call "story competence," which allows them to recognize a story as opposed to an endless chronicle of events; I'm taking all sorts of risks here, but I'll say it's somewhat akin to the "linguistic competence" which allows children to "know" what a sentence is, even if they speak ungrammatically. I'm trying to access that competence, to provoke it into playing a part in the reading experience of readers from the most naive to the most sophisticated. Anybody can use this data, for any number of pedagogical or ideological purposes. I've made studies, myself, of preclosure patterns in stories from different periods.

Siebert: I remember an article where you discuss this. I found it really interesting and I couldn't imagine why it would be that the early period and the contemporary period are very similar in their stylistic features.

Lohafer: Yes.

Siebert: And whether there are cultural connections behind the stylistic parallels.

Lohafer: Yes, that is exactly the kind of question that, in my mind, connects what I'm doing with other kinds of discourse, other kinds of inquiry more popular in the academy. For example, someone might look at stories written by women and stories written by men. One could look at initiation stories written by women and initiation stories written by men. One could take any kind of in-use category. For me as a critic, the most exciting studies have been of stories which clearly violate normal expectations of storyness. Does the reader's competence fail, or impose itself in some new way?

Siebert: You're creating a really inviting opening for somebody to take, I think, to look at, say, differences in men's writing and women's writing. That's talked about so much with no clear sense as to why.

Lohafer: Oh, absolutely. There have been some books in the commercial press about men's and women's speech . . .

Siebert: Deborah Tannen, yes.

Lohafer: But those studies have been done using conversation, other forms of spoken discourse. I confess I'm one of those strange people for whom words come alive on the page almost more than in the mouth. I don't want students to miss that excitement, so I try to keep them from making the story simply a tool, a term in a larger discourse. As I said, I think there is always a danger of cannibalizing the story, turning it into a utility for some other purpose. People will argue that there's a danger that's going to happen to all of literature, not just the short story. If "short story" is an empty qualifier, so is "literary" in many circles. I simply mean that, in my experience, the short story is one of the most vulnerable forms of imaginative prose. It's gobbled up all the more easily because it's bite-sized.

Siebert: That's interesting. I see critics going right up to the edge of seeing the importance of short story itself when they happen to be discussing a story text for larger purposes—and then there'll be a turn in the paper and they'll say, maybe it's because of the short story form, or they will say it is because of the short story form, but the argument never really comes out except as an aside.

Two years ago there was a fine paper at this conference delivered by Barbara C. Ewell on Southern writing, Southern women's fiction. If I recall, she was looking at the marginality of Southern writing, women's writing, and the short story form in relation to one another. She seemed to be getting at how the story is a marginal form and why it absorbs those marginal interests. And yet, I felt like she was writing around that question the whole time and never quite got there. Maybe that wasn't her intention. It makes me think of the proposition in your talk the other day about gender in Mansfield's story that there's a difference in the short story, and then what are those differences, or why are they there?

Lohafer: You mean that what I was talking about with the Mansfield story could also be done with a novel?

Siebert: Well, I didn't think it could be, and I thought you were close to saying that there was something about the story form that revealed those gender differences.

Lohafer: I'm not sure.

Siebert: Maybe I just wanted you to say that.

Lohafer: Let me see if I can clarify this point, because it's an important one. I wouldn't want to say that the short story, by virtue of being a short story, is particularly useful or revealing for a study of, say, the plight of charwomen in the first decades of the 20th century in London. Rather, I'd say that the short story, by virtue of its brevity and singularity of focus, could be more easily *used up* in a discussion of that topic, as a sort of exemplum (which is, of course, one of the forms of modular discourse from which the short story developed). Novels, from the sheer mass of their fictional worlds, and poems, with their surface deformations, resist attempts to subsume them too quickly or easily into discussions of issues—although, of course, it can be done and *is* done in classes with a high-profile ideology. Of course, I have an agenda, too: I want my students to see how even the most sophisticated, *avant-garde,* issue-laden story taps into a resource they already have, a powerful readiness-to-perceive, a . . .

Siebert: Sense of storyness?

Lohafer: Yes. And after I've activated that sense, I'm interested in teaching systematic ways of identifying and organizing impressions generated by attentive reading, and in careful, step-by-step ways of moving from this data to a discussion of the larger questions of interest in our day—and I think these continually change. I'm back to the point I started with—I want to be sure we don't leapfrog over the text on the shoulders of an "issue."

I'm not ideologically at war with the scholars who think formalism is reactionary; in fact, it rather amuses me to think that, by virtue of my interdisciplinary and genre-based work, I am "marginalized" on the map of the humanities. In today's academy, that is a position of some influence, considerable freedom, and, I like to think, new access to the future. Does that sound like a stopping point?

Siebert: That's great, you're the expert on closure.

Charles E. May

Susan Lohafer

Charles E. May was born in Kentucky in 1941. He received his Ph.D. from Ohio University in Athens, Ohio, and was an assistant professor there from 1966–67. With his 1976 volume, *Short Story Theories,* Charles May became one of the most influential scholars in the field of short fiction studies. His other works include *Edgar Allan Poe: A Study of the Short Fiction* (1991), *The Modern European Short Story, Twentieth-Century European Short Story* (1989), and *Fiction's Many Worlds* (1993). His much-revised collection, *The New Short Story Theories* came out in 1994. In addition to his books, he is a prolific contributor to such journals as *Style* and *Studies in Short Fiction.* Charles May is a professor of English at California State University, Long Beach, where he has developed the use of software in the classroom as a way of teaching the short story form. May claims that situating short fiction in a spatial context helps to uncover meaning, as well as demonstrating how meaning is constructed within a fictional setting.

Lohafer: I'm going to ask you to make a long story short, and tell us a little about how you got interested in the field of short fiction theory. You're welcome to start with "In the beginning . . ."

May: Well, I was one of those country boys in a small town in the mountains of Kentucky who somehow got interested in reading books. Who knows how such things happen? My father read Mickey Spillane, and because those books were available, so did I. I also read all that good stuff like

The Three Musketeers, Robin Hood, Tom Sawyer, Robinson Crusoe, etc. I read comic books, I read men's magazines, I read everything I could get my hands on. Like so many others like me, I read Poe. I would like to do a study someday about how many writers first decided to be writers because they read Poe. I bet it is considerable. I know I could include Barth and Borges and a slew of others.

Lohafer: And I've always wondered how many short story theorists started out as short story writers. Obviously, you did.

May: I wanted to write. Didn't we all at some time? I wrote stories in high school and people liked them. I went to college and was named "Most Promising Fiction Writer" at a writers' conference. I got a fellowship to do graduate work at Ohio University and went there and had a lovely time. It was fun to spend my time reading and writing about what I was reading and talking to others about what they were reading. SO . . . six years out of high school I had a Ph.D. and got a job in California and started teaching. My field of expertise was Victorian lit., but the place I got a job had enough Victorian specialists (why they hired me, Lord only knows), so I taught other things—American lit., writing, and, then I started teaching a General Education course call The Short Story. It was for nonmajors—students who needed a GE course in humanities, but knew that novels were too long and poems were too hard. Short stories were, after all, short. How hard could they be?

So I started teaching the short story, bent on showing students that they were hard. And I started developing some interpretations of some stories and after that the interpretations seemed to be related in some ways, and then I started trying to understand why they were related. I discovered that there were no real "experts" on the short story and no one was doing much work with the form, although literary theory was beginning to blossom. I literally read everything that had been written on the short story and put together the *Short Story Theories* book based on that reading.

Lohafer: When my students read your work, they find that your discussions of the short story are usually framed by a "history of ideas" approach, an overview of relevant philosophical and psychological theories about reality. They ask me whether these interests are a function of your previous training and interests, or of the peculiar demands of short story criticism. How should I answer them?

May: I am glad that your students recognize my efforts to place my modest ideas about the short story within a psychological and philosophical framework about the nature of reality and knowledge. All of my research and writing springs from my teaching in the classroom, and I simply cannot teach fictions as if they were the province only of literature teachers. If short stories do not have to do with the most basic issues of what it means to be a human being, then I want nothing to do with teaching literature.

I always try to get my students to get at the most basic ontological and epistemological ideas (without using those terms) about who they are, where they are situated, how they think, what they desire. Because of this classroom need to ground stories in some notion of what it really means to be really human, it is inevitable that when I write about short fiction I also try to understand stories as a means of understanding reality.

Lohafer: Let me interrupt a minute to play devil's advocate. I think some people might argue that you are taking an "essentialist" position here, particularly when you talk about what's "*really* human." Are you perhaps using "human" as a code word for what you believe are essential characteristics of human experience—regardless of race, gender, social context, or historical period?

May: Reality is the result of human making. The one thing that makes human beings different from any other kind of life form that *we* know about is that they're inveterate "meaning-makers." They can't leave things alone. And making things mean something, creating fictions in order to make life meaningful—that process of just not being content with reality-as-found (whatever that means)—that process seems to me to be the essential one.

Lohafer: So, what you're talking about is an essential *process* (of meaning-making), NOT an essential *thing* or *quality*? That brings us back to your interest in epistemology and psychology.

May: I am really most interested in the human need to tell stories and how stories create what we take to be reality. Consequently, I am interested in all psychological and philosophical approaches to this most basic human need. Although I have been fascinated by philosophical ideas since high school (I think I was the only person in my hometown of 4,000 people who was reading Bertrand Russell), except for a minor in philosophy in college, I have no special training in the area. As for psychological approaches, again, I have no special training. But for a number of years back in the good old sixties, I taught a course here at Long Beach called Love and Sex in Literature (almost got fired for daring to use the F- word in class and for discussing pornographic material). My interest in that class focused on the basic issue of how literature affects the reader, by focusing on sexuality, which often directly affects the reader and creates an hallucinatory affect in which the reader seems at one with the fantasy created by the material. I did a lot of study of dreams, fantasies, hallucinations, etc. for that class, and that too has spilled over into my study of the short story; everything fits together somehow, doesn't it?

Lohafer: How, then, would you describe your method? Eclectic?

May: I guess I am a classic, country-boy example of what Claude Lévi-Strauss calls the *bricoleur.* I take a look at the resources available to me and make what I can out of them. It is the difference between the way my wife and I handle the cooking chores. She likes to find recipes, make a list of the ingredients she needs, go to the store and get them, and then methodically follow the instructions. I, on the other hand, ferret through the fridge and the pantry to see what I have and then put something together based on what is available. In short, I use whatever works. I don't classify myself as a thinker of any particular stripe; I just love to try to make some sense out of my experience.

Lohafer: Many of us who still talk about the aesthetics of short fiction find ourselves on the defensive against contemporary critics who debunk any kind of formalism in general, and genre theory in particular. You've already explained your interest in the formal features of short stories, but since this is such a central issue in the profession, perhaps you'd like to elaborate further?

May: I don't feel on the defensive against the current anti-formalist approach. For me there is no content without form. Stuff just doesn't lie out there, waiting for Samuel Johnson to stub his toe on it. Mere stuff doesn't interest me; what is human interests me, and humans, God bless 'em, cannot get hold of anything without some formal framework embedded unconsciously (or consciously) within their means of perception. So, if I look at stories more formalistically than a lot of critics do, who are more interested in stories as containers of social ideas, or reflections of social ideas, it's because—whatever those social ideas are—they're still the result of some artifice, some fiction-making, some creative process.

Lohafer: It sounds as though you're approaching a borderline between philosophy and cognitive science—in particular, the study of how we create meaning through various cognitive strategies—perhaps those very "form-making" compulsions you've been talking about.

May: To me, it's the basic difference between "noise" and "information." Information really means noise formed or structured into some sort of humanly acceptable pattern. So, I don't know how one could ever avoid dealing with form or structure in looking at literature. To ignore that, to leapfrog over it—as if you could just reach your hand in and find raw content! For me, the "really human stuff" is constructing and making, building and perceiving structure. Or developing structure and then *thinking* we've perceived it.

What I want to do is understand how it is that we experience anything. I am sympathetic with those who wish to examine social issues vis-à-vis multiculture experience and sexist assumptions. However, I have never believed that I can teach my students the real significance of literature by focusing on the mere "content" of it. It is easy to rap about race or fume about feminism; few disagree that many people have been excluded from the canon by a bunch of dead (and living) white guys. However, it is hard to really understand how we understand. Unless I can get my students to get beneath the surface of things and examine what they are used to accepting without examination, then I don't feel I am teaching them anything about the mysterious magic of fiction.

We have all watched critical fads come and go; we know that New Criticism replaced historicism and that structuralism replaced New Criticism, and that deconstruction replaced structuralism and that historicism has replaced deconstruction. That is all fine with me. But, regardless of what fashion dominates, for me, it is just not human to avoid trying to understand what it is that makes us human.

Lohafer: And, of course, that understanding is the writer's goal, too. As we mentioned earlier, many short fiction theorists have a special regard for the writer's perspective. Would you agree?

May: If readers want to understand fiction, then they need to understand something of what writers understand. I was pleased but not surprised at the recent Short Story Conference that writers from different ethnic groups were less interested in being identified as ethnic writers than as "artistic" writers. Writers are most interested in form because they know that form is what makes literature. How can we as readers ignore this?

Lohafer: In your recent book on Poe—the original "practitioner-theorist" in our field!—you conclude that, although his vision may be "narrow," it is undeniably "primal and profound." With the help of distinctions like "sacred vs. profane," you have tried to identify a kind of primal experience or way of knowing that is a generic feature of the short story. Can you say anything more about the "primacy" of the experience captured in short stories?

May: My use of such terms as "basic," "primal," "sacred," etc. to identify generic characteristics of the short story derives from a distinction I have always tried to make between the novel and the short story. The real question is, "What is real reality?" Or, put another way, "When are we really us?" Or, "What do we really want?" I mean, if mere experience were enough, even broad experience, then there would be no need for religion, for art, for love. To be really human means to be dissatisfied as we are in the everyday profane world of eating our cornflakes, mowing the lawn, washing the dishes—just getting through the day. There is always DESIRE, isn't there? I don't mean desire for some specific thing, but desire for something that always evades us. It seems to me that most great short stories deal with basic human desire, basic human fear. As far as I can tell, most short stories are not really interested in defining human beings in social terms, but in more transcendent terms.

Lohafer: Ah! That sounds like the traditional romantic stance—a concern for the individual struggling toward a transcendent reality . . .

May: Critics and writers have been saying for years the same thing Frank O'Connor said in *The Lonely Voice*—and Elizabeth Bowen said it, too—that short stories are different from novels because, in short stories, characters are placed alone on the human stage, and not in a social context. They're cut loose from the social context. And for some strange historical, and maybe epistemological reason, that's always been the case. Part of it may be because the short story, the way we know it, got its jump-start in the Romantic Period, when that was the prevailing point of view.

But writers today are still just as much, if not more concerned with the universals of human experience than with the particular circumstances of a time and place. For example, take Toni Cade Bambara's little story "Lesson." The social issues here are simple enough: "it just isn't fair that some white folks have lots of money and lots of black folks have little money." But that is not what the story is about; that's only an excuse for Bambara to explore the mysterious nature of how we learn something that we fight against learning even as we know simultaneously the truth of what it is that we learn. Bambara wants to explore how readers can both sympathize with the speaker of the story, while simultaneously finding her obnoxious. You want to squeeze her and kick her backside at once. This is a basic issue about how human beings are attracted and repelled simultaneously, not a surface social issue that can be taken care of by social welfare or increased job availability, or racial integration, etc.

I agree with many writers in the past who have recognized that short story writers deal with humans caught in the most complex and paradoxical dilemmas of what it means to be human and alone. Bartleby cannot be helped by getting a better job and Roderick Usher cannot be helped by a shrink, and Goodman Brown cannot be helped by New Age theology. Things are more complicated than that. As the young girl says in Mansfield's "Garden Party," "Isn't Life . . . Isn't Life . . ."

Lohafer: As teachers, we are always trying to get our students to realize that "things are more complicated than that." I'd like to ask you now about a special teaching instrument you've developed, one that helps students learn to recognize and respond to the many levels of a literary text. *Hyper-Story* is an interactive software program which accompanies *Fiction's Many Worlds,* the short story anthology you edited for D. C. Heath. Does *Hyper-Story* represent a new direction for you, or just an application of principles embedded in your earlier work?

May: My work with computers and my development of *HyperStory* is a result of my natural inclination to explore new approaches and ideas and my basic formalist approach to the short story that seemed a natural for the formalist approach necessary to understand and exploit the way that computers can process data and create information. I bought a computer back in the mid-eighties, taught myself to use it to do word processing, data-base management, etc., got a grant to teach other teachers how to do what I had learned to do, developed a course to train teachers to use computers in the classroom, started to try to develop some applications that would help my students learn how to read short stories in the way I thought they had to be read. I think that there is much to be learned about how computers can help students learn reading and writing skills. I am pleased with the success of *HyperStory* in my own classes. Practically every student that has used it has found it valuable in helping them to learn short story reading skills.

Lohafer: Obviously, short stories are widely taught, and no doubt always will be. Yet few graduate students in English prepare to go on the market as specialists in short fiction studies. Why do you think that is, and what advice would you give to someone interested in specializing in this field?

May: I was very pleased at the recent Short Story Conference to meet colleagues who had recently finished their Ph.D. degree by writing a dissertation on the short story. Many of them told me how difficult it was to get faculty to sponsor such research. I am currently serving on a committee for a candidate at a university in Florida who wants to do a dissertation on the short story but was having trouble finding faculty there interested. Anyone familiar with the short story knows how snobbish many academics have been about the form. There are lots of reasons for neglect of the form and I won't rehearse them here. But it seems to me that this is changing now.

My best advice to students who want to specialize in the short story and still be able to find a job is to focus on some traditional area for course work and thus be a specialist in Am. Lit., some area of British lit., etc., but yet do a dissertation on the short story within those more traditional areas. I don't think there is ever going to be specialists in the short story per se, but then there are few specialists in the novel, poetry, etc., in our period-bound conservative academies.

Lohafer: What do you think is the single most pressing problem facing short fiction theorists today?

May: Lord, I don't know. I suspect that it is still trying to get a basically conservative profession to accept seriously something that they have dismissed for years.

Lohafer: Here's a final, rhetorical question for you. . . . Are there any unanswered questions about the short story as a genre?

May: There are so many unanswered questions about the short story as a genre, but for me the most basic one is: How do stories that are short differ in what they capture and how they work from stories that are long? But there are many related subsidiary questions: What is the difference between the tale à la Poe and the short story à la Chekhov? What does psychological obsession have to do with short stories? (I am working on a paper on this now). Why do short stories have to be so highly unified? Why is form more important for the short story than for the novel? Why do people have to tell stories? What would life be like without stories? How are stories like dreams? Lord, there are many, many more. I hope I have the time and energy to try to answer some of them.

Bharati Mukherjee

Beverley Byers-Pevitts

Born in Calcutta, Bharati Mukherjee attended the University of Calcutta and Baroda where she received a master's degree in English and Ancient Indian Culture. In 1961 she came to America to attend the Writer's Workshop and receive both the M.F.A. and the Ph.D. in English from the University of Iowa. Mukherjee represents and writes about the (in her words) hybridization of the new American. In examining this new identity, she says she wants to explore the consciousness of those who are not of one ethnic group or another, but of many different ethnicities. She is the author of two volumes of short stories— *Darkness* (1985) and *The Middleman and Other Stories* (1988), for which she was awarded the National Book Critics Circle Award—and of four novels—*The Tiger's Daughter* (1972), *Wife* (1975), *Jasmine* (1989), and most recently, *The Holder of the World* (1993), a postmodern meditation which she researched for eleven years. She is also co-author, with Clark Blaise, of two nonfiction books— *Days and Nights in Calcutta* (1986) and *The Sorrow and the Terror: The Haunting Legacy of the Air India Tragedy* (1987). The recipient of Guggenheim, National Endowment for the Arts, and Woodrow Wilson Fellowships, she currently teaches English at the University of California at Berkeley.

Byers-Pevitts: In 1992, when you were in Iowa for the Second International Conference on the Short Story in English, I was enchanted with your reading/presentation; also, I had read *The Middleman and Other Stories, Jasmine,* the novel, and *Darkness,* the first short story collection. There was a wonderful interview I heard on NPR with you discussing the ethnic cultural impact of your stories and your concern about multi-culturalism. In our interview, I'd like to focus on several areas, one of them being the cultural diversity of the numerous populations revealed in your work. But first, will you give a description of your philosophy of writing, how you arrived at that philosophy and a statement of what it encompasses?

Mukherjee: I know what my aesthetics are; I don't have a philosophy. But book by book, I've learned how I write, how I see stories within the text of life. To be totally honest, when I'm actually writing, I'm not conscious of the calculations but I'm just either going with a character who's taken over my whole mind or I'm hearing a voice. Short stories start for me in so many different ways: the birth of the idea for the short story may be just a line or a title I want to use. For example, because I don't drive, I'm more alert to things inside cars: "Objects in the mirror might be closer than they appear." Phrases like "objects in the mirror . . .," speak to me in unclichéd ways. So, the genesis is either an idea, an image, a phrase, a character, a compelling voice. Some stories I do in one or two sittings, others may take *months* to find the right voice. It's in the thickening process, the revision process, and I love revising stories, where I make the aesthetic calculations.

Byers-Pevitts: Normally, how long does it take to revise a story? Do you take a different time to write and revise each story depending on the subject?

Mukherjee: "The Management of Grief," the one which is most anthologized, I did in two sittings. Almost all of it was written in one sitting because I was so ready to tell that story. Clark [Blaise] and I co-authored a nonfiction book on the event that's not mentioned, specifically, the terrorist bombing of an Air India jet, so all the feelings for the characters and the details of what happened in the hospital (I'd visited the hospital), were all at my fingertips ready to find their way in at the right moments of the text. Then there are others, like "The Middleman," the title story, the most autobiographical of my stories, in some way, because it came directly out of my having been stuck in Costa Rica among rather complicated, difficult people. That I wrote and wrote and wrote in the third person and then I realized that having a Bengali woman there, even though true, was totally implausible in the story. It wasn't until I found the first-person voice, this character of the Iraqi Jew, the middle-man, that the story wrote itself in one sitting.

Byers-Pevitts: Once you had the voice.

Mukherjee: Yes. So mine are all voice stories and it (the writing) is in finding the voice. And sometimes, it comes to me ready-made. I wake up hearing this character *yell* inside my head and there are other times when I know to put the manuscript away . . .

Byers-Pevitts: . . . and wait. In the revision process, for example, in "The Middleman," did you do much revising after it became right? After you had found the voice?

Mukherjee: Some cutting.

Byers-Pevitts: Do you do cutting as you revise?

Mukherjee: Yes, some, and sometimes only one sentence will remain because I don't look at the last draft.

Byers-Pevitts: So it is a revision and rewriting process.

Mukherjee: It is rethinking. I want to start again. I'll open a new "file," in other words, rather than going back to add into the old "file."

Byers-Pevitts: Are many of your stories autobiographical?

Mukherjee: All my fictions are, in a sense, in a very loose and large sense, autobiographical, because they're about emotions or ideas or situations that matter to me, and I'm very comfortable, unlike a writer like Clark [Blaise], writing *directly* about my life. And so, for me, art becomes, or fiction writing becomes, a matter of finding the most compelling metaphor, the most precise metaphor. The hardest thing for me is to write about my family, about myself, without any of that evasion or wall.

Byers-Pevitts: So you work and weave for the subtlety, for the change, and the metaphor to apply for meaning.

Mukherjee: Right.

Byers-Pevitts: Do you feel that you always write with metaphors in mind? Any metaphor for this particular idea?

Mukherjee: Well, if you asked me the first question now, I would say my philosophy is: all fiction is metaphor. It is about disguising in order to reveal the essential truth of an experience or of an emotion.

Byers-Pevitts: How did you develop your voice as a writer? How do you see your progression?

Mukherjee: Well, I started writing very early. I was a precocious reader and, from the age of four and five I was reading, not just Bengali novels, but European novels in Bengali translation. And I was an obsessive reader. There was nothing else that I could do or enjoyed doing. The world of books was more real to me than the people in the world around me. As a result, it seemed to me the most natural thing as a shy young girl in a very crowded household of forty to fifty people, to then make up my own world because I knew how to write faster than most people.

Byers-Pevitts: And you found your solitude in that, too.

Mukherjee: Yes, and I started my first novel when I was eight to nine years old. But now, thinking back, it would seem the most natural thing to do at the time, but that was for "self," in order to find the privacy that I couldn't get in a crowded household, rather than for telling a story. Story by story, that became for me the way of fighting the problems in the world or understanding, decoding the world. I got them published in magazines from age twelve. It was a given to me, the way other people decide at age three they're going to be bus drivers; I knew I was going to be a writer. In my adult life, I came to the University of Iowa Writers' Workshop because I wanted very much to come and also, because, accidentally, we heard that this was the only place in the world that offered writing within the university so you could get a degree for writing and go back home with something to show. And book by book, now, I realize that these are stages, these are sort of chronicles, if you like, of the stages of changes that I have made, or been forced to make, within myself. These are the transit stops or crosses, stations, in my process of Americanization. I'm talking about not only what I think of the story, but what issues overwhelm me, obsess me as story material and sentence structure. And so (I'm going to talk about some of this in the evening lecture), if language is identity, then I can see how language and therefore, identity's changed, novel to novel or book to book. And I have invented my own version of American English. And that's why I feel comfortable (with my American English writing) instead of mimicking Richard Ford or Ann Beattie or mimicking as we were taught to do by the nuns when very small children in Calcutta. Write British English, write like Dickens, write like Jane Austen.

Byers-Pevitts: Write like this good person who writes.

Mukherjee: But British.

Byers-Pevitts: But, very British.

Mukherjee: And with whole sentences with many clauses.

Byers-Pevitts: Would you talk about finding the way to write sentences, the development of the voice through those writings?

Mukherjee: Well, simple things, like, in my first novel, an omniscient narrator was the most natural way because I saw the world as having that kind of order. I was in control of class, category, and character states, just as my life was being controlled by an order up *there*. And I could think in those kinds of multiple clauses with semi-colons and so on. And it is, bit by bit, as I've lost that wisdom, that distance, and become closer to my material or allowed my feelings, and just my own life, to be expressed instead of always having to be as I was trained, to cover, to dissemble, to be polite. The choice of point of view has become first person. That's the most comfortable to me, as opposed to that god-like omniscience. And just the energy of the sentences; they're sentences now full of energy and emotion which I would not allow myself because I had been taught by the British education in independent India that that was uncivil.

Byers-Pevitts: Is that part of the up-bringing that you had to escape to develop your own structure and voice?

Mukherjee: Yes. Yes. And, in a sense, my love of America is really my rebellion against British colonialism. It is a liberation from structure. Because we don't have that same direct history between India and the U.S. as India does with Britain.

Byers-Pevitts: When looking at your work, thematically, I see some emerging influences or themes. One is what I call a feminist theme. I apply the label "feminist" because the viewpoint is frequently a woman's point of view, as related to women, sisters, friends, mothers, daughters, the wife, the dominant voice in the story other than the male, the daughter, the prominent focus. And also, themes and stories of family oppression, stories of societal oppression being told from a female point of view emerge throughout your work including one's search for autonomy as a female.

Mukherjee: Yes!

Byers-Pevitts: Do these female voices, and these feminist themes come from conscious decisions to write about women and to also write about race?

Mukherjee: They are. They're not conscious, but they are dominant issues in my own life and in my own growth. I grew up in a very traditional genderist, or sexist society where even the law, when I was a little girl, did not allow women many rights. Women couldn't inherit property, they couldn't divorce, and so it was an extremely hierarchical, sexist society. And I saw, up close as a child, incredible wife-beatings and abuse of women, daughter's dowry batterings. And so, that anger of my mother's, for example, I shared and I have found another way of expressing in fiction. A less dangerous way, perhaps, of expressing or getting redress. It was not a conscious decision, like a thesis that says, "I'm going to take on and expose men," but these (themes) are what formed me. These are the oppressions and concerns, emotions, rages, hopes that formed me; therefore, they're somehow going to shape, color, whatever I write. The autonomy, a woman looking for autonomy, I realize even in my staying on in the U.S. I came as a student, I was supposed to go back after two years, marry a traditional Bengali . . .

Byers-Pevitts: An arranged marriage?

Mukherjee: Yes. "Falling in love" is, of course, about hormones, neuro-chemistry, whatever emotions love is all about. The phrase I like to use is that those kinds of accidents are, really, fulfillment of unacknowledged de-sire that I wanted to stay. I knew that if I went back, I would, again, be controlled by those other forces. To stay on in the states, even though we were poor, desperately poor, living in quonset huts for graduate student housing in Iowa City (ramshackled places) and *still* liberation. And I'm one of those who have chosen to be American. Chosen to make my life here, not because there's economic betterment, I've taken an *enormous* social and material demotion. But, because of the psychological reinforcement, the space, the grieving, I can be who I want to be and make mistakes and that's alright, because I'm accountable for my mistakes.

Byers-Pevitts: They're yours.

Mukherjee: I can't blame others.

Byers-Pevitts: That's an autonomous decision for you . . .

Mukherjee: Yes. So the female autonomy that you said is absolutely accu-rate. And I'm not sure that even with *The Tiger's Daughter* or *Wife* I realized what the characters were doing. All these characters, male and female, are versions of myself. But in the later books, *Darkness,* for example, for me, there was a real breakthrough. In 1985 it was too early in the history of U.S. publishing for a book about non-European communities, so the U.S. publishers said, "It was a marvelous book, but we are not going to be able to sell it because no one wants to read multi-cultural fiction."

Byers-Pevitts: Oh, yes.

Mukherjee: You see? So it's only less than ten years in which things have changed.

Byers-Pevitts: And *now* people are saying, "We want to use . . ."

Mukherjee: Yes! *Now* they want to reprint. They want . . .

Byers-Pevitts: "We want her to visit our university and to read her stories here and to speak to our students and work with them. And we want her books here as part of the literature that our students can read."

Mukherjee: Right, this book *was* a breakthrough in a sense that I was writing about people who, whether they liked it or not, whether they succeeded or not, knew that they had made that move; that there was a split in their life between country of origin and country of residence. All these characters in *Darkness* are about salvations, Pakistanians, Indians, Singhalese. But with *The Middleman,* I felt confident enough, now, to write about both sides: European or traditional Americans, as well as new-comers like me and the change the country is going through as a result of this new influx of non-traditional influence. So they became about America—*The Middleman, Jasmine*—rather than about new influence.

Byers-Pevitts: And the placing of oneself into America out of this other culture which then, of course, is what America is all about.

Mukherjee: Except that we've forgotten that. See, I see my work as being a little different and this may have been included in the NPR interview, different from the Italian-American fiction, the Chinese-American fiction, or the Greek-American fiction. All that is in the tradition of the second-generation, third-generation writing, imagining the country of origin of their ancestors. We haven't had real immigrants writing about the immigrant experience in a long, long time, because, either they haven't had sufficient English or they've been engineers, doctors, and devalued exercises of imagination. And so, I am, in a sense, in that very first group to write; immigrants writing about the immigrant experience and not as diary, not as anthropology, but, I hope, as work of art.

Byers-Pevitts: And not as a second-generation voice, but as an artist's voice outside that experience.

Mukherjee: I see myself as having very much affinity with the Eastern European immigrant women who went into the midwest.

Byers-Pevitts: What other authors do you relate to in that sense?

Mukherjee: Well, a lot of Willa Cather. And there are so many people that I feel very close to even though their writing is totally different, the backgrounds are totally different, like Flannery O'Connor. I connect to that kind of moral energy where the invisible world of good and evil is made manifest in fiction. I loved Flannery O'Connor who, I didn't know when I first came to the workshop, was an Iowa workshop graduate.

Byers-Pevitts: Did you ever meet her?

Mukherjee: No. But I wish I had discovered her earlier.

Byers-Pevitts: And her undercurrent sense of violence . . .

Mukherjee: Yes! Yes.

Byers-Pevitts: . . . is prevalent, and I find that in some of your writing, too.

It is the thing that's just under the edge and is about to explode that makes that voice so important.

Mukherjee: Urgent. And, I want to think, there's a moral center in my work, but that that moral center doesn't always coincide, in fact it often collides, with the socially accepted set of rules.

Byers-Pevitts: And the world at large.

Mukherjee: Yes.

Byers-Pevitts: How do you connect that with the work that some people are trying to do to make this a more de-racist society? In other words, I would use that terminology to eliminate the sense of "haves" and "have nots" with, in the sense of owning race, owning self, the authority of being the superior. How do you connect that in your writing?

Mukherjee: I'm going to . . .

Byers-Pevitts: You're going to talk about that tonight.

Mukherjee: Very much so! We're going to zero in on that.

Byers-Pevitts: Well, they're going to love that. Good. That's what I see in your writing which I think is so important.

Mukherjee: Yes. The salient points I want to make in response to your questions are: I think, like Salman Rushdie, that for a fiction writer, there should not be any monopoly of ethnicity or gender. You can write in any gender, any race, any class, if it is persuasive as fiction. If you can make the reader *believe* in that story, the world of that story, then that's the criterion for value or failure. I'm against commodification and commercialization of ethnicity and race, and I'm against politicians and academics, especially Marxist theorists, whom I'm calling in my lecture tonight, assassins of the imagination, who insist on devaluing literature, reducing novels and stories to straight sociology and anthropology. They want to omit the literal; they don't even bother to read the text, but they want to know the class of the author, the gender and race of the author, and judge the work according to, "Does the author have rights?" So, I'm against literature of revenge, and I'm against politics of hate. And I'm going to counsel tonight, plead tonight, that we all let go of that part of our history that is about anger and desire for revenge which creates a reverse racism.

Byers-Pevitts: Yes.

Mukherjee: . . . and reverse oppression, and instead, that we work together to re-formulate what it is. What is that social contract that we, as a community of Americans, want. And if the old social contracts are no longer relevant, let's remake one. There has to be a sense of community of all of us together as opposed to aggregates of antagonistic self-sufficient groups. Good writing cannot come out of writers who want to create characters who are representative of entire groups. *Jasmine* is only Jasmine. Jasmine should not be the spokesperson for *all* Indians or *all* non-white immigrants into this country. Then I'm writing propaganda. Then I should be writing political pamphlets. And that's where I think an awful lot of ethnic studies theorists for self-serving, careerist reasons have appointed themselves as spokespersons for their entire communities and as oppressors of fiction. But I'm going to go into that later.

Byers-Pevitts: What kind of response have you gotten on your latest work, the novel, *Holder of the World*?

Mukherjee: Some are saying it is re-imagining the Puritan history of colonial Massachusetts and that community, out of which Hawthorne constructed a very constipative, not constipative, but restrictive Puritan tale. I'm saying how multi-cultural those times were, how exuberant. It's a postmodern meditation on the making of America through a pre-American, looking at the life of a pre-American, American woman. It uses virtual reality as work because I didn't want to do a straight historical novel. And I wanted virtual reality, because many of the new immigrants are involved in that kind of technology, twenty-first century technology, and I wanted people to be able to experience history rather than have pallets of history, tombs of history, limp data, laid on them.

Byers-Pevitts: It also becomes almost a metaphor of the virtual reality for their lives.

Mukherjee: Yes. Yes. There was a lot of interaction we're finding out, through non-fiction books that have come out just in the last few months, how much interaction there was between colonial families and Indians, American-Indians. And how one of those, Reverend Williamson's daughter, didn't want to come back after she'd been kept hostage and had married an Indian, how people had to wear Indian leather bands if they did return (to their own society). That kind of contact between different cultures also took place because those were the times when Massachusetts, through the British East-Indian Company, had enormous trading traffic with the coast.

Byers-Pevitts: How long did it take you to write *Holder of the World?*

Mukherjee: It took me eleven years of research and much of it was done in the University of Iowa libraries and of course, every library that I've been to, including archives in England and Holland and France and India.

Byers-Pevitts: What are you working on now?

Mukherjee: On a novel that I hope I'll finish by the end of the spring semester on the Vietnamization of America, but it's about a woman serial killer.

Byers-Pevitts: What is her ethnicity? Or, I should not ask that?

Mukherjee: Yes, because I want to talk about—as I see my children growing up or as I see the hybridization of the New American, I want to explore the consciousness and relationship with American identity of those who are not securely of one ethnic group or the other, and that who are not African-American, who are not confidently Latin-American or Asian-American, but who are many, many different ethnicities together, which is the real America.

Byers-Pevitts: Which is the real thing. It is the point of the whole thing.

Mukherjee: Yes. I mean, in a sense, trying to go beyond that kind of tyrannical identity with ethnicity, biologically—trying to go beyond biological identity.

Simon J. Ortiz

Mary Lindroth & Kathleen Anderson

S imon J. Ortiz was born in 1941 in Albuquerque, New Mexico. An Acoma
Pueblo Indian, he is best known for his poetry, yet he has had a successful
career as a prose writer also. His honors include National Endowment for the
Arts, 1969 Discovery Award, and Humanitarian Award for Literary Achievement. His works of poetry include *Going for the Rain* (1976) and his Pushcart
Prize-winning collection *From Sand Creek* (1982). More recent publications
from Ortiz include *The People Shall Continue* (1988) and *Earth Power Coming:
Short Fiction in Native American Literature* (1983), an anthology of Native American short fiction. His latest works include *Woven Stone* (1992) and *After & Before
the Lightning* (1994).

Anderson: Your stories emphasize both a universal, communal Native
American identity, and the importance of specific tribal and regional roots
(Clyde in "Woman Singing" is one example). Do you consider any characteristics of your fiction to be "Native American" in a general sense, and
others to be Acoma Pueblo?

Ortiz: The question is universal. There's always a universality in any story.
I believe that is the basis for what story means, in general. And in specific,
for Native American people, story enhances and engenders what one's connection is to the rest of the world. And is an expression, a human expression, of what is the world. So in that sense, there's a universality that is
specifically Native American. As to whether there's something that's explic-

itly Acoma, in contrast to Native American, there's really no distinction because Acoma Pueblo (which is where I come from and whose culture I was raised within) is of the Native American world. Obviously, there are cultural distinctions, which include language, location in New Mexico, and certain social traditions that are distinct from those of Native Americans who live in South Dakota, like the Lakota Sioux people, or the Cherokee people who live in Oklahoma and North Carolina. Linguistic and social traditions. So those kinds of differences exist, yes.

Anderson: Can you think of specific aspects of your stories that distinguish them as Native American? Speaking in more concrete terms of your stories themselves, what characteristics would you see as Native American?

Ortiz: Culture is a very strong and basic element in any people's outlook on life. Obviously, everybody has a culture: indigenous people such as the Native American people, or people who come from Paris or live in New York City. Everybody has a culture or a way of life. A view that the people live by. In the story you mentioned, "Woman Singing," the basis of the story has to do with Clyde's connection with and concern for his own people back home while he is away working as a migrant potato picker in Idaho, which is the case for many Native people. Not so much now as it used to be, although people still follow the crops . . . you know, from New Mexico, to Colorado, to Idaho, to Oregon, Washington. And of course, Native people, who are too often known as "illegal immigrants," come from Mexico, from Guatemala, all the way up to Washington state, and probably all the way up to New York state, following agricultural production. Anyway, in this particular story, Clyde has a very explicit concern for his community and what he feels is his responsibility towards his cultural spirit, there in the Idaho farming community. That kind of cultural connection is important for me, as a writer who knows a source, who knows a cultural knowledge as his source, in which this story is set.

Anderson: That leads well into my next question. What do you see as your "literary identity," and how does your ethnic identity affect it? I ask this because characters in your stories often mourn over their and their people's displacement. For example, the protagonist in "Loose" says, "Going nowhere. Coming from nowhere. It's scary to think about it." Do you feel displaced as a writer, or rooted and "at home?"

Ortiz: Well, your question is really in two parts. One, about literary expression in general, and the second, about Native American people and literary expression, or myself, personally as a writer. I'm a writer because I value and love language, and story really is the main way in which any kind of cultural discourse is allowed, or is opened and is verbalized. By and with the oral tradition, which includes information or knowledge about everything in life. Without the oral tradition for indigenous peoples, there's really no cultural continuity. And so, I very definitely relate this to what my own work is as a writer: I'm a writer, I'm a person who has come to language through love and then uses this love in a specific way, with my cultural background as someone from Acoma Pueblo who is Native American. And the second part of the question is . . . I forgot what the second part is.

Anderson: Well, you've kind of answered it already. I was wondering if you felt displaced as a writer.

Ortiz: OK, no, I haven't answered it enough. Well, as an Indian person (I use the term "Indian" interchangeably, don't let it bother you) . . . as an Indian person, in the present day America, after 500 years of invasion by non-Indians, Indian people do feel displaced. And I am a writer who uses even the language that the invaders have brought, and I use it fairly well because I've learned it fairly well. I mean, someone who has been within the invasion comes to use it quite skillfully. And so, there've been so many instances, too many instances, of actual physical displacement, cultural, social and political displacement, and so forth. As a writer, from within colonialism and as a child of colonialism, I do speak as a person who has been affected by colonialism. And so, you could say that I am displaced. I do not necessarily call it displacement. I see my voice and I hear my voice as an urgent, insistent expression of hope. Some people say that I'm more optimistic than the general modern-day climate deserves. And I am hopeful, but I'm only hopeful if I as a writer, and other writers, or artists, are going to continue to struggle. In that sense I'm not a displaced person. Do you see what I mean?

Anderson: Yes, that makes sense. The dedication of your short story collection, *Fightin'*, ends, "Only by fightin', often fighting back, do we maintain a necessary vital life; this is our victory." How do you fight or fight back as an artist, through your short stories? What and how are you fighting now?

Ortiz: I guess the previous answer, even though it wasn't intended to be, fell spontaneously in correct order.

Anderson: I'll ask you a related question, then. I noted your optimism as well, and there's a remarkable absence of malice or venom in your stories, despite the oppression reflected through them. And I wonder, how does a person "fight" without becoming a tyrant oneself?

Ortiz: At the core, Native American culture insists on one's humanism. And not just humanism as an ethno-centric or people-centric concern. We're not the only ones, but rather, we have a bondage, linking, an absolute connection to all things and all people. And so, it's necessary to express oneself. It's necessary to live, even under the most oppressive conditions, with an absolute commitment to humanity and its relationship to all things. The story "Loose" is based upon my meeting one guy, who came into this coffee shop and lurched against my table as I was sitting there, and he wanted to get a quarter off of me. I asked him where he was from, and he didn't say anything but that he was . . . "Loose." He didn't give me his name, nothing except "Loose," whatever his name was—Henry, Bob, Tom, or whatever. And the story concludes by implying that even people like Loose (a victim like the children starving, Native children in Ecuador or other parts of Central America or Africa or South Dakota) are actually the salvation of a society which for the most part ignores them. My own book, *Fight Back,* is an insistence on "emii i hanoh, amoo o hanoh"—compassion and love for the people. The complete subtitle of *Fight Back—For the Sake of the People, for the Sake of the Land*—is a statement of compassion and love for the land and the people. This is a principle, a value and a very clear statement of spiritual commitment and responsibility that is very material and practical.

Anderson: You emphasize your belief in the importance of a human family as well as a Native American family. Your preface to *From Sand Creek* concludes, "I hope . . . we will all learn something from each other. We must. We are all with and within each other." And your view of the human family and of authorship seem strikingly similar. Your dedication to a 1977 poetry collection and the recent *Woven Stone* collection both have a similar dedication. I'll read the '77 version of it: "The stories and poems come forth / and I am only the voice telling them. / They are the true source themselves. / The words are the vision / by which we see out and in and around." Why is this statement important to you? Do you see a relationship between your view of the human family and of authorship?

Ortiz: I'm not only a human person, but rather, I'm one of the living, I'm one of the items, one of the beings in all creation. There are some creations that are people like us, other creations that are hippopotamuses, and other creations that are the Andes Mountains or the sky. In that respect, I'm a part of all creation. I cannot remove myself from that, and I have to remind myself that I'm part of that all the time. Sure, it's very convenient to avoid that outlook because Western cultural education is often, too often, competitive, which alienates the individual from his family and from his community; and the kind of government that the U.S. and other world governments have categorizes, and creates destructive class systems, racism, sexism, and so on. And so, I have an insistence that we are more than just competitive, male chauvinistic, sexist people. Instead, we truly are spiritually or sacredly bound to something much more important than we are. And of course, I do refer to family in my other dedications or in my poems. I talk about my children, my mother, and my sisters, because I believe we all can relate to those kinds of relationships. And I also specifically refer to cultural tradition, which considers the family, community and land as elemental. I have to honor and respect that, although in some of my poems and stories, I am also very angry at the attacks upon the family, land, culture and community.

Anderson: I have a question related to that. Environmental destruction is effectively criticized in your writing (such as the effects of oil-drilling, mining and pollution). Characters' agonized responses to unnecessary deaths of animals in "Distance" and "The End of Old Horse" are particularly vivid to me for some reason. My question is, are you drawing a parallel between the plight of Native Americans and nature—such as that both are expendable in the eyes of western society?

Ortiz: Yes. The site for the first atomic bomb explosion was New Mexico. And nuclear weapons are still developed and experimented with at Los Alamos National Laboratories in New Mexico, which are located on the hills just a few miles above San Ildefanso and Santa Clara Pueblos. Some of the Native people work there. The destruction through modern-day technology, of the landscape, the natural terrain, through the mining of coal, oil, gas since the 1920s, on a large, large scale in the Southwest, is mostly or largely done on Native lands. When I got out of high school in 1960, I worked for Kerr-McGee, so I wrote my book *Fight Back* twenty years later, as a reflection, insight, a portrayal of what was happening socially and politically to the people who are indigenous (that is, the Acoma Pueblo, and the Laguna Pueblo people, and the Navajos, who live right in the midst of the uranium development region). And so, I do make a parallel, more than just a parallel, since Native American people and their culture are absolutely connected to the land itself. It's as if uranium ore or coal and oil development were taking place upon the soul of the people. In that respect, industrial development doesn't only affect the land but affects the communities as well. Especially at Laguna Pueblo, where the Jackpile Mine, operated by Anaconda Corporation, was active from 1951 or -52 to 1980. Now it's just a great big hole out there. That's Laguna novelist Leslie Marmon Silko's homeland. And the strip-mining that's taking place out in the Four Corners area—that's Navajo or "Dineh" people's land. Or, on Black Mesa—that's Hopi and Navajo land. That's as if it were taking place right in your soul, in your heart, in your bosom.

Anderson: My last question seems to come naturally here. The "suffering artist" is a common stereotype. Do you believe there's any truth to this stereotype? Especially considering all that you've mentioned, and that your stories contain a lot of suffering. How has your suffering influenced your literary craft?

Ortiz: Well, I try to have a good humor about it. Suffering is not necessarily the power behind any art. I said earlier that language, and love of the oral tradition, for me, as an "Aa-quumeh hahtrudzai" (an Acoma man), is the real soul and spirit and heart of what I write and have written over the past thirty years. Suffering obviously is the experience that for five hundred years Native Americans have endured because of the loss of land, culture, children and so on. Some of the stories, poems, newspaper articles, or magazine articles that I have written, as well as the film documentary narrative that I did in 1992 ("Surviving Columbus"), speak of the result of this loss. I know and other people know what this suffering has resulted in. And so, the suffering artist is kind of an archetype, but I think it's more than that. It's the artist who loves his people. Well, we exist because we mean something to ourselves. And when something attacks that, or threatens that, or injures it, we're going to hold on to our humanity as fiercely, and as lovingly, and as much as we can. So, I guess that's why I write, or how the writing comes about.

Lindroth: I want to talk a little bit about certain elements in your stories and specifically the narrators in your short stories, who I noticed tend to be observers or listeners to stories. (The narrator in "The Killing of a State Cop" hears Felipe's version or the narrator in "Kaiser and the War" relates various observations on Kaiser's actions.) And I think of your suggestion that words and stories are not owned because they come from a community of people. And I'm wondering if this detached narrator is meant to draw attention to the storyteller/artist figure as a conduit rather than an owner of language and stories who passes on as best he can the details he observes?

Ortiz: The narrator in "The Killing of a State Cop" is the first person, a first person seeing and hearing what is happening around him. And it's based on a true story. In 1952, the two young men from Acoma Pueblo, Willy and

Gabriel Felipe, killed a state cop. This state patrolman had been known to harass people. And the boys, or young men (one was a Korean war vet and the other was somewhat older) decided to take it upon themselves to "get rid of this guy," I guess. And so that's what they did. They went up to this small non-Indian town, a white town, near Acoma, enticed this patrolman on to the Acoma Pueblo reservation, they made sure he followed them, and they ambushed him. So, that story is based on fact. I wrote it in the first person point of view not necessarily as a factual story, because it's fiction. But I felt it was the most immediate and intimate way for me to tell it in first person, and have that be the way in which the reader could experience the story. I feel a great deal that, as I said to Kathleen, the oral tradition and the effective power of oral tradition is the intimacy and the immediacy of language. If you read that story out loud or if you were being told that story out loud, there's much more of a sense of presence, rather than something you merely read as lines on the page and then turn the other page until you finish with the story. Good storytelling, orally told, is very effective, is very powerful.

Lindroth: That brings me to a related question. You're very interested in storytelling and in "good storytelling" and a number of images come to mind: storytelling as a performance, or storytelling as a journey meant to bring all people together across distances. And I'm wondering if there is a more effective way to think of story. Is it more effective to think of story as a performance, or as a journey, or both?

Ortiz: Both. Both, actually. Before I wrote stories, before I *wrote* anything down, there was language. There was oral language. I didn't speak any English until I went to school. But I already knew the power of story, of language in story. And I suppose that power comes from the way a family is. You know, all the connections between family—mother and father, siblings and other people—and things that you do in a community. So, I knew that and had that. And when later I began to write, I felt that, not immediately of course, I felt that it was important just to, just to get words out, just to know that words meant something to me. I didn't really know what writers did. And it was not until much later, although I wrote for quite a few years, that I even began to fantasize what writing was. I mean, I fantasized maybe when I was 16, 17, 18 years old. But before that I was already writing, like in journals, and I would compose little songs. And of course I would tell stories. My mom always used to tease me and say, "You used to tell some tall tales." Children are good at that. Of course, children love language, and they know what they're saying simply because it's experience. And I think when writing came along for me and I turned that from experience into written expression, I wanted to keep that experience immediate and intimate as much as possible. This relates to that choice of first person point of view, which I believe is so effective. I know that scholarly and academic writing loses some of that quality because it's a remove. It's more than just one remove. I think it's several removes from that intimacy and immediacy because objective observation, so-called scientific observation, which is supposedly the basis of scientific analysis and study, requires it. Whereas the oral language of storytelling doesn't necessarily mean analysis and study, but experience.

Lindroth: I'd like to pick up on that note of experience and talk about another element that I sense is important in your stories: the experience of prayer. And, what I felt was an incredible moment in your piece entitled "Hiding, West of Here" when your narrator (the West Virginian miner) begins by what he thinks is surreptitiously spying on a ceremony, and ends up feeling that his presence has been anticipated by the two Native American men. He says "I'd come up here just to be by myself because, well because I like the quiet and the thinking that I do and sort of studying things. I guess it's praying of a sort, yeah. And then it seemed like I was sort of part of what they were doing, like they wanted me to even though they didn't know I was there." How is the experience of participating in prayer different from the experience of participating in storytelling?

Ortiz: I'm glad that you picked up on that. I've never heard anybody really give it any kind of discussion as you have before. Ultimately there's no difference. The experience of storytelling and the experience of praying or meditation is not any different. Because story, in essence, is source of existence. And prayer, in essence, is also the source of existence. It's like a consciousness of ourselves. It's a consciousness of mankind's history and how he came to develop an understanding of his reality or existence, through language . . . such as the emergence or origin stories of Native American people. Prayer, in the same way, because it is language and it is meditative expression, confirms that existence. And it also does bring ourselves into reality. It's not as if we're only praying that things will be good, but praying within even the moment that may not be so good. A consciousness or awareness of story and prayer are I think the same. I've said before in other contexts that poetry is prayer. Really poetry and prayer are one and the same. I think that Western cultural knowledge and Western cultural theory of language may differ with that because language is not prayer. As an Acoma person, how I use language is intended to show that I exist, that I'm thankful for my existence, and that existence, then, is always related to other things. If I deny that this microphone before me is here, then by that same token I wouldn't be acknowledging my own existence. It would be as if there were nothing around me. So language through story and language through prayer is really one and the same.

Lindroth: You've talked about language and stories and language and prayer. There's another form that you talk about in your stories: song. Characters are constantly singing to themselves or hearing others singing. You just defined for us what you thought was a consciousness of prayer and storytelling. How would you define song?

Ortiz: Well, song is a specific form of language. I grew up in a family that was traditional in some ways (that is, in the traditional Acoma Pueblo way of life) and also non-traditional in another way of life. My family was expressive, expressive in the traditional ways, but also changing—by the late '40s and '50s as all people were affected by just pretty drastic change. And so my father spoke Spanish and he used to sing in Spanish. And also my mother she was a churchgoer so she sang Catholic Church hymns. And it was a mixture of singing that was part of my own background as an artist. Pueblo people were agrarian people. We were farmers, traditionally. And if you're farmers, you sing in order to make your life meaningful to what you're doing. Planting corn and helping the corn grow or asking as a prayer for rain, for conditions to be good and for your family to feel good about what they were doing. And so singing was for that and ceremony always has songs. And then later on I think that songs for me also became an expression of my poetry. I used to like country and western music. I used to listen to it once in a while. I think I even wrote lyrics to country and western, gosh, when I was 12 or 13 years old. And sometimes I say that's really where my poetic writer beginnings took place.

Lindroth: Do you feel that your song shapes, features differently in your poems than it does in your short stories?

Ortiz: They are a part of each other. Sometimes I tell stories about the songs and songs are a necessary part of that story. There's this one song that I did and I can never remember all the lyrics to it. I was coming from Phoenix I think it was and I was going through Cottonwood, Arizona, on the way up to Flagstaff. And me and this Apache guy were sitting in a bar and he was telling me about his uncle who had some land some miles outside of

Cottonwood, and he was Yavapai Apache. And his uncle had some cattle and above that land was a white rancher who had shut off the stream of water which ran through. And it was a real hot, hot year some time before then and so he had damned that small creek up so that there was no more water. So the Apache man went and cut the fence so his cattle could go up and drink. He felt that water which his cattle needed justified, for him, cutting that fence. So he was brought to court. He and I were talking about this, so later on I wrote this song called "Yes, You Honor, Judge." [Sings.]

> Yes, You Honor, Judge
> Yes, You Honor, Judge
> Yes, You Honor, Judge
> You Honor, You Honor, Judge.
>
> Where's my life, Judge?
> Where's my life, Judge?
> Where's my life, Judge?
> Where is my life, Judge?
>
> Where's my land, Judge?
> Where's my land, Judge?
> Where's my land, Judge?
> Where is my land, Judge?

and then there are more verses, and then it concludes:

> Yes, Your Honor, Judge.
> Yes, Your Honor, Judge.
> Yes, Your Honor, Judge.
> You have no honor, Judge.
> You have no honor, Judge.

He was told that he had to pay a $50 dollar fine, the songs says in the middle part of it, or else go to jail for 50 days. And he did not want to, he said, "No way, I'm not going to go." Yes, your honor, you have no honor. Anyway, yes, song and story are part of each other.

Lindroth: I want to ask if there are any questions that you want to answer that didn't get asked?

Ortiz: I think I'll ask this. Let's see, how would I say this. I'm wondering if there would be a question that would be posed this way: "Why do you think, Mr. Ortiz, that there is considerable interest in Native American Literature by non-Native Americans? Especially contemporary readers of American Literature."

Lindroth: And how would you answer? Or would you?

Ortiz: Well, I think there's a lot of interest because of two things. One is the environmental issue and the environmental catastrophes. Whether it's water or the air or the trees or the great plains. People are beginning to really look at Native American culture knowledge of this. That's one of the reasons. And two, there's a strange, I don't know, element in the psyche of non-Indians, especially white people, who are immensely curious about the . . . I don't know what it is . . . an element that's unclear to me. They want to know something so deeply about that other, other person, other. I don't understand quite the concept of the "Other" entirely. But they want to know about Indian people because they want to know, I think, about themselves, about themselves. I have a poem, in fact, which says, "I let you see into me in order that you may see yourself." I think that kind of searching, as long as people are also responsible for what they find about themselves, not about the "Other," but about themselves, that that kind of searching is good and I think it's healthy.

Mary Rohrberger

Susan Rochette-Crawley

Mary Rohrberger, a New Orleanean by birth, attended Newcomb College and Tulane University where she received her Ph.D. in 1961. She is author or editor of a dozen books, seven chapters in books, and more than 350 articles, reviews, etc. Almost all her work has been in the area of prose fiction, the bulk of it in the short story. She is founder and editor of the journal *Short Story,* founder and Executive Director of the biannual International Conference on the Short Story in English, and fiction editor of *The Journal of Caribbean Literatures.* She retired from the University of Northern Iowa in late December, 1996, to take up a position as professor of English in residence at the University of New Orleans. She is currently at work on a critical study of the fiction of Shirley Ann Grau.

Rochette-Crawley: Professor Rohrberger, to place this interview on a time line I would like to begin with the present, move toward the past, and then return to the present. The International Conferences on the Short Story in English are deservedly premier events in the history of the development of the short story and its criticism. Would you speak about how the Conferences came about and how they have evolved over the last six years?

Rohrberger: I first heard about the Conference when it was going to be held in France, in 1989 or thereabouts. However, the announcement was late in getting to me, so I was unable to attend. I did write to Claire Larierre, a French short story writer, critic, and editor who was putting it together in

France. When there were no further Conferences, it occurred to me that there was no reason why it couldn't be moved from France. At the same time I had taken a job here at the University of Northern Iowa, in part because Susan Lohafer was at the University of Iowa, and I thought the two of us together might be able to do something about putting together a conference for 1992. When Claire Larierre agreed we were started. Professor Barbara Lounsberry of the University of Northern Iowa was our first director and an excellent job she did. We also enlisted the help of Steve Pett, at Iowa State University. The conference is a spectacular, magical occurrence, although it's very costly to us, both in time and in money. But, my belief is that it needs to be continued: both to reinforce the idea that the short story is a separate genre and, in addition, for what has become a more recent interest—to establish diversity as this issue comes more and more into prominence. It appears that most peoples begin by writing short tales. And, as we look to the history of short stories in English from more recently emerging cultures like the aborigines in Australia, it appears that their short stories began, as ours did, with tales, many of them coming out of the fairy tales of the people. It seems a logical consequence that we should move in the direction of multiculturalism and diversity at this particular time.

More importantly, perhaps, for myself, the short story genre is a genre that needs to be studied. I find that, more and more, the genre is being swallowed up in theories of narrativity or being taught by people who don't have the vaguest idea that there is a difference between longer and shorter fiction. It is a fact that the short story is being taught in most of our schools as simply typical of novels by important persons; and this kind of misreading has a great bearing on our understanding of the genre because genre expectations dictate our habits of reading.

Rochette-Crawley: That leads into the next question I would like to ask. You, along with Charles May, Susan Lohafer and others, have devoted much of your critical interest to the short story. Could you speak about how you first became interested in the genre and maintained your commitment during times when the short story was not receiving much critical attention as a genre?

Rohrberger: I read short stories, of course, along with every other genre. I was weaned on the New Criticism. I learned very early how to read closely. I had, as my advisor, through my Master's and Ph.D. work, Richard Fogle, who was interested in the British Romantics and the American Romantics like Hawthorne and Melville. So, I gave quite a bit of attention to those writers, Hawthorne, Melville, and Poe. And I thought I understood how they put their stories together. As it happened, after I finished my M.A. degree, I chanced into a class that was being taught by John Husband at Tulane. It was called just "The Short Story," and it was the only formal course in the short story that I came close to, but it also did not discuss genre but rather individual stories. It was a summer class, and I sat in on it.

I was struck by how gripping the discussion was, and it struck me also that perhaps one of the most interesting characteristics of the short story was that it does not "say" what it means. And, as I mulled over that, it seemed to me that a dissertation based on the relationship between Hawthorne's stories and those of more modern writers would be of some interest. There was a correlation there. It seemed to me especially to be true of Hawthorne. So I started to read as many short stories and theoretical articles as I could find. Many of the theoretical statements came from the writers themselves. I extracted critical statements from Hawthorne's work as I could, and I found that there were remarkable similarities in the theories of various kinds of writers of short stories. And I began to look at the structures of Hawthorne's stories and found that there were remarkable similarities between the structure of his stories and those of other writers. So I concocted a definition that I have been refining every since. It said, in effect, that the short story is based in a different kind of metaphysics, that it is based in the romance tradition, that it assumes that there is more to the world than can be apprehended through the senses, and that there is an element of mystery, that directs the movement of the story by means of various kinds of symbolic patterns. And, as I say, ever since I have been refining it or trying to.

I, perhaps unfortunately, published the book that derived from my dissertation through Mouton at the Hague. And that was fine, except that maybe it didn't get the kind of wide reading that everyone hopes to have. As a result, most people who have come to recognize my work have done so mainly through a summary chapter that Charles May printed in his book, *Short Story Theories*. This has been a problem because people don't understand the real amount of work or documentation that I put into it.

I think that many scholars don't understand that I tie the short story so closely to the metaphysical and the aesthetics deriving from an embracing ontology. Later I looked again at Poe's influence and I recognized that in the beginning I did not give him enough credit because I didn't read closely enough those important words having to do with "kindred art" and not so obvious meanings; "undercurrents," Poe called them. And these are factors that I believe most everyone else ignores in Poe. I think that he's been downgraded too much and thought of in terms of the "well-made" story. I'm not sure this is the way Poe intended it to go. The "well-made story," for me, is something like stories by O. Henry and Maupassant.

Rochette-Crawley: This misunderstanding of the actual depth of your work is interesting and leads me to wonder if there is a possibility that your work, *Hawthorne and the Modern Short Story,* can be reprinted?

Rohrberger: I have not made any particular effort to do that, but perhaps it will happen.

Rochette-Crawley: The next question that I have pertains to the collaborative effort that you and Dan Burns made in writing the essay, "The Short Story and the Numinous Realm." How did the two of you come to collaborate, and do you see the short story as a genre that invites collaborative work among critics?

Rohrberger: Dan was one of my students in a class on the short story. He is remarkably gifted in writing. And he managed to take what I said and set it down in a very effective way, and I looked at what he did and suggested that we revise and publish it together. That's the only collaborative work that I have done with him. I have done collaborative work with other people, mainly in the line of my looking for somebody who complements my abilities. For example, I hate detail; so, I look for someone to work with me who likes detail. And I had a very good working relationship with a colleague at Oklahoma State.

I haven't published any other work with students, although I think that's a good thing to do. Somehow or another, our field has got the notion that solitary work is preferable, and there's no reason for that. In the same way, our field has got the notion that authors who help to pay for publication are behaving odiously—without realizing that some*body* is paying for publication. You know, some university or some department, somewhere, is paying for the publication of all scholarly work. I think we could ease our publication problems if we realize those two facts, as science scholars have already done.

Rochette-Crawley: In Susan Lohafer's *Short Story Theory at a Crossroads,* you give an excellent recapitulation of recent theory on the genre and the problem of definition by saying, "We simply go on from where we are, somewhere between shadow and act." I'm interested in why you chose the phrase "between shadow and act," used earlier by Ralph Ellison. Do you see connections between the condition of minority status and the state of short story theory these days?

Rohrberger: One of the ways I characterize the short story is in terms of its metaphoric content, and I think I really like the form because I think in terms of metaphor also. I happened to be reading Ellison's criticism preparatory to another article at the time you mention, and it seemed to me to be a particularly apt phrase in its metaphoric implications. In so far as my own definition of the short story, I think that somehow or other the short story does fall between shadow and act; as a matter of fact, that it is a combination of the two because I think that the short story—in its questionings—merges antitheses. You come to the end of a short story and you say, "Well, what did that mean?" And you try to answer it and then you say, "No, no, that's not it." And then you go back and try to answer it in the opposite way. That I think is most characteristic of the form, that it merges antitheses, dismisses dualities.

Rochette-Crawley: Just recently I had a conversation with someone who said that while the short story might be considered a "minor" genre in Western literature, in Japanese and Arabic cultures the short story is given precedence over the novel. I was wondering if you could say a little bit about how the short story and the novel work, or don't work, together.

Rohrberger: I think the people who give the short story less stature are novices in the genre and don't know how it operates or what it is. I think most fiction writers realize that writing a short story is much more difficult than writing a novel. In many cases they will make statements such as Faulkner did, that the poem is the hardest thing of all to write and the second is the short story and then the novel. It seems to me that the novel is looser in structure. There is more room for error, more room for vagaries. I teach novels in translation all the time but I wouldn't translate a poem and equate it in any way with the original. Always, in talking to my students, I speak of the novel and the short story in terms of knitting, and tell them that the novel is something that is created with very large knitting needles and heavy yarn, and that the short story is created with much smaller needles and thinner thread. And that the poem is made, probably, with the smallest of needles and the thinnest of thread.

Rochette-Crawley: Thank you, that's a very good analogy. Moving more into the present, could you comment on how you chose "Voices of Diversity" for the focus of the most recent International Conference on the Short

Story in English, and perhaps speak a bit on the connection between the short story and cultural diversity?

Rohrberger: I don't know that I could say much more to elaborate that. It was time. During the first conference—the Second International Conference, the first one in Iowa—we brought canonical figures, some women, but mostly men. These were the people who had established directions in the short story, people who had made some contribution to the short story form, John Barth, for example, whose *Lost in the Funhouse* is significant to the development of the postmodern short story. This is not to say that we had all of the most important writers, though we did have excellent representation.

One of the things that has spread extremely rapidly in academia has been the notion of diversity and multiculturalism. Four years ago, at most universities, "diversity" was just a word. Now it's a reality. And it was about four years ago that I began to think about what the next conference would be. To me it just seemed that it had *to be,* "Voices of Diversity." We had to bring together as many people as we could, from as many different ethnic backgrounds, who wrote in English. We had not paid any particular attention to gender and to race, and chose all writers, all of them fine writers, nevertheless we chose them with reference to diversity. I think another thing in operation was that our international visitors, during the second conference, wondered why we didn't have more Americans of different ethnic backgrounds. And that was a hard one to answer, because w had made no special effort in that area. So this time we went out to find not only writers from other cultures who write in English but also our own ethnic minorities.

As I said before, all peoples seem to begin with narrative, whether or not it is in the form of prose or poems. And all peoples seem to move in the same direction: starting with the mythologies, and moving often to matters of social realities that "bother" them the most. Often, in emerging cultures, an interest in the latter leads to social realism, where irony is the base for the emergence of meaning. It's only after that, that people begin to move to the symbolic realm, and once in that mode, chronology can disappear. I think that peoples of different cultures with literature in different stages of development can be of great use to each other.

Rochette-Crawley: In addition to the conferences, you have been the founder of the Society for the Study of the Short Story, the four S's, which publishes the journal, *Short Story* carrying interviews, stories, and criticism pertaining directly to the short story. Could you speak on your role in the formation of the journal and perhaps offer some of your insights as both editor and critic of the short story?

Rohrberger: As journals go, we are pretty young. Basically the journal was just started when I moved to the University of Northern Iowa. Fortunately the University of Northern Iowa saw a reason to support it. The four S's was formed as a support group by means of which the short story conferences and the journal could help to be funded. This University has been remarkable generous in seeing the value of our work, as have the other Regents' Universities in Iowa. Also, I must not forget the great contribution to the journal made by the University of Texas at Brownsville, where our managing editor is housed.

Rochette-Crawley: The last question I have to ask pertains to your book, *Hawthorne and the Modern Short Story*. Until it is reprinted, what are some of the main ideas from the book that you would like people to know?

Rohrberger: Well, I've published a lot in other places, too. I tried to reference some examples of what I have written in the last article that I wrote from Susan Lohafer's book. In effect, while summarizing what other people have done, I also summarized what I have done and indicated in the endnotes where to find it.

Charles May and I are very similar in our thinking about the metaphoric, but my book, of course, preceded his, and I don't know if my work had any influence on his. A major difference between us is that May tends to ignore stories that don't fit into his definition, while I try to deal with them. I actually make a division in stories that are short and short stories in terms of how meaning emerges. If meaning emerges primarily through simple irony, the story is likely an example of social realism, and it probably exists mainly on surface level, and is probably chronological. In what I call a true short story, meaning emerges through multivalence resulting from patterns of images that create symbolic substructures, meaning is never so clear as to be easily summarized, and plots, or the lack of them, are simply one aspect of meaning.

Rochette-Crawley: Is this connected to your idea, in the book, of the difference between short story and simple narrative?

Rohrberger: Yes, that's right. I never did like that phrase "simple narrative," but I couldn't think of any other way to describe certain stories, and I still can't. It is a phrase, though, that I find very helpful to describe stories that are primarily in an ironic mode. Maupassant, I think, writes in a mainly ironic mode; somebody like Nikolai Gogol, who was contemporary to Hawthorne, constructs his best pieces around metaphors. Writers who formed the modernist movement, people like Anderson and Mansfield and Joyce, clearly write in the metaphoric realm, though their surfaces are realistic. I will say here something that I mean to develop in an article as soon as I get the chance. It seems to me that the epiphany, which is generally attributed to the modernist short story can be found also at least as far back as Hawthorne, that the epiphany in Hawthorne comes at the end of the stories, that the climax is a false climax, and that the questions arising at the very end of the stories point to meaning. This structure would make an interesting kind of graph, if we tried to draw what I am describing. We'd have an overlap of traditional and modernist plot structure something like this:

    false climax   epiphany
            (space where "yes" and "no" meet)

The margins of the "yes" and "no" create the resonance peculiar to, say, "Young Goodman Brown," by Hawthorne. There the false climax appears at the line: " 'Look up to heaven and resist the evil one' "; the epiphany on the last phrase: "and his dying hour was gloom."

Kirin Narayan

Minoli Salgado

Kirin Narayan was born in Bombay in 1959. After schooling in India, she came to the United States for higher studies. She received a Ph.D. in anthropology from the University of California in 1987 and is currently Associate Professor of Anthropology and South Asian Studies at the University of Wisconsin. Narayan is author of *Storytellers, Saints and Scoundrels: Folk Narratives in Hindu Religious Teaching* (1989), which won the 1991 Victor Turner Prize and the Elsie Clews Parsons Prize for folklore (co-winner, 1990); and of *Love, Stars and All That* (1994), a novel. She is a co-editor of *Creativity/Anthropology*. Her study of women's songs and folk narratives from Kangra, Northwest India, entitled *Mondays on the Dark Side of the Moon: Himalayan Foothill Folktales* (1997), was published after the following interview was conducted.

Salgado: I'd like to ask you first about your recently published novel, *Love, Stars and All That*. I understand that it was begun as a short story. Tell me something about how that evolved.

Narayan: Well, I started writing that short story in the Spring of 1987 when I was finishing my dissertation at the University of California at Berkeley. I'd been writing stories since the time I learned how to write—from about the time I was three or four years old. My mother still has old notebooks in which I scribbled about fairies sitting on lotuses and so on. As I got more and more sucked into graduate school the occasions for writing fiction were becoming fewer, and while finishing my dissertation I felt this enormous urge to assert that this part of myself would not be altogether left behind. I was moved to write a short story that compared different expectations of romance in India, as I knew it, and in America, as I'd come to know it. So this story was really about clashes of expectations. For a long time my friends had been saying that I should write a story called "An Arranged Affair." So I wrote this story about two characters called Ajay and Gita. Gita has a very doting Aunty, Saroj Aunty, who sets her up with this guy called Ajay who works at Bell Labs, at a time that both Gita and Ajay are over in Bombay from America. Once I wrote the story everyone I showed it to felt as though they owned the characters. They had very clear opinions about what different characters would be saying or doing, and I began to just fold in their commentaries. So the story began to just grow and grow and eventually became a 45-page 'short' story! I had become very attached to the characters and so I thought back, "Who is Gita? How did she land in this predicament?" The novel grew from that.

Salgado: You've just said you folded in the comments of your first readers. How did you do that?

Narayan: Yes. I was especially affected by the views of my closest friends. And throughout the writing of this book I felt it had open margins and open bindings. So if someone suggested I should include something, I thought "Well why not?" For example the hot-tub scene was suggested by a good girlfriend of mine in Berkeley who is Goan and has lived in America for about twenty years. We were taking a walk and she said I must include a hot-tub scene. A lot of my story-telling impulse comes from oral story-telling and the influence of interesting conversations with my friends.

Salgado: I'm interested in this interactive element that feeds into your fiction. Do you think it might be related to your academic interest in folk narratives which belong to this oral tradition and which you focused on in your academic study, *Storytellers, Saints and Scoundrels?*

Narayan: Very much so I think. Both of them are linked by my voracious appetite for the well-told story. I delight in having a professional excuse to work on folktales: being able to listen to beautifully told tales seems like a terrific luxury! In creative writing I've been able to pick up some of the stories I've most loved retelling through the years and put them into a form that can reach people who don't know me face to face.

Salgado: Can you think of any other ways in which your interest in folk-narrative influences your writing?

Narayan: The most obvious element is that in the novel and other things

I've written, some of the folktales. I've come across are brought into the literary text. The tale as a whole is transported into the work.

Salgado: I noticed that the story about the king and his minister which you referred to in *Storytellers* came up again in your novel. In addition to this insertion of the folktale into a literary text, it occurred to me that, as your work really gains from being read aloud (something which came across in your reading yesterday), your emphasis on dialogue might be something that draws upon the folk narrative tradition. Your literary style is fast-paced and uses short sentences. It lends itself to being read aloud. Some of these elements are evident in Bharati Mukherjee's work. Do you think this is a feature of Indian writing from the United States?

Narayan: I think that my greatest influence for writing in that fast pace and having every sentence short enough that it can be read aloud in one breath was Grace Paley who taught me in Sarah Lawrence College. She would make students read their work aloud. That's where the emphasis on hearing work spoken comes from. You'll notice it in her writing as well—it's always as though someone is having a conversation with you when you read her short stories.

Salgado: Which writers do you most admire?

Narayan: I guess the writers who are most on my mind depends upon who I've read most recently. I think the writer who has had the greatest enduring influence on me is J. D. Salinger, and I am definitely following Seymour's dictum to his younger brother, Buddy, of "write what you most love to read." I think it's important to communicate that joy.

Salgado: Yes, you certainly convey it in your writing particularly through the use of humour which seems to come very naturally to you. Are there any Indian writers who have influenced you?

Narayan: I love the novels of R. K. Narayan. And more recently I have been impressed by Amitav Ghosh who is also an anthropologist. His work has subtlety, polish, a compassionate portrayal of the people, a sense of multiple cultures coming together and intertwining through the lives of the characters.

Salgado: If I could go back to the relationship between your creative writing and folk narrative: do you feel your creative writing might draw upon some of the symbolic patterns found in folk narratives?

Narayan: This is a difficult question to answer. I did try to craft certain sections of *Love, Stars and All That* according to various symbolic themes and this may be influenced by the close literary analysis of folktales. But ultimately the creativity that sweeps through and helps you get something written overrides the more rational use of symbolism.

Salgado: The novel struck me as something of a quest narrative.

Narayan: Actually, I consciously split the book into two parts. The first part is the quest narrative, and it's a critique of the narrative that has structured so many women's lives: the quest for the perfect hero who is going to make their lives whole. This narrative exists more in European fairy tales than Indian ones. As folklorists like A. K. Ramanujan have pointed out, very often in Indian folktales that focus on marriage, a woman starts by being married, then loses her husband and goes on a quest to regain him. This contrasts with the European model—for example Cinderella was single and then finds a husband at the end. This has to do with different cultural systems where marriage can be an assertion of free will or is arranged and adapted to. South Asians like ourselves have psyches that are so overlaid with Western narratives—our education was so steeped with British literature—so we are influenced by both sorts of stories. So the first part of the book is a quest narrative, showing up its emptiness. Gita does end up with the man she is going to marry by the end of this part, but it's clear to the reader that this is a big mess. The second part is much more open-ended. Instead of looking for happiness through someone else, she realizes she must take responsibility for that herself. So she is free from the idea that romantic love will bring her fulfillment, and comes to understand that there are many different shades of love that can enrich life.

Salgado: This relates to Gita's view that perhaps *jori* isn't destined but is instead determined by human mediation. Are you challenging the concept of destiny which is so prevalent in Southern Asia?

Narayan: The premise of the book is that Gita's Aunty has summoned her astronumerologist for predictions and he tells her that Gita will meet the man she will marry on a certain date, March 1984. At the end he himself admits that if you love someone you can't do good predictions for them because you are so eager for things to happen to them. Gita's saying that maybe *jori* isn't destined but that you make it happen is less a matter of discarding the concept of a destined partner or *jori* altogether and more an affirmation of the human vigilance and work that goes into making a good relationship. It's never clear as to whether Firoze did come on the scene in March 1984 or not.

Salgado: Can you explain the concept of *jori* for people who aren't so familiar with it?

Narayan: I am speaking now not as an anthropological scholar but as a person who grew up with the notion. A *jori* is a pair, a perfect match. For example a set of shoes is called a *jori*—they match each other and are the same size and same fit. It involves the notion of a person having their perfect match somewhere out there that should be brought together through an arranged marriage in particular. When I do my field work in Kangra, women often talk about a *jori*.

Salgado: I'd like to take you back to an idea that you deal with in your study, *Storytellers*—the idea that some of the folk narratives you study affirm that everything is for the best. I was wondering whether you felt this view might encourage a passive approach to life, an approach that is a central subject for many writers from India.

Narayan: Other people have asked me about this. As I saw it work in people's lives it was less that they accepted everything blindly but that in retrospect they would try to come to terms with something in a way that enabled them to go on. Obviously if someone dearly loved dies tragically, it is not for the best. But you have to find something in the situation that can provide you with the guidance that can take you on in your life. That is what I saw happening in the case of Swamiji in *Storytellers*. It's a question of sifting through the past in order to take something that is of value out of it and move onward.

Salgado: I am very interested in the character of Gita and have heard that you felt as though she was your younger sister. There are so many parallels between Gita's situation and yours, I did wonder how much of you there was in her.

Narayan: Well like all characters that one writes about there are fragments of one's personality there, and what's more characters become part of one-self as one knows them so well. This includes the characters who aren't so lovable. Gita's experiences are not mirrors to mine. For example I was never seriously involved with a professor at Berkeley, thank God, and I think she is a little more timid than I am, a little more earnest—especially in the beginning. I am very fond of Gita but I don't feel that Gita is me.

Salgado: At one point in the novel you say that one of the things that binds Gita and Ajay together is "a common past." How important is that to you?

Narayan: I think it's become less and less important to me as I've gotten older because I've come to understand that you can interpret your past across differences. You can share elements of who you are with other people through translation.

Salgado: Do you feel that this side of you has developed as a result of living in the United States?

Narayan: I am sure it has. And of course working in anthropology, where cross-cultural interpretation is central. And it's also the result of being more and more secure in who I am—not needing external affirmation so much, especially since I am half-Indian and half-American. When I was younger I thought I must definitely be with an Indian man to be affirmed as Indian in some way. I'm now married to a Russian Jewish man who I've found I can tell my choicest stories to about India. He is willing to enter my imaginative world with me.

Salgado: One thing I found of special interest was the form that you adopted in writing your book, *Storytellers*. It's digressive, fluid, personal and has that quality of an oral narrative. Was this a conscious break from the conventions of academic discourse or is this approach often found in anthropological texts?

Narayan: I was writing my dissertation during a time in the late eighties when there was a great deal of upheaval in anthropological conventions of ethnography, that is writing about other cultures. There had been several books out that challenged some of the ways in which anthropologists had been writing: that is in an objective, generalizing fashion, often negating the elements of time, of variation, of inequality. So as a result of this literature I was able to convince my committee that I could write a different text. I chose the narrative form largely to embed the power of narrative while presenting and interpreting the stories. Both the theme and the form mirror each other in my study.

Salgado: When listening to Swamiji's stories, you sometimes express unease with your role as an academic. Do you feel that analysis can work against creativity? Vikram Seth has said that "analysis is the death of the novel." How would you respond to that?

Narayan: I am quite fortunate in not having to analyze my own fiction except for an interview like this. I am often left aghast at the conclusions that critics come to but it can be rather entertaining if you distance yourself from it all.

Salgado: Do you feel a tension between your roles as a creative writer and as an anthropologist?

Narayan: So far I have felt that the roles are mutually complementary. It's like having two different lenses that you can apply to the same situation. As a writer I am very interested in the personal, the subtle nuances, the minute details, and as an anthropologist I am often drawn to the larger structures, the cultural patterns, the social themes and the historical baggage that shape people's lives. I think that bringing each to the other has enlivened both my anthropological writing and my fiction writing. The main problem is finding the time for both and striving to do both well.

Salgado: Earlier you mentioned that your novel began as a very short story. Do you find the compact form of the short story poses difficulties for you? Perhaps the novel offers you a sense of freedom—the ability to expand a theme—that agrees with you more.

Narayan: That is definitely true. In fact when I was first introduced to my agent I had several short stories each between thirty and fifty pages long. She told me that the stories that get published are really short—ten or fifteen pages long—and that I had a novelist latent in me. She advised me to let loose and write a novel. But I must confess that last week, to avoid the packing up of boxes as I leave New Mexico, I sat down and wrote a short story that is only eighteen pages long. I think that this might be my first truly short story because I have nothing else to say about this character. The story covers an incident that happened to someone I met just once when I was visiting professor at a small east coast college. For the last six years I'd been musing over the incident thinking it would make a hilarious short story. I had asked the person concerned whether I could write about the incident and was told I could help myself, and as I knew him only slightly my imagination has run riot.

Salgado: Do you find writing a release of some sort?

Narayan: I love writing and possibly because my academic work is demanding and serious I tend to move toward the more frivolous and entertaining in my fiction.

Salgado: One of the developments in Indian writing in English is that there has been a general move away from the public and the political toward a concern with more personal issues such as marriage. Vikram Seth also dealt with marriage, though in a historical context, in *A Suitable Boy.* Do you feel you are part of this broader movement?

Narayan: I just wrote what I had to write. I was not aligning myself with any movement. In fact I was stunned when Vikram Seth's novel came out as there were so many parallels between it and my novel. I was relieved that my novel was already in page-proof otherwise people might have suspected that it was derivative. I have slipped in some political details in my novel but, as I was writing, the political situation in India just seemed too complex to take on. I felt I could not be a spokesperson in that mode.

Salgado: That's true. This development I've just mentioned does seem to be linked to a general inability to comprehend in a single, unified way the apparent chaos that is India.

Narayan: Yes, but you could say a novel like *A Suitable Boy* or some of the work of Rohinton Mistry—though on the face of it appear very psychological and inward-looking—also directly address the communal strife that is found in contemporary India.

Salgado: Would you be reluctant to put your work into some sort of political frame?

Narayan: In *Love, Stars and All That* the political frame is primarily that of gender politics. It looks at the different ways in which women perceive themselves. Gita is disempowered by some traditional Hindu ideas that are overlaid with Victorian middle-class Indian prudery.

Salgado: You refer to a "cultural self" in *Storytellers*. How might you relate this concept of a cultural or national identity to your novel?

Narayan: A national identity is a cultural artifact of a modern nation state. In South Asia I would say regional identity and class identity are more important. And increasingly one finds people of mixed identity, who are negotiating many different notions of what it takes to make a decent person and perhaps I represent that.

Salgado: How has your book been received in India?

Narayan: It hasn't come out yet. It should be out any day. Penguin India is bringing it out.

Salgado: What are you working on now?

Narayan: I have just finished an anthropological book on one woman's folk narratives in the Himalayan foothills. And I am supposed to be beginning another anthropological work on gender representations that exist in women's songs from the Himalayan foothills.

Salgado: Your mention of songs reminds me that you are clearly interested in literature as performance. I was wondering if you had thought of dramatizing your novel.

Narayan: I didn't think of this when I was writing it, though I would be quite open to someone adapting it for the stage or the screen if they want to. It makes me think of the difference of mediums and the economy of words and images; it's only the dialogue that could stay constant.

Salgado: You do seem to be leaning toward a dramatic form in the novel and I was wondering if it might be something you would consider experimenting with in the future.

Narayan: Perhaps, but not yet. I am now taking notes towards another novel. Since I exist in the culture of academe, it is a form of survival for me to write academic parodies. I think that my next novel will involve an American woman anthropologist who is a missionary's child, culturally mixed, and who goes to India and does field work in the villages.

Salgado: One of the main subjects of this conference has been how people identify themselves. How would you say you identify yourself?

Narayan: For me there are multiple planes of identification that are evoked in different contexts. If I am in India dressed in Indian clothes with my father's relatives I feel very Indian. If I am in the States in a miniskirt with a troupe of American friends I feel very American. Sometimes I feel in-between. At other times I realize that both "Indian" and "American" are conglomerate terms that don't have that much weight or particularity. My father is really not just Indian, he is Gujarati, and not just Gujarati but from Kutch—the desert region. Our identification cannot be unified: there are twisting strands that make a very rich skein of identity.

Sonia Sanchez

Danielle Alyce Rome

Sonia Sanchez, an acclaimed African-American writer, has written several books of poetry, numerous plays, children's literature, and short stories. The influences of her literature range from the political, with such figures as Malcolm X, to the musical, with the influences of Billie Holiday and John Coltrane. The subject matters for her writings are those which unify the members of the human community by the commonality of the human experience. Her works include *The Adventures of Fat Head, Small Head, and Square Head* (1973), *Homecoming* (1969), *Homegirls & Handgrenades* (1984), *It's a New Day: Poems for Young Brothas & Sistuhs* (1971), *I've Been a Woman* (1987), *A Sound Investment and Other Stories* (1993), *Under a Soprano Sky* (1987), *Wounded in the House of a Friend* (1995), and *Love Poems* (1973).

Rome: I've read your definition of a poet as a creator of social values, a manipulator of symbols and language images. Does this definition coincide with your perception of a writer and artist of other literary genres as well?

Sanchez: I do believe a poet is indeed a creator of social values and I maintain that it could move on to other genres also. Certainly writers are manipulators of words and language images. Writers can also maintain the status quo or also talk about effecting change. I believe poetry is also, what I call, subconscious conversation. It is as much the work of those who write it as those who listen. So it is not by chance to sometimes hear people say, "Um hum, yeah right." It is that subconscious conversation. We are dealing with those subconscious images already planted in the psyche of people by the society or by people's culture so that they can do a call and response then and say, yes I understand or yes I am moved by that or they will cry out in the night as they sit in bed some place and read your poetry. I get letters from people that will say to me I was reading your book at midnight and I starting crying and that letter comes from India, that letter comes from Italy, that letter comes from France, that letter comes from many places where people say yeah. And what they're saying is what the writer is actually saying, we all have a common experience but my face is blackly black and your face is whitely white or pinkly pink or yellow or brown or whatever. But within that experience, that culture, we all have a common experience and that common experience is one of humanity, one of love, one of disdain, one of respect and that's the great joy about writing. You give the poem to the world and people look at it and say, yes I understand that experience, yes I've had it, I understand that love poem, I understand that cry of help, I understand it, I've lived it, I've tasted it. And that's why I personally believe poetry is the greatest genre on the planet Earth.

Rome: When you write another genre, say the short story or drama, does your approach to the writing itself differ?

Sanchez: I don't think so, although the manifestation of it might be a different one when I write plays and the short story. When I write plays I am very aware of my characters. I am very much aware of their movements on the stage. I'm very much aware of a story I'm telling in a different fashion and therefore, a different writing comes about. The concentration is certainly on dialogue, the concentration moves the dialogue and moves the people. I'm very much more aware, when I write plays, of lying, that is telling a story. Once, in a play writing class I taught, a student had to bring in a piece, a dialogue. He brought in a dialogue of parents arguing and separating and he had heard this when he was a child. As he read the piece he cried, but as we listened we didn't. And he looked at our dry eyes and he couldn't understand, "Why aren't you upset, why aren't you crying?" The students said, "Well, we weren't involved." He said, "How could you not be involved?" because he was really crying. But the point is those were his parents and he really was there, but the way he wrote it he didn't involve us with it, so we never cried. And he said, "But it happened just in that fashion." I said, "That's partly the problem, so write it in another fashion and bring your imagination in and lie a little bit and perhaps we will become involved with it."

Rome: Does your emphasis of the transmission of truth shift or become more focused from one form or another?

Sanchez: I think that's what you're hearing about that play and also about the short story. Sometimes because I start a piece off with the "I" then people assume it's personal, but it is the collective "I" I'm talking about. The collective "I" of many women, or the collective "I" of a certain culture, or the collective "I" of all men, or whomever. It has nothing to do with me personally but I use the "I" to bring you into the story and the immediacy of bringing you into the story saying, "Come in and taste this immediately." And, yes, quite often I realize when I write a piece, even when I do poetry, I write it and say this is how it happened. But as I write I realize that how it happened is not necessarily interesting. So I have to, in a sense, come back and embellish and invent or bring the imagination in to bare on the piece. And the imagination is not necessarily involved in whether this is true or not.

Rome: Do you constantly maintain the same level of truth to yourself in your writing? Regardless to the genre, do strive to relay the African American female perspective in your writing?

Sanchez: I do that in many ways but its not always necessarily one in which the person is always the "shero." I mean, when we're talking about truth people have to look good always or you have to be a "shero" as opposed to a hero. Therefore, the truth might be where I show a damaging aspect of the African American experience. My new book is called *Wounded in the House of a Friend.* In it I have a poem about a young African American woman, this young black woman who takes her nine-year-old daughter to a crack house for a fix. That's a horrible truth that's there, but if I ignore that truth and say now I'm gonna do this story about this woman who takes her nine-year-old daughter to the zoo; there are women who take their daughters to the zoo, parents who take their daughters to the zoo, but there are also women now where crack has wiped out the whole concept of history, of family, of motherhood, of peoplehood, of whatever. And I read that piece to a group of homeless women who were now staying in this little house in Philadelphia and when I read one of the women said, "That's right, you can't do that anymore." And that cracked my skull. She didn't say, wow, isn't that something, listen to that story, and isn't that interesting, she said, "I can't do that anymore." My skull cracked and I sat there crying because I knew that what I hit on, what I wrote about was very real. You can't deal with something as addictive as crack and expect to stay human or to have human ideas. The whole point of allowing people to become addicted in that fashion means that you break the pattern of motherhood, and you break the pattern of being human.

Rome: I've often read that critics consider you to be a radical. Do you consider yourself to be a radical or are you a realist?

Sanchez: I don't know what it means to be a radical. In this country people will call you a radical to demean you, but they will turn around and call a Latin writer or another writer from another country a radical writer and it'll be okay. I think I am a writer who attempts to deal with what it means to stay human, with what it means to be a human being and sometimes I do it in a rough fashion. Sometimes I do it in a lyrical fashion. Sometimes I sock you in the eye and say, "Look up, look up. You must not walk this walk." You can say radical if you want to. You can say lyrical if you want to. You can say committed if you want to. You can say whatever, the point is that I write because I must write. I write because I must bring attention to what is happening in the world. A new piece that I have just begun talks about bodies floating down the river Rwanda. And at the same time, I juxtapose next to that bodies floating the river of 125 St. going for drugs. They're different deaths, but the same death.

Rome: In your writing you portray things that are very real cross-culturally. Does it matter in which community or just the human community itself?

Sanchez: The human community, right.

Rome: In your writing, does your approach to the short story differ from your approach to the poetry or any other genre that you write?

Sanchez: I used to tell my students that if you can write poetry, you can write a short story, then you can write a novel or you can write a play. That you should call yourself a writer, not just a poet, not just a short story writer, not just a novelist. I do believe that we can really do that. It probably depends upon where you want to concentrate. I came into writing a story because I was writing a long poem, I realized that I wanted to say more about it and that's how I moved into the genre of short fiction. Sometimes I call my short fiction prose poems because it takes up six pages and I do it poetically. And I take a slice out of someone's life at some point and put it on paper. So I do make use of the short fiction or the short story when it suits my purpose and I have something else to say and I need to say it in that fashion and I gravitate towards it. I don't always know why I do but I do.

Rome: Do you find that one genre versus the other lends itself more to a manifestation of power. In poetry you have more immediacy and you can say what you want more effectively quickly. Do you find that the short story deters from the power of writing?

Sanchez: No, I don't. I never have any problems, any discussions, or any arguments about which is easier, which is better, which is more powerful. I've read some powerful short stories that have made my flesh crawl. And then at the same time, I've read some powerful poems, understanding that each line is a paragraph sometimes that has turned my body inside out. I love literature and as a consequence we should teach our students and ourselves that there is not one better than the other. Sometimes we fixate ourselves at one genre because we get used to it, you get fixed at it, you get truncated there and you assume that's where you belong. But we're all probably Renaissance women and men, which means we can move in and out of various genres with ease and joy.

Rome: In the creation of a new piece of literature, what is foremost in your mind in regards to any specific piece? Is there one message that you set out to permeate your piece?

Sanchez: I'm finishing up two books. A long poem to my brother, which is almost like a short story. It has all the trappings of a short story because when you have a poem that is book length you're telling a story. It's a ballad, this is rhyme royal. You're telling the story and you have to grab people's attention the way a short story has got to with the same few lines. And in order to do this I felt myself dividing it up as I would do if I were writing a short story sometimes in terms of movement into the piece. This story is about my brother who died of AIDS, and I found myself doing it chapterlike of short story like. This is a section, this is a section there, this is the climax, this is a confrontation, this is the denouement, this is how I'm ending it. All of that came into play in this long poem and I found it was interesting how I had to construct this piece. It was a very difficult piece to write because I think there was a transcrossing. All the knowledge you have about literature comes into play, although with the rhyme royal I had to fixate myself with rhyme because it requires that it has a certain form of rhyme that you have to deal with. But at the same time, I'm aware of telling the story within the rhyme. There's always the fighting to tell the story and coming to the poetry form for the rhyme to happen. There's a real struggle that goes on sometimes that's fascinating. I'm very grateful to the various forms they move you to write, they move you to see overlapping. The greatest novels or short stories that I have read have been very poetic, very lyrical, the ones that have made me sore. And the ones that have dealt with a lot of imagery and those short stories that have made me think and didn't tell me we're at this point now, we should be thinking this or now you know you're at the climax here, now you're ready to experience this. The ones that let me wander in and out in a stream of consciousness. Those are the ones that I've enjoyed.

Rome: Once a piece of yours goes through its preliminary phases, what does your revision process entail?

Sanchez: That is always the hard work. The easiest work sometimes is getting it down and then the revision and sometimes discarding lines that you like. Or putting in another book for another piece because you know it doesn't work but you like it so much that you decide to keep it. Revision is a mother. I teach my students by bringing in one of my poems. The first regurgitation then the finished product. Then I have on xeroxed paper the second revision, third, fourth, fifth, sixth, seventh, and eighth revisions where I've written why didn't I stay with the first revision of the poem because you are depressed by then. You've pulled all the juices out. But it's at that eighth or ninth revision that something happens and the juices begin to pour back in at some point. They pour back in and there's the final product. And there is a difference between the first regurgitation and the last and there are similarities also. They need to see that and know that it is the going through all of those revisions that you finally come back full circle to what you need to keep and what you need to discard and how you get the juices to flow. The same thing happened with a short story I wrote called "After Saturday Night Comes Sunday." I had started that piece with a different voice, a male voice, and half way through it I realized it was the wrong voice and that it had to be the female voice. I had had the male voice telling the story of his dissent into drugs and how it affected the children, and it was the wrong voice. I had to go back and change it, and I made it the female voice telling the story although it was the man's story. Sometimes, in writing the short story, it's the wrong voice, it's not the first person but the third person and then, all of a sudden, it works when you do that. That only happens sometimes when you've finished the whole thing and nothing gels, nothing works. And then, all of a sudden, with a change in the voice, it works.

Rome: I've noticed one of the things you use in your writing is Black English. How do you feel about that form? Do you feel it lends more realistically to what you're trying to say?

Sanchez: Sometimes it does; I can weave it in and out. Sometimes when characters speak, they speak Black English and what are you going to do, whiten it? Change it or lighten it? Educate them? And also, in doing that you would deny that people speak in that fashion, you say that its not worthy of a place in literature. *Their Eyes Were Watching God,* there's Black English in there and it's a great book. And it's when you understand that that you're writing literature, that people who speak in Black English have great thoughts also and they're worthy to be drawn as characters in novels, and short stories and poems also. You put them in there and you say, "Look at this, this is how I speak and contrary to what you think I'm human with these human ideas, these human thoughts. Here I am and listen to it, it's a viable way of talking and speaking."

Rome: There is a pressing need for people to align themselves with certain theoretical camps nowadays, it's sort of the in thing to do. Do you align yourself specifically with any of these camps?

Sanchez: What theoretical camps are you referring to?

Rome: Postmodernism, multiculturalism, ethnicity, etc.?

Sanchez: You don't have to align yourself because people will pull you to their camp and you go and you tell them what you think. I think the following about this. I think that we're so willing to put tags. When I teach something, I don't put a name on it quite often until the end of the semester. The whole idea that the students think they can't figure out a story or a poem, so we read a poem and I ask them, "What do you think about this?" and we have a long conversation. Then I say go read what Jane Schmoe said about it, and they come back and say she said the same thing I said about it. Yeah right, you can think, you can figure out a poem, you can say the same thing. And then we assume, when we give a poem or a section in literature, we say read that and see what Jane and Joe Schmoe say about it cause we assume the student can't figure it out and I don't. I make no assumptions, I know my students are just unpublished critics, and I know they can think because they've had to live eighteen years. When I get an eighteen-year-old and a twenty-year-old and a twenty-two-year-old in my class, they have maneuvered Philadelphia, or California, L.A., N.Y. City, and they've had to think about that. They didn't do it easily; it is not easy living in modern day society. So they have had to figure out ways to deal with mothers, fathers or no mothers, no fathers, which means they had to think critically before the point of sitting in my classroom. So, I expect them to think when I give them something, and we come back and discuss it. I say casually, this certain person said the same thing and I read. They look at themselves and say, "Ha, ha, I figured that out myself," and this is the joy about teaching as far as I'm concerned. It's that nothing you say in this classroom will be considered stupid, will be considered dumb, will be considered too far out. I've had some students who have taken criticism far out. Their analysis of some things have been so far out everybody stopped and looked, but it's possible. And because it is possible, because all criticism is your idea of what the text is all about, I say this is possible and this is viable. Then you allow them to understand and consider what other people have said, and to consider this critic who is the critic par excellence on this person. And what do you think about his ideas? And then because you've released the whole idea they say, "Well, it's okay but it's not as good as mine." And I love that because that's the way it should be, they should know about what other critics say, but they should not demean their own sense of what that text was all about. That's what learning is all about.

Leslie Marmon Silko

Florence Boos

Leslie Marmon Silko is noted for her haunting stories based on Laguna folktales, *Storyteller* (1981), and for the compassion and epic vision of her novels, *Ceremony* (1977) and *Almanac of the Dead* (1991). A MacArthur Foundation Fellow, Leslie Silko has also published *Laguna Woman* (1974), a book of poetry, *Sacred Water: Narratives and Pictures* (1993), and many individual stories and poems. However, Silko, a distinguished contemporary writer, is most well known for her compassionate novel, *Ceremony* (1977). It was the generous reception of this book that launched Silko headlong into fame, as well as giving her older stories new recognition. The most recent work of Silko's is *Sacred Water: Narratives and Pictures* (1993).

Boos: Do you consider yourself primarily a writer of stories or a novelist?

Silko: I've never tried to categorize what I do according to generic labels. I'm a writer, and I love language and story. I started out loving stories that were told to me. Growing up at Laguna Pueblo, one is immersed in story telling, because the Laguna people did not use written language to keep track of history and philosophy and other aspects of their lives.

Imagine an entire culture that is passed down for thousands and thousands of years through the spoken word and narrative, so the whole of experience is put into narrative form—this is how the people know who they are as a people, and how individuals learn who they are. They hear stories about "the family," about grandma and grandpa and others.

When I started out at the University of New Mexico, I took a folklore class, and began to think about the differences between the story that's told and the literary short story. I started writing the "literary" short story, and tried to write it as closely as I could according to the "classical" rules which seemed to manifest themselves in my reading. I wanted to show that I could do it. But I've turned away from this since and haven't really written a short story in the usual sense since 1981. From 1981 to 1989 I worked on *Almanac of the Dead,* and so I don't think of myself as short story writer. Yet stories are at the basis of everything I do, even non-fiction, because a lot of non-fiction reminiscences or memories come to me in the form of narrative, since that's the way people at home organize all experience and information.

I found the rules of the "classical" short story confining. I think you can see why the post-modernist narrative and the contemporary short story went off in another direction. They're trying to escape the strictures of the formal story form.

I've now tasted the freedom one has with a novel, so I wonder if I'll turn back to more structured forms. I've written one short story, "Personal Property," which I'm going to read tonight, and which purposely breaks some of the rules of the classical short story. Maybe I'm not done with making trouble with the short story form!

Boos: How are your poems related to your stories?

Silko: For me a poem is a very mysterious event . . . my poems came to me mysteriously. I started out to write a narrative, fiction or non-fiction, and something would happen so that the story would organize itself in the form of a narrative poem rather than a short story.

In fact, that happened with "A Story from Bear Country," in *Storyteller.* I intended to make a note about a conversation I had had with Benjamin Barney, a Navajo friend, about the different ways our respective Navajo and Pueblo cultures viewed bears. I started a narrative of our conversation, but something shifted abruptly, and before I knew it, I was writing something that looked more like a poem. At the very end of that poem a voice comes in and says, "Whose voice is this? You may wonder, for after all you were here alone, but you have been listening to me for some time now." That voice is the seductive voice of the bears. Benjamin Barney and I had been discussing the notion that if humans venture too close to the bear people and their territory, the people are somehow seduced or enchanted. They're not mauled or killed, but they are seduced and taken away to live with the bears forever.

So I don't have control [over whether my tale becomes a tale or a poem]. I set out to narrate something—either something which actually happened or a story I was told—and after I begin the piece sorts itself into whether it will be a poem or a short story. I find a mixing of the two in "The Sacred Water," a piece that I wrote a couple of years ago—a wanting to have the two together—so that there's really no distinct genre. This story also contained a bit of "non-fiction." I wanted to blend fiction and non-fiction together in one narrative voice.

So I am never far away from oral narrative, storytelling and narration, and the use of narrative to order experience. The people at home believe that there is one big story going on made up of many little stories, and the story goes on and on. The stories are alive and they outlive us, and storytellers are only caretakers of the story. Storytellers can be anonymous. Their names don't matter because the stories live on. I think that's what people mean when they say that there are no new stories under the sun. It's true—the old stories live on, but with new caretakers.

Boos: You present yourself as a narrative writer, but it struck me as I read *Storyteller* that you also think visually. How do you decide where to put the words on the page?

Silko: I'm a very aural person. On the other hand, my father was a photographer, and when I was a child, I would go in the darkroom, sit quietly on the stool, and watch as the images of the photographs would develop. As I've written in *Storyteller,* there was this old Hopi basket full of snapshots. One of us kids would pull a photograph and say, "Grandma, who's this," or "what's this?" A photography would be tied to narration. And when I was a child walking in the countryside, I'd see a certain sandstone formation of a certain shape, or a certain mesa, and someone would say, "Look, see that hill over there? Well, let me tell you . . ."

Through the years I've done a lot of thinking about the similarities and differences between the "literary" story and the story that's told. I began to realize that landscape could not be separated from narration and storytelling. One of the features of the written or old-fashioned short story was the careful, detailed description of its setting. By contrast, in Laguna oral stories, tellers and audience shared the same assumptions, a collective knowledge of the terrain and landscape which didn't need to be retold. That's why something an anthropologist or folklorist has collected may seem sparser than a literary short story; sometimes the oral short story can seem "too sparse." I realized that all communities have shared knowledge, and that the "literary" short story resulted when all over Europe—and all over the world—human populations started to move. People didn't have this common shared ground anymore.

Boos: *Storyteller* seemed to evoke a whole context related to your deep kinship with your family. Even the shapes of the stories seemed to arise from your identification with those telling the stories.

Silko: Right. One of the reasons that *Storyteller* contains photographs was my desire to convey that kinship and the whole context or field on which these episodes of my writing occurred. The photographs include not only those of my family, but of the old folks in the village and places in the village. I started to think of translation [from Laguna]. I realized that if one just works with the word on the page or the word in the air, something's left out. That's why I insisted on having photographs in *Storyteller.* I wanted to give the reader a sense of place, because here place is a character. For example, in the title story, "Storyteller," the main character is the weather and the free, frozen land itself. Or in the story I'm going to read tonight, "Private Property," the community itself is a character—although places and communities are not ordinarily characters in the "classical" literary short story. I felt a need to add in these other [visual] components which before were supposed to be extraneous to the narrative, but which existed at Laguna Pueblo as visual cues—a mountain or a tree or a photograph.

Boos: When you advise your creative writing students, what suggestions do you give about choosing topics or about technique?

Silko: Usually I tell them just to think about a good story, not to think consciously about topic or theme. I tell them that their stories should contain something that they don't know, something mysterious. It's better not to know too much, but to have just the bare bones of an idea, and let the writing be a process of enlightenment for them.

I often say, "Well, you can tell me the idea for the story, so why can't you write it down?" There's a large difference between speaking and writing. But when I'm writing, it's as natural to me as if I were speaking, though the results are different. The most difficult element of writing to teach the student is that ease—writing as if you were talking to yourself or to the wall.

Students are traumatized by the writing process. I've noticed the traumatization begins right from the first grade. Usually kids withstand it till around the seventh or eighth grade, and then they experience a real terror of failure and scolding. People who can talk, who can tell you things, freeze when they sit down in front of a blank piece and a pencil. It shouldn't be difficult to make the transition from speaking to writing, and I blame the United States educational system for the fact that it is.

Boos: Though you speak of an oral narrative tradition, you also remark that you speak and write differently. What's different about the writing process for you, and why do you value that?

Silko: I was conscious that I wasn't as good a storyteller as the storytellers at home, for the people at home are so good at this. An oral performance is just that, so I needed to go off in a room by myself to evoke that same sense of wholeness and excitement and perfection that I seemed to hear all around me [during their performances].

Also, when I'm writing I'm alone. When I'm speaking to an audience, by contrast, I'm very sensitive to what people want from me or expect from me, whether the audience are becoming restless or whatever, and I'm anxious to please and to serve, putting the comfort of others ahead of my own. When I write I'm alone with the voices . . . with the people in my memory. Some of the voices that I'm alone with might even be those of people still living, so that I could go and talk to them outside that door, but when I'm alone in the room writing, a connection with the older voices occurs, which cannot happen for me when I'm storytelling.

Boos: Writing isn't just inscription of stories, then, but something that requires solitude as well?

Silko: Being alone allows me to hear those voices. I think it's aloneness to be able to hear Aunt Susie's voice, for example. If I were in a room with her I would only listen, not write or speak, but solitude enables me to hear [and transcribe] her very distinctive voice. I think it was meant to be distinctive so that I could never forget it.

I've thought a lot about this distinction between oral narration and writing. Storytelling was done in a group so that the audience and teller would respond to each other, and be grounded in the present. As I said, I'm not as good at that, but I learned that it's also dangerous to go into the room alone and hear the voices alone, because those are voices from spirit beings who have real presence . . . and bring dangers . . . There's a real danger of being seduced by them, of wanting to join them and remain with them. I'm forty-six, and things are becoming clearer to me, things that before I had only heard about and hadn't experienced, so I couldn't judge.

But now I'm beginning to understand. Old Aunt Susie used to say that when she and her siblings were children, her grandmother started storytelling by bidding the youngest child to go open the door "so that our esteemed ancestors may bring in their gifts for us." But when we tell the stories of those past folks telling stories, they are actually here again in the room. It's therefore dangerous for a storyteller to write in a room alone without others, because those old ancestors are really coming in.

In writing *Almanac of the Dead,* I was forced to listen . . . I was visited by so many ancestors . . . it was very hard. It changed me as a human being. I came to love solitude almost too much, and it was very frightening.

Boos: Don't you ever fear that the presences of the dead might view critically something you wrote?

Silko: No, I've never been afraid. I know the voices of the storytellers, and I know that if you tell their truth and don't try to be self-serving, they aren't dangerous—in fact, they bring great protective power—*great protective power.*

Boos: How do you know what is true rather than self-serving?

Silko: I can tell. One method to avoid self-serving is to use a male protagonist, as in *Ceremony.* I wrote two stillborn versions of *Ceremony* now in the [Beinecke] Library at Yale—though I suspect that the rest of the university may had thought I was the Anti-Christ, so maybe they're not even catalogued! If anyone is interested, they can read the two stillborn drafts—each about sixty pages long—that lead up to *Ceremony.* "Stillborn" is of course such a grim term, but before I sold them to Yale University I looked at them again and saw that they're not really "stillborns" at all, but a necessary part of writing the novel. This gave me new confidence in the process of writing, and all young writers should understand that even those things that we throw in the trash can are necessary to get us to where we want to be. The first two stillborns had *female* protagonists.

Boos: Why would changing to a male protagonist have enabled you to transcend yourself?

Silko: When the characters were females, I identified too closely with them and wouldn't let them do things that I hadn't done or wouldn't do. It's not good to identify too closely with [one's own characters]. All this happened when I was very young; I started writing the "stillborn" versions of *Ceremony* when I was twenty-three.

Boos: Did you start to write short stories before you published poems? You published the poems of *Laguna Woman* quite early.

Silko: I wrote stories before I wrote poems, but the poems were easier to get out. That was because in writing stories I found myself too connected to the main character. Even though I wanted [her] to be a separate character,

[she] wouldn't be. When on the third draft of *Ceremony,* I created Tayo, and I was so liberated by working with a male protagonist.

Also, in a matriarchy the young *man* symbolizes purity and virginity— and also the intellectual, the sterile, and the orderly. The female principle was the chaotic, the creative, the fertile, the powerful.

Boos: *Ceremony* struck me as a book about the bonds between men, very deep bonds. Why would it be liberating for you to deal with male bonding and the recovery of a man's sense of himself?

Silko: When I was a little girl, I hung around adults. I was always the kid who wouldn't go off and play with the other kids, but liked to watch and eavesdrop on adults. I come from a culture in which men and women are not segregated, and so I had a great deal of opportunity to listen to the men talking. When I was really small, I listened to World War II and Korean War veterans. They had drinking problems and lacked regular jobs, but they had good souls and good spirits. Perhaps tragedy and anguish and trouble attracted me right away as a little girl, more than the easier parts of life.

Also, the Laguna people lived in a matriarchy, and in a matriarchy one is more afraid of what women may say and think about oneself. Children feel less powerful than their mothers, and men seemed more interesting to them because they too had less power and were more like themselves.

Needless to say, women are a lot happier in a matriarchy than in a patriar- chal society. Also those elements that had given women their strength and continuity were not nearly as shaken by outside pressures as were those reserved for men. I think this was mainly because when outsiders came in, they didn't realize the women's power, and so they left them alone. They stopped more of the things that men did traditionally than those that women did. So you see the men were more broken apart by the invasion. The government imprisoned men for practicing the Pueblo religion. Then of course war came, and the Second World War and the Korean War were devastating for men.

The Pueblo world is the reverse of Anglo-American and mainstream cul- ture, where the final word is the man's word. In the Pueblo world, women have the final word in practical matters. This is a simplification, but women own all the property, children belong to their mother's clan, and all the mundane business—quarrels, problems—are handled by women. The fe- male deity is the main deity, and in the Kiva ceremonies, man dress as women. But formerly the matriarchy was more evenly balanced, for the men were responsible for the hunting and religious ceremonies.

Boos: On the other hand, I've heard the theory that because the Euro-American legal system was so patriarchal, it destroyed certain aspects of Indian life that favored or protected women (by enforcing nineteenth-century laws, for example, which gave a married woman's property to her husband). If so, imposition of foreign laws sometimes diminished women's authority.

Silko: Well, we're only seeing that starting with my generation. It's taken that long for western European misogyny to arrive in the Pueblo. It's true that the conquerors negotiated only with Pueblo men, ignoring the clan mothers, but in the long run, when they destroyed what they thought was important, they left behind the authority of women.

Yet it's true that women are sometimes disadvantaged. A lot of tribal councils were established which didn't give women the right to vote, even though tribal organization was matriarchal. But that's a superficial level of damage, when you think that if the Conquistadors had really understood how important women were, they might have tried to [undermine their power]. Patriarchal attitudes have touched the Pueblo people only in a superficial way.

Boos: Does your identification with Tayo perhaps suggest that an author should try to identify with someone of the opposite sex as a way of moving towards a full presentation of reality?

Silko: Totally. When I was growing up, for a long time I felt that I was "just me." That was easy to be in a matriarchal culture, where women have access to the wide world. Women are everywhere and men are everywhere women are. There isn't this awful segregation that you find even now in the Anglo-American world . . .

Boos: In university life!

Silko: Yes, in university life. In the Pueblo, women crack dirty jokes to men who aren't their husbands or close relatives. There's a lot of banter, and a real feeling of equality and strength within the community. There weren't places where a little girl was told, "Oh, you can't go there!," or things of which a little boy was told, "Oh, you shouldn't do that!" I wasn't told that because I was a little girl, I had to dress or act a certain way. So for along time, although I didn't think I was *really* a boy, I kind of . . .

Boos: . . . didn't learn *not* to identify with men.

Silko: Yes, I didn't learn not to identify with men. I had a horse and was kind of a tomboy, and I was glad of it. Although I was intensely attracted to men and males, I saw that as a part of being interested in them and watching their activities.

I finished writing *Ceremony* in 1977, when it was still not politically correct for a woman novelist to write from a man's point of view. Feminism in America was still so new that feminists wanted women to write of their own experiences, not those of men. Perhaps too, because my name is Leslie, which is kind of androgynous, they may not have realized that I was a woman author. For awhile I didn't hear anything from the feminists. I felt I was punished for using a male protagonist, but that was the only way I could write.

Boos: I'd like to ask you about some of your fellow contemporary women writers who have written novels about their own cultures—Michelle Cliff, Toni Morrison, and Maxine Hong Kingston among them. Are there contemporary women writers whose works you've read a great deal, or whose works you believe resemble yours in any way?

Silko: Of course Toni Morrison's work has been important to me, and that of Maxine Hong Kingston. Both women have encouraged me to believe that I'm on the right track, and that we share something—that it's not so lonely, for there are other women and other people thinking and writing about the same sorts of things.

Boos: It seemed to me that you portrayed discrimination profoundly from within, not preaching about it, but analyzing its different layers and guises. Might I ask you to comment on contemporary Native American political issues and conflicts?

Silko: I'll tell you what's happening in terms of history. The largest city in the world is Mexico City, and officials don't really know its population. The uncounted ones are the *Indios,* the Indian people. A huge, huge change is on the horizon, indeed it's already underway—and there's nothing you can do.

A couple months ago at sundown, a freight train came up from Nogales through Tucson, covered, crawling with human beings. People were sitting on top, people were hanging on the side—and so the great return to Aztlan which the Chicano people talk about is coming to pass in a big way. The Zapatista uprising on January 1st, 1994, was one of the most important signalings of what is to come. After that small demonstrations were held all over Mexico and the United States and Canada, showing the solidarity of Native American people throughout the Americas. We sense that the rising on January 1st was a sign of this awakening.

The most important thing right now which people must watch out for it jingoism and hysteria about immigrants and immigration. [The U.S. government] is building an iron curtain, a steel wall—Rudolfo Ortiz calls it the Tortilla Curtain—but it's ugly. They're trying to seal off Mexico from the United States. But [those they are sealing off] are Indians, Native-Americans, American Indians, original possessors of this continent, and [those who hate them] want to create a hysteria here so that it will justify U. S. troops opening fire and shooting and killing. The future could be a horrendous blood bath and upheaval not seen since the Civil War.

Right now the border patrol stops [Indian] people. I've been stopped three or four times, and have had dogs put on me.

Boos: Oh!?

Silko: This happened to me on my way from Albuquerque to Tucson. Many people in the rest of the United States don't understand that the U.S. government is destroying the civil rights of *all* citizens living near the border. Something terrible is developing, and it's being sold to the American people, or shoved down their throats through this hysteria over immigrants and the fear that their jobs will be taken. But I see a frightening collision on the horizon! I'll tell you something—the powers that be, those greedy corrupt white men like Rostenkowski and all those criminals in the United States Congress—their time is running out very soon! The forces from the south have spiritual power and legitimacy that'll blast those thieves and murderers right out of Washington, D.C.

Boos: Are there particular Native-American groups that you see working effectively against government wrongs?

Silko: Ah, ah, this change that's coming will not have leaders. People will wake up and know in their hearts that it's beginning. It's already happening across the United States. The change isn't just limited to Native Americans. It can come to Anglo-Americans, Chicanos, African-Americans as well. Every day people wake up to the inhumanity and violence this government perpetrates on its own citizens, and on citizens all over the world. That's why the change will not be stopped, for it will be a change of consciousness, a change of heart.

We don't need leaders. They can't stop [this revolution.] They can shoot some, they can kill some—like they have already—but this is a change that rises out of the earth's very being—a Hurricane Andrew, a Hurricane Hugo, an earthquake of consciousness. This earth itself is rebelling against what's been done to it in the name of greed and capitalism. No, there are no groups which bring change. They aren't needed. This change that's coming is much deeper and much larger. Think of it as a natural force—human beings massed into a natural force like a hurricane or a tidal wave. It will happen when the people come from the south, and when the people here [in the North and Midwest] understand.

One morning people will just wake up, and we'll all be different. That's why the greedy powerful white men will not be able to stop what happens, because there will be nothing to grab onto. There are no Martin Luther Kings to shoot, so the F.B.I. can give up on that!

There's no one that can stop us, because [the return to Aztlan] will be a change inside of *you!* It will happen without your knowing it. And this won't happen because someone preached at you, threatened you with prison, put a gun to your head. No, you'll wake up [yourself]. It will come to you through dreams!

Boos: No Martin Luther King will have helped bring about change, but what about Leslie Marmon Silko? How do you see yourself contributing to this movement?

Silko: Just be telling people—"Look, this is happening!" As I tried to make clear in *Almanac of the Dead,* you don't have to do anything, for the great change is already happening. But you maybe might want to be aware of what was coming, and you might want to think about the future choices that you might have to make. Though as I said, in your heart, you will already know.

Boos: Amen, and thank you.

INDEX